Foucault Now

Theory Now

Series Editor: Ryan Bishop

Virilio Now, John Armitage
Baudrillard Now, Ryan Bishop
Rancière Now, Oliver Davis
Sloterdijk Now, Stuart Elden

Foucault Now

Current Perspectives in Foucault Studies

EDITED BY
JAMES D. FAUBION

polity

First published in 2014 by Polity Press

Polity Press
65 Bridge Street
Cambridge CB2 1UR, UK

Polity Press
350 Main Street
Malden, MA 02148, USA

ISBN-13: 978-0-7456-6378-4
ISBN-13: 978-0-7456-6379-1(pb)

A catalogue record for this book is available from the British Library.

Typeset in 11 on 13 pt Bembo by
Servis Filmsetting Ltd, Stockport, Cheshire
Printed and bound in Great Britain by TJ International Ltd, Padstow, Cornwall

For further information on Polity, visit our website: www.politybooks.com

Contents

Acknowledgments

Ian Hacking's essay in this volume is reprinted from a 2011 issue of *The History of the Human Sciences* (**24**[4]: 13–23) with the kind permission of Sage Publishers.

The excerpt of an interview that Benjamin Hans-Dieter Buchloh conducted with Gerhard Richter, which appears in Paul Rabinow's essay in this volume, has been reprinted from Richter, G. (1986) *Gerhard Richter (October Files)*, Buchloh, H. (ed.) with the kind permission of MIT Press.

Michael Lucey has translated Didier Eribon's essay in this volume from the French.

Contributors

Didier Eribon is professor at the School of Philosophy and Social Sciences of the University of Amiens. He is the author of the first biography of Michel Foucault (1989; third edition, revised and enlarged, 2011) and many other books including *Insult and the Making of the Gay Self* (2004), *Une morale du minoritaire* (2001), *Retour à Reims* (2009) and *La société comme verdict* (2013).

Eric Fassin is Professor of Sociology in the Political Science Department and the Gender Studies program at Paris 8 University (after 18 years at École normale supérieure and 5 at New York University), also affiliated with research center IRIS (CNRS/ EHESS). His work focuses on contemporary sexual and racial politics in France and the United States, and their intersections (in particular concerning immigration in Europe). He is frequently involved in French public debates on issues his work addresses – from gay marriage and gender parity to the politics of immigration and race. He is the author of *Le sexe politique* (2009), and co-author (with the collective Cette France-là) of four volumes on French immigration policies (2008–12). He co-edited *De la question sociale à la question raciale?* (2006). His latest book is *Démocratie précaire. Chroniques de la déraison d'État* (2012). He is currently working on

Actualité d'Aimé Césaire (to be published by La Découverte) and *The Empire of Sexual Democracy* (to be published by Zone Books).

James D. Faubion is Professor of Anthropology at Rice University. Publications representative of his interests include *Modern Greek Lessons: A Primer in Historical Constructivism* (1993); (ed.) *Essential Works of Michel Foucault, Volume 2: Aesthetics, Method and Epistemology* and *Volume 3: Power* (1998, 2000); *The Shadows and Lights of Waco: Millenarianism Today* (2001); and *An Anthropology of Ethics* (2011).

John Forrester is Professor of History and Philosophy of the Sciences at the University of Cambridge, author of *Language and the Origins of Psychoanalysis* (1980), *The Seductions of Psychoanalysis* (1990), *Freud's Women* (with Lisa Appignanesi, 1992), *Dispatches from the Freud Wars* (1997), and *Truth Games* (1997). He is completing (with Laura Cameron) *Freud in Cambridge*, a study of the reception of psychoanalysis in the 1920s. He has research interests in reasoning in cases in science, medicine, and law and also in the genealogy of the concept of gender, particularly in the work of Robert J. Stoller. He is Editor of *Psychoanalysis and History*.

Ian Hacking is a Canadian philosopher with many interests. His books include work on experimental physics, philosophy of language, probability, multiple personality, social construction and (forthcoming) the philosophy of mathematics. *The Emergence of Probability* (1975) was his first major contribution to be influenced by Michel Foucault; see the Introduction to the 2006 edition. *Historical Ontology* (2002) develops many themes that are derived from Foucault. He is an emeritus professor at the Collège de France and the University of Toronto.

Lynne Huffer is Samuel Candler Dobbs Professor of Women's, Gender, and Sexuality Studies at Emory University. She is the author of *Mad for Foucault: Rethinking the Foundations of Queer Theory* (2010); *Maternal Pasts, Feminist Futures: Nostalgia and the Question of Difference* (1998); *Another Colette: The Question of Gendered Writing* (1992); and numerous articles on Foucault, feminist philosophy, queer theory, post-structuralism, and French and Francophone literature and film. Her newest book, *Are the Lips a Grave? A Queer Feminist on the Ethics of Sex* (2013), explores the ethical stakes of queer versus feminist politics, practices, and thinking about sex.

Colin Koopman is Assistant Professor of Philosophy at the University of Oregon. He has published two monographs, one on genealogy: *Pragmatism as Transition* (2009); and *Genealogy as Critique* (2013). His published scholarship on genealogical thinkers has appeared in *Philosophy & Social Criticism*, *Foucault Studies*, *The Review of Metaphysics*, *Journal of the Philosophy of History*, *Critical Inquiry* and *Constellations*, and Wiley-Blackwell's *Companion to Foucault*. His current work involves issues of philosophical methodology beyond metaphysical philosophy, and the status of emerging norms and forms of power.

James Laidlaw is currently Head of Social Anthropology at the University of Cambridge and a Fellow of King's College. His regional interests cover South and East Asia (India, Bhutan, Inner Mongolia, and Taiwan). His books include *The Archetypal Actions of Ritual* (1994), *Riches and Renunciation: Religion, Economy, and Society among the Jains* (1995), *The Essential Edmund Leach* (in two volumes, 2000) and two edited volumes of essays on the anthropology of religion: *Ritual and Memory* (2004); and *Religion, Anthropology, and Cognitive Science* (2007). His latest book is *The Subject of Virtue, An Anthropology of Ethics and Freedom* (2013).

Laurence McFalls is Professor of Political Science at L'Université de Montréal, where he is co-director, together with Mariella Pandolfi, of the *Groupe de recherche sur les interventions militaires et humanitaires* and where he is Montréal director of the International Research Training Group "Diversity: Mediating Difference in Transcultural Spaces." His recent research and publications have elaborated the concept of "therapeutic domination," based on a cross-reading of Foucault and Max Weber. In addition to his critical work on humanitarian interventions in collaboration with Pandolfi, he has worked on Weber's epistemology and social theory, on the cultural aftermath of communism in eastern

Germany, and on winegrowers in the south of France. He was co-founder and longtime director of the Centre canadien d'études allemandes et européennes.

Toby Miller is the author and editor of over thirty books and 150 essays. His latest books are *Greening the Media* (with Richard Maxwell, 2012) and *Blow Up the Humanities* (2012). You can follow his adventures at www.tobymiller.org.

Mariella Pandolfi is Professor of Anthropology at L'Université de Montréal and co-director of the *Groupe de réflexion sur l'image dans le monde hispanique*. Her previous research on the anthropology of the body developed through a dialogue between psychoanalytic and phenomenological approaches to ethnopsychiatry. In the last decade, through her work in the post-communist Balkan territories (Bosnia, Albania, and Kosovo), she has delved into a complex terrain marked by the breakdown of communist regimes and the explosion of violence and armed ethnic conflicts, exploring the moral and political boundaries of humanitarian aid. Her theoretical tools revisit the concept of biopolitics and elaborate new critical perspectives on neoliberalism and crisis. Having served as consultant for the United Nations to Vienna and for the International Organization of Migration in Kosovo, she has stimulated critical debate in the international community and the media. In 2004 she received the "Woman of Distinction Award" from the Women's Foundation of Montréal and in 2012 The Order of Merit of the Italian Republic.

Paul Rabinow is Professor of Anthropology at the University of California, Berkeley. Of his many publications, the most recent include *Designing Human Practices: An Experiment with Synthetic Biology* (with Gaymon Bennett, 2012), and *Demands of the Day: On the Logic of Anthropological Enquiry* (with Anthony Stavrianakis, 2013). A more complete list of his work can be found via anthropos-lab.net.

Cary Wolfe is Bruce and Elizabeth Dunlevie Professor of English at Rice University, where he is also founding director of 3CT: The

Center for Critical and Cultural Theory. His books include *Animal Rites: American Culture, the Discourse of Species, and Posthumanist Theory* (2003), *What Is Posthumanism?* (2010), and *Before the Law: Humans and Other Animals in a Biopolitical Frame* (2012). He has also participated in multi-author projects involving J.M. Coetzee, Cora Diamond, Stanley Cavell, Paola Cavalieri, and others. He is founding editor of the series Posthumanities at the University of Minnesota Press.

Abbreviations

References to many of Foucault's works are identified in abbreviated form, as follows:

Abnormal: A
Archaeology of Knowledge: AK
The Birth of Biopolitics: BB
The Birth of the Clinic: An Archaeology of Medical Perception: BC
The Courage of Truth: CT
Critique and Power: CP
Discipline and Punish: The Birth of the Prison: DP
Dits et écrits 1994. In 4 volumes: *DE (1–4)*
Dits et écrits 2001. In 2 volumes: *DEii (1–2)*
Essential Works of Michel Foucault, Vol. 1: Ethics, Subjectivity and Truth: EW1
Essential Works of Michel Foucault, Vol. 2: Aesthetics, Method, Epistemology: EW2
Essential Works of Michel Foucault, Vol. 3: Power: EW3
Folie et déraison: FD
The Foucault Effect: Studies in Governmentality: FE
Foucault Live: FL
Le gouvernement de soi et des autres: GSA1

Le gouvernement de soi et des autres II: le courage de la vérité: GSA2
The Government of Self and Others: GSO
Herculine Barbin: HB
The Hermeneutics of the Subject: HS
History of Madness: HM
The History of Sexuality, Volume 1: An Introduction. The Will to Know: HS1
The History of Sexuality, Volume 2: The Use of Pleasure: HS2
The History of Sexuality, Volume 3: The Care of the Self: HS3
Histoire de la folie à l'age classique: HFAC
Il faut défendre la société: IFDS
Naissance de la biopolitique: NB
Naissance de la clinique: NC
Madness and Civilization: MC
The Order of Things: An Archaeology of the Human Sciences: OT
Politics, Philosophy, Culture: PPC
Power/Knowledge: PK
Psychiatric Power: PP
Remarks on Marx: Conversations with Duccio Trombadori: RM
Sécurité, territoire, population: STP
Security, Territory, Population: STP(E)
Society Must Be Defended: SMBD
Technologies of the Self: A Seminar with Michel Foucault: TS
La volonté de savoir: VS

Complete references of these works appear in the bibliography. Several of the contributors to the volumes have provided their own translations of Foucault's texts. In such cases, citations of the corresponding pages of published English translations, in brackets, follow the citations of the French originals.

Introduction: The Use of Foucault

James D. Faubion

In the aftermath of the publication of the last of Foucault's works ever likely to see the light of day, this volume has its chief ambition in coming to fresh terms and making fresh work with the conceptual details and the broader scope of the programmatic dimensions of Michel Foucault's thought. A topical compendium, *per impossibile*, it is not. But nor is it a mere sampler. Instead, it offers an analytical clarification and several practical illustrations of the promise and the productivity of a methodological and critical project that, for all its twists and turns, aimed squarely at revealing the contingency of what conventional wisdom would construe as necessary, essential, forever written in stone. The project had its limits; no mere mortal can do everything, after all. It also had an enduring focus. Above all, it was aimed at revealing the historical and sociocultural contingencies of conceptions of the human – however necessary, essential and written in stone they might seem to be to those who have embraced them (or continue to embrace them). In "What is Enlightenment?" (*EW1*, 303–19) – which reads pointedly as a retrospective self-formulation of what had always been at the heart of his labors – Foucault deemed his project a critically oriented "historical ontology of ourselves." This volume seeks to elaborate on and add to that historical and historicizing ontology. This is its specific difference from all the other collections on Foucault – and there are a great many – that one might encounter.

Foucault has been cast as "anti-humanist," occasionally as "post-humanist" – but these are hazy and often polemical epithets. Whatever else, Foucault was dubious in principle of doctrines presuming or purporting to reveal that human history was not merely a matter of contingencies but also an expression of the human as such – pan-historical, supra-historical or the effective telos of the historical process as the case may be. Such doctrines are legion. In the France of Foucault's formative years, psychoanalysis, Marxism, phenomenology and Jean-Paul Sartre's (psychoanalytical, Marxist and phenomenological) existentialism were their leading academic representatives. Foucault joined many other thinkers of his generation in being dubious of them. His cultivation of his doubts nevertheless remains unique – terminologically, conceptually, and methodologically. It was a restless process. It was sometimes self-revisionary. Its valences could be positive as well as negative. It was by no means a merely academic exercise. Throughout his career, Foucault was at pains to demonstrate the close connection between essentialist construals of the human and their practical consequences – some of those consequences quite invidious. The topics he pursued have broad collective import. They were also close to his own heart.

(Paul) Michel Foucault: Notes on a Life's Work

Foucault was born in Poitiers, France, in 1926. At the age of 20, he was admitted to the École Normale Supérieure – one of the great training grounds of the French academic and intellectual elite. He studied psychology and philosophy. He completed his doctoral thesis in 1960. Entitled *Folie et déraison: Histoire de la folie à l'âge classique* (Madness and unreason: History of madness in the classical age), its prevailing argument – now famous – is that an abrupt shift occurs in Europe at the end of the eighteenth century in the conceptualization and treatment of the mad, of "fools." Previously regarded with some mixture of amusement and awe, odd and wise and perhaps even divinely touched, they came rapidly to be recast as a sort of breed apart, spouters of nonsense, dangerous to themselves and to others and in need of special confinement. The "asylum" is thus born. In this volume, Ian Hacking reviews the strange fortunes of the various editions and titles of *HM*; Lynne Huffer revisits and takes a clear stand on the controversy that it ultimately provoked.

Through the mid-1970s, Foucault also writes a number of essays on literature and painting. Following more closely in the footsteps of *HM*, however, is *Naissance de la clinique: Une archéologie de regard médical* (*The Birth of the Clinic: An Archaeology of Medical Perception*), also published in 1963. Grounded in the same historical periodization that informs its predecessor, it focuses on the transformation of the theorization of disease. What was formerly understood as a condition tied to the particularities of the environment in which it emerged, disease – once again rather abruptly – came instead to be conceived as a condition of the body, a "case." It rapidly came to have another institution of confinement – the clinic – as its putatively proper home. Its successor, *Les Mots et les Choses: une archéologie des sciences humaines* (titled in its English translation *The Order of Things: An Archaeology of the Human Sciences* [*OT*]), made Foucault famous. "Archaeology" in the subtitle again. Imagine a khaki-clad explorer treading through what looks to begin with like a perfectly natural landscape. Then, all of a sudden, indications of organized life begin to appear – traces of the foundations of edifices built and razed, pottery intact and in shards. In short, the explorer discovers a field site. It's a site on the surface, but it promises other sites, a stratigraphy of previous settlements, below. Replace "the foundations of edifices" with the "rules of formation" of those "discourses" (medical, economic, biological, linguistic, and so on) that are in part or whole about the human, the human as such. Replace "pottery" with "inscribed pronounce-ments" (*énoncés*). Replace the explorer's digging down into the earth to discover the layering of distinct settlements of times past with Foucault's digging back into the archives to unearth distinct settlements of conventional wisdom past (and perhaps still lin-gering in the present). Then you'll begin to have an idea of the mission of Foucauldean archaeology. For a more complete idea, see his *Archaeology of Knowledge* (*AK*) – the first of many subsequent reprises of work already accomplished.

In 1970, Foucault was granted a chair in "the history of systems of thought" at the Collège de France. In 1975 and 1976, he published two books that remain his most broadly referenced: the first published in English under the title *Discipline and Punish: The Birth of the Prison* [*DP*]; the second under the title *The History of Sexuality, Volume 1: The Will to Know* [*HS1*]. These latter works are sometimes regarded as the inauguration and maturation of Foucault the "genealogist." Inspired by Friedrich Nietzsche's *The Genealogy of Morals* (originally published in 1887), Foucault the genealogist looks to have shifted his attention to the continuities between the relationships of ancestors – theoretical and practical – to descendants in roughly the same domains at least as much as to the differences between them. There's much to be said about whether this shift is fundamental, or simply a shift in emphasis. At this point, it is enough to note that with "Nietzsche, Genealogy, History," Foucault makes explicit a critical enterprise that was previously left for his readers to infer (or distort). He is conducting a "history of the present."

The turning of the eighteenth into the nineteenth century is once again the stage setting for *DP* and *HS1* alike. The former traces the discursive and practical shift, or relative co-adjustment, between two modes of the exercise of power. "Sovereign power" was still the dominant mode in the eighteenth century. The monarch – a figure of law incarnate – was its typical point of reference. It was a messy business that in the course of a few decades gave way to "disciplinary" power and yet another distinctive institution of confinement – the prison as we now know it. Protestants led the way, with the Dutch Calvinists and the Philadelphia Quakers at the forefront. They decried the brutality of the sovereign's gallows. They abhorred the sovereign's public spectacle of taking vengeance on the perpetrator of criminal acts. They were reformists, and what they sought to reform was a relatively novel presence in the penal arena – the souls of what physical anthropologists and criminologists soon began to characterize and classify as "criminal types." They forged a "gentle way of punishment," removed from the public gaze and devoted to guiding the offender to make penitence for his or her delicts (hence the prison as "penitentiary").

The trouble was that the prison didn't work very well. Only a bit more than a decade after the first of them was erected, reformists widely recognized they were leading to ends absolutely contrary to the ends they were supposed to serve. Putting criminals together in penitentiaries was turning out to produce more clever and skilled criminals, not saved souls. Then why had they endured so long? Why had they come to seem so natural and inescapable a part of the social landscape? Why, for that matter, did such human sciences as physical anthropology and criminology endure along with them, in spite of what Foucault had argued in *OT*: that they were not merely unreliable but also grounded in paradox? Foucault's answer was "power/knowledge" – the entanglement of moral-juridical judgment with fact, of "ought" with "is," of strategic intervention with epistemological authority.

Power/knowledge is also central to the analysis of *HS1*. The human scientists who deemed themselves sexologists are its fulcrum. The emergence of the concept of sexuality as most of us still know and use it is a leitmotif. *HS1* is also the locus of Foucault's introduction of a third modality of power, "bio-technical" power or "biopower" for short. It stands in contrast to its sovereign counterpart, definitionally if not as a matter of historical fact. The signature of the latter is the right or privilege of "letting live or making die." The signature of biopower is the right or privilege of "making live or letting die." The bedrock of its legitimacy rests on linking together security, well-being and health; its historically most complete realizations are European welfare states.

Foucault initially intended *HS1* to be the first installment of several subsequent volumes, all focused on the nineteenth century. Things didn't turn out that way, for many and complex reasons (a more complete account can be found in Eribon 1992). First is Foucault's gradual development of the concept of governmentality, which in its later articulations serves as a common umbrella for two distinct aspects of what Foucault came to conceive as governance in general: the conduct of conduct. On the one side, we have political domination, economic exploitation, and characterological (e.g., racist) subjugation. All are direct modes of governance. All are coercive. In the absolute, they are incompatible with anything that might be conceived of as freedom. On the other side, however, are "arts of government." They function as incentives, tips, guidelines, and rules as thumb, not merely for adjusting to being governed but also for developing ways and means of governing oneself. They leave room for the exercise of freedom, which Foucault comes to render straightforwardly as the capacity to pursue behavioral and conceptual and emotional alternatives in any given situation. Freedom for Foucault is very much a thing of this world and it is never absolute. Even in situations in which we are objectively capable of pursuing options, we always also find ourselves enmeshed in "power relations." In such relations, one party typically (though not always) has more of a capacity to act on another's action than the other party does. Even so, power relations are not relations of coercion. They constrain. They also leave open possibilities. They are not in a mutually exclusive relationship to freedom. They condition our freedom. They are also liable to being conditioned and reconditioned by it.

The domain of power relations is the domain in which Foucault locates ethics. He characterizes ethics in such locutions as "the reflexive practice of freedom." It won't do as a definition (a serial killer, for example, is capable of exercising the reflexive practice of freedom), but it does provide Foucault with an analytical orientation, in what finally turn out to be the second and third volumes of *The History of Sexuality*, to the ancient Greek and later Hellenistic and Roman philosophers. Why go back to the ancients? Once again, the reasons are complex, but the response that Foucault himself offers in the opening sentences of *HS2* will do in summary: unlike the Christians who followed them and so unlike a tradition that is still very relevant to any history of the present, the ancients did not have any conception of "the flesh" as the substance of inherent evil, to be addressed only to be neutralized, even negated, in the interest of the purification of the soul. A fourth volume of the *History of Sexuality*, on early Christian monasticism, is available in snippets in Foucault's last publications, but was never finished. In early 1984, the complications of having contracted the AIDS virus sapped Foucault of his resources. He died in June of the same year.

Receptions and Applications

I don't . . . consider these Wednesday reunions as teaching activities, but rather as sorts of public accounts rendered of a work that I
am left to do more or less as I want. In that respect, I consider myself
absolutely obliged, in effect, to tell you more or less what I am doing,
where I'm coming from, in what direction the work is going; and in
that respect, just as much, I consider you entirely at liberty to do what
you want with what I say. These are tracks of research, ideas, schemas,
stipples, instruments: do with them what you want.
                                  – Michel Foucault, *IFDS*, 3–4 [*SMBD*, 1–2]

So Foucault introduces the lectures he gave at the Collège de
France in 1975 and 1976. If the introduction invites the impression Foucault's lectures are more disorganized than they really are,
it's still a fair enough self-assessment. The 1975–6 lectures and
many of his other lectures at the Collège are exploratory, often a
sort of testing ground for and complement to the monographs he
was writing in tandem with them – all of which were revised and
revised again before appearing in print. It's a fair enough assessment as well of the vast majority of engagements with Foucault's
work, which are now too numerous to count and, if anything, are
appearing with increasing pace and in increasing numbers. The
tenor of the more recent installments might be critical, though
rarely as vituperative as the tenor of many of those of his earlier
readers, who were certain that they were in the face of an unre-
pentant bourgeois, a moral decisionist, a neo-conservative, an
anti-modern, a malcontent without any grounds for his acidic
remonstrations other than his own petulance (and so on). Their
arguments and the disciplines from which they proceed are
increasingly wide-ranging. (For a survey, see the Postscript to this
introduction.) This alone might justify yet another volume on
Foucault. He remains very much alive and well. His vitality shows
no signs of abating. His accounts rendered are still very much
being taken into account – and not merely, it would seem, because
his literary executors have been careful to release his corpus only
gradually instead of at one fell swoop.

As previously indicated, however, this volume claims its justification, distinction and point of departure in underscoring that
Foucault was not merely a provisioner of tracks of research, ideas,
schemas, stipples and instruments, however fruitful all of these
might and surely will yet be. To borrow one of his own favorite
turns of phrase, there is more. Nor is there much need for interpretation here: the multifariousness of his tracks of research, ideas,
schemas, stipples and instruments, aside, Foucault's enterprise is
more than a piecemeal enterprise by Foucault's own reckoning.
He was in fact regularly inclined to give retrospective diagnoses
of what he'd actually been doing of a distinctively systematic sort.
As already noted, *AK* is the earliest (and also the most lengthy)
of these. Many other reckonings unfold in assorted (and carefully
edited) interviews.

One of the most systematic of such reckonings appears very
close to the end of Foucault's career and life. Appearing in the
1984 edition of the *Dictionnaire des philosophes* (Dictionary of
Philosophers), the entry "Michel Foucault" is credited to a certain
Maurice Florence – which is a pseudonym for the actual author,
Foucault himself. Foucault begins by relegating himself to the "*critical* tradition of [Immanuel] Kant," a "critical history of thought"
(*EW2*, 459). In particular, he follows Kant in pursuing the analysis of "the conditions under which certain relations of subject to
object are formed or modified, insofar as those relations constitute
a possible knowledge [*savoir*]" (459). In his Three Critiques, Kant
sought to establish the formal conditions that made judgment and
knowledge possible (in the first Critique, scientific knowledge; in
the Second, the exercise of practical reason; in the Third, aesthetic
judgment). Foucault is interested instead in the rules and strategies
of what he often calls "games of truth" – which can be, and almost
always are, played with the utmost seriousness. He is not, however,
interested in any and every game of truth that has appeared on
the historical radar screen. His focus is restricted instead to those
games "in which the subject itself is posited as an object of possible
knowledge" (460). An enquiry of three "segments" is the result,
though each historically overlaps with the other. We have already
met them: one segment concerning the formation of the "human
sciences"; another concerning the construction of the criminal

"deviant"; and a third concerning the history of "sexuality" (460–1). In vivid contrast to Kant, Foucault's research is grounded in "a systematic skepticism toward all anthropological universals" (462). A first methodological imperative thus has its rationale: "insofar as possible, circumvent the anthropological universals (and, of course, those of a humanism that would assert the rights, the privileges, and the nature of a human being as an immediate and timeless truth) in order to examine them as historical constructs" (462). Two other principles accompany it. One of these consists in a reversal of "the philosophical way of proceeding upward to the constituent subject which is asked to account for every possible object of knowledge in general" in favor of "proceeding back down to the study of concrete practices by which the subject is constituted in the immanence of a domain of knowledge" (462). The other consists in addressing "'practices' as a domain of analysis," approaching the study "from the angle of what 'was done'" (462).

In "What is Enlightenment?" – published in the same year, but posthumously – Foucault (no pseudonym this time) addresses the same effort through a somewhat different lexicon. The title of the essay is a translation of the title that Kant – writing at some remove from the Kant of the Three Critiques – gave to an article published in a journal targeting the lay educated public of Berlin in 1784. Commentators are in near consensus that the essay is Foucault's self-reflective response to Jürgen Habermas' accusations that his French contemporary had been plying a critical course in the absence of any discernable critical principles. It's a response that hinges on the articulation of the principles of a distinctly modern "philosophical ethos," whose realization and dynamics consist of "a critique of what we are saying, thinking, and doing." It's a critique wrought precisely through a historical ontology of ourselves" (*EW1*, 315).

It should be noted immediately that most philosophers of the philosophical mainstream would likely find the very idea of "historical ontology" a paradox. In the mainstream, ontology – otherwise known as metaphysics – has nothing to do with history. Or to be more precise, it has nothing to do with history as the contingent, accidental, particular flow of events, the sort of history that Foucault has in mind. But then, Foucault doesn't belong to the philosophical (or the historical) mainstream. His critique is what Hacking has deemed "another way of doing philosophy" (and it's another way of doing history as well; see Hacking's essay in this volume). It is genealogical in its design, and so does not try to "deduce from the form of what we are what it is impossible for us to do and to know." It rather separates out, "from the contingency that has made us what we are, the possibility of no longer being, doing, or thinking as we are, do, or think" (*EW1*, 315–16). It is archaeological in its method, and so does not "seek to identify universal structures of all knowledge or of all possible moral action," but instead "to treat the instances of discourse that articulate what we think, say, and do as so many historical events" (*EW1*, 315; Faubion 2012, 68–9).

Choose one lexicon or choose the other. In Foucault's oeuvre, the ahistorical and essentializing ontology of the subject dear to philosophers (Western and not so Western) gives way to the design and methodology of a critique that has as its primary object of interrogation just that ahistorical and essentializing ontology – and the compulsion to put it into practical effect (thus power/ knowledge). Such a critique is programmatic, which is to say that it offers a systematic procedure for formulating questions about and pursuing diagnoses of the structure and the consequences of one or another authoritative but historically variable version of what it essentially is to be human. It isn't, however, a program; it doesn't restrict the themes and sites of inquiry in advance. It doesn't demand that we continue to attend only to those segments of the historically variable "truth of our being" to which Foucault himself attended.

All of the authors collected in this volume would likely agree on this much. Gary Gutting has put forward much the same claim in his introduction to *The Cambridge Companion to Foucault* (Gutting 2005), but his and his contributors' emphasis on the divigations and heterogeneities of Foucault's tracks of research, ideas, schemas, stipples and instruments stand – to reiterate what has already been reiterated – in contrast to our emphasis here. That said, the contributions to come do not follow one early commentator in judging either the range or the pretensions of Foucault's critical history of thought as of the same order as such "grand theorists" of the past as Karl Marx, Friedrich Nietzsche, or Sigmund Freud (Philip 1985). True, Foucault himself once asserted – or at least suggested – certain affinities between their procedures and his own. In particular, he offered a reading of Marx, Freud, and Nietzsche as methodologically committed, in principle or in fact, to the undecidability of the phenomena they addressed (*EW2*, 269–78). It's a contestable reading in each case – but it does sound a note of epistemological modesty that all of the contributions to come implicitly or explicitly endorse. Whatever else, dogmatism is out of the question.

Our contributors are in accord on four further fronts. They agree that more use can be made of Foucault than has yet been done – and many of them offer exercises in and avenues on which to pursue some of what they have in mind. They agree that some of the use to which Foucault has so far been put runs the risk of and occasionally amounts to misuse – not the appropriation that Foucault invited but instead a misappropriation of the sort that he would likely have rejected. (Granted, it's a bit over-reaching to anticipate Foucault's reactions, even with the wisdom of hindsight.) They agree that readers should engage Foucault's full corpus (which by some reckonings of the notion of what constitutes a corpus we will never have) before daring to venture altogether confident pronouncements on what Foucault meant at any particular moment in his career, on what he embraced or didn't embrace, on whom he admired or didn't admire, on what if anything he definitively stood for, on who or what, in short, he was. Not at all least, they agree that every further encounter with Foucault's corpus – whether in reading what had not previously been available or in rereading what has already been published – is more likely than not to provoke and even demand a revisiting of interpretations already formulated, conclusions already drawn, uses already devised.

It's worth dwelling a bit on the second of these points of accord. That Foucault has occasionally been misused and misappropriated is not always a matter of the cruel slings and arrows of bitter fortune, to be sure; not all the slings and arrows of fortune are infelicitous. Then again, some are. Take "sexuality" – and all the more so because it is a topic that a number of the authors in this

volume visit, though only a few (Eribon in particular, though see
also Fassin) visit as a central thematic. In its translation from French
into English, sexuality has tended to lose the contextual specificity of Foucault's conceptualization of it and drift instead toward
decontextualization and recontextualization, with three results.
The most unfortunate of these is imputing to Foucault oversights
and falsehoods of which he was not in fact guilty (a phenomenon
of course hardly unique to Foucault). Almost as unfortunate is
the loss – sometimes severe – of analytical precision and substantive content. More constructive is the adjustment of a concept's
scope to suit investigative and analytical projects of greater reach
than Foucault's own. The latter often amounts to what I might
self-indulgently call the "anthropologization" of Foucault. Paul
Rabinow's work offers the most sustained example (Rabinow
1989, 1999, 2003; Rabinow and Bennett 2012; Rabinow and
Stavrianakis 2013), though it is not limited to certified anthropologists alone.

Sometimes, indeed, sexuality has come into English with its
parameters well intact even as it has been extended to other climes
and times. Judith Farquhar's concise summary of Foucault's critique of the repressive hypothesis in her China-focused *Appetites*
is illustrative:

> The repressive hypothesis was [in fact] the occasion of a huge linguistic
> effusion . . . speaking endlessly of sex while adopting a proper socio-
> logical code for its various practices. This order of discourse, which
> placed sex at the center of experience, is constitutive of the discourse
> of sexology wherever it may appear. Natural sex, made up of needs and
> drives, influenced by society but subject to self-control, is the object of
> this science. (2002, 239)

Farquhar appropriately highlights that Foucault's analysis falls
within his broader ambitions as a historian of those nineteenth-
century concoctions, the human sciences. Among those sciences,
sexology is instrumental in objectifying sex as a natural kind, a
kingdom of genera and species, the species of the homosexual
among them (*HS1*, 43). In Foucault's own words: "As defined
by the ancient civil or canonical codes, sodomy was a category

of forbidden acts; their perpetrator was nothing more than the *juridical* subject of them. The 19th century homosexual became a personage, a past, a case history, and a childhood, in addition to being a type of life, a life form, and a morphology" (*HS1*, 43; my emphasis).

The homosexual of the sexologists is historically novel precisely in its being among the subjects of a (would be) natural science. As Farquhar seems well aware but contrary to what the majority of Anglophone readers have presumed, Foucault is not claiming here and does not claim elsewhere that nothing like the notion of homosexual preference or orientation can be found anywhere in Western history before the nineteenth century. Nor – and again contrary to what a vast number of readers have presumed – is he claiming that what was at issue prior to the nineteenth century were merely homosexual acts and never the subjects of those acts. His claim is quite different: that prior to the sexological nineteenth century, the scrutiny of such ancestral figures of the homosexual as sodomites fell under the purview of the domains of explicitly nor-mative authorities – those of the church, of the law. Within such domains, the sodomite could thus be conceived as someone who was a "habitual sinner" (Foucault's phrase: *HS1*, 43) or breaker of the law. Only with the ascendance of sexology, however, could the "homosexual" – whether the sodomite or any other sub-species – also be conceived as having a characteristic anatomy and physiology, a "singular nature," a biochemical essence that the positing of a "gay gene" is only one among many latter-day attempts to capture.

Even in *HS1*, Foucault uses the term "homosexuality" to refer to one in the long list of the sorts of sins and offences that canonical and jurisprudential courts were pleased to condemn and punish from the establishment of Catholicism forward (e.g., *HS1*, 38). He uses it much more freely in *HM*, though largely in those parts of the book that did not appear in the much abridged version on which Anglophone readers have until recently exclu-sively had to depend. One of this volume's contributors, Didier Eribon, has found a "contradiction" between Foucault's usage in *HM* and *HS1* (Eribon 2004, 9). I do not, but still agree with another of this volume's contributors, Lynne Huffer, that having the complete version of the former text would much have affected the Anglophone reading of the latter, especially in the United States. Huffer points to both of the presumptions that I have just visited as distinctive of what we might call the Americanization of *HS1*, and further provides an astute account of their appeal. That account centers on the text's reception within the stormy horizons of a scene that had no French counterpart at the time that it was written – the scene of gay and lesbian identity politics. Huffer provides a subtle and compelling argument that the scene in question may have affected the very translation of the text (though it might be mentioned that the translator, Robert Hurley, is not gay). I leave Huffer's full argument aside in favor of one of its central moments. It concerns a passage in the text of which I offered above only an excerpt. In that passage, Huffer notes, Foucault deploys in French the terms *individus* (in the plural), *personnage*, and *figure* in reference to the homosexual. These are the terms that name, as Huffer puts it, "a phenomenon of emergence that Anglo-American readers have interpreted, again and again, as identity," and identity in its politicized sense as connoting "group belonging or affiliation" (2010, 70). Huffer reminds us of Foucault's own skepticism of a politicized identity so construed, but follows with a note on the revisiting of Foucault in his native country. She is in accord with yet another of this volume's contributors, Eric Fassin:

> since the 1990s, French philosophers like Alain Finkelkraut and Frédéric Martel have reclaimed, "recycled," and repatriated Foucault as a "titular figure of French republicanism" and as a philosophical force of "individual" French resistance against what is viewed, sometimes homophobically, as the scourge of American identity politics: the "communitarian wind that blows in the U.S.," as sociologist Irene Théry so derisively puts it. (Fassin 2005b, 226; quoted in Huffer 2010, 71)

I don't wish to place my own interpretive allegiances with the communitarian Foucault any more than with the regallicized republican Foucault, but simply to emphasize that his conceptual transatlantic round trip is a cardinal case in point of the decontextualizations and recontextualizations that conceptual apparatuses are fated to suffer – or enjoy – in their travels.

The moral of this very brief and partial cautionary tale (which could be supplemented by a review of the fate of the circulation of Foucault's conception of discourse) consequently is not that one inevitably misuses Foucault in not following his tracks of research, ideas, schemas, stipples, and instruments to the letter. The moral is rather that, whether agreeing or disagreeing with him, appropriating him or amending him, one is well advised to be as sure as possible of what one is actually doing.

The Order of Things to Come

The scholars collected in this volume do not agree on every point. They have diverse analytical and substantive orientations. They hail from diverse disciplines even as they do not hesitate to cross disciplinary boundaries – with Foucault and by means of him. This said, they devote themselves neither to hagiography nor to mere commentary. Instead, they demonstrate – sometimes more, sometimes less polemically – the many respects in which Foucault's project of a historical, critical ontology of ourselves, in our presence, remains generative and continues to yield compelling insights. They further demonstrate that such an ontology of the present is restricted to no particular terrain, but instead ranges widely and on paths that frequently intersect.

The six essays that constitute the first part of the volume address the question of the use – and abuse – of Foucault in general terms James Laidlaw offers a sustained consideration of what Foucault's thinking through of the co-constitution of freedom, relations of power, and the historical and sociocultural contingency of the subject has to offer to the foundations of an anthropology of ethics – and how additionally it is in danger of being distorted almost beyond recognition. His argument reaches well beyond the domain of the anthropology of ethics alone. In his reflections on the notion of *déraison* (unreason) in *HM*, Ian Hacking provides us with a lesson on one way to read – and a few ways not to read – the relations among Foucault's terminology, analysis and rhetoric, from *HM* forward. In doing so, he reminds us of one of the most crucial elements of Foucault's skepticism of anthropological universals – a skepticism toward the unity of reason as such. Lynne Huffer further pursues the historical and conceptual dynamics of the relations among unreason, madness, and reason itself in *HM* and beyond in her critique of what to her mind is Jacques Derrida's fundamental misreading of, and indeed failure to notice, the undermining at once of Cartesian and Hegelian rationalism that Foucault undertakes from the very first pages of his first major book through *HS1*. Through a juxtapositon of Roland Barthes' *Lover's Discourse* and *HS1*, Didier Eribon underscores at once the intellectual power and the present relevance of two friends' and fellow travelers' undoing of the axiomatics of the "Freudo-Marxist" humanism reigning in France when they were at the height of their careers. He further throws down the gauntlet (Huffer joins him) before scholars who would in one way or another attempt to reconcile Foucault and the psychoanalytic tradition and its distinctive brand of humanism, whether Freudian or Lacanian. Colin Koopman ventures into what are in fact the currently vexed philosophical territories of the debate over whether Foucault should be read as an heir to the transcendental analytics of the Kant of the Three Critiques or as an heir to the empirical tradition of the historicists. My own introductory taking of sides in that debate is obvious. Koopman, for his part, doesn't seek to resolve the debate, but rather to suggest a pragmatic alternative – Foucault as the forger of a path of "critical empiricism" that may come as close as Foucault ever came to what he hoped his critical ontology of ourselves might produce – a new figure of truth. Adapting Foucault's conceptualization of biopolitics in conceptualizing our currently pervasive "infopolitics" and what becomes of us in its midst, he offers a compelling illustration of what such critical empiricism can illuminate. John Forrester offers a robust portrait of Foucault as the muse of desubjectivation – a must if we're to get beyond the ossifications of the subject that surround us and so inhibit our very capacity to engage in a critical, historical ontology of ourselves. For Forrester, Foucault is a muse who, should we attend to him carefully, takes us beyond such ossifications, not least among them our petty academic (and not so academic) preoccupations with our particularity, our individuality, our distinctive stamp, our conviction that we are indeed an island all our own in the mocking waves of a common sea.

The contributions that follow in the second part of the volume capture in more substantive detail the most salient of the many analytical purposes to which the Foucauldean corpus is currently being put – or could be put – in the name of a critical ontology of ourselves. Like Eribon, Eric Fassin follows Foucault in addressing sexuality as an inescapably political issue, and as inescapable as it is because it is at the core of biopolitical technologies of power. Would Foucault have been amused or merely bored by the current debates in France surrounding "gay marriage"? Fassin entertains both possibilities, linking them to Foucault's relative disinterest in, or perhaps suspicion of, the normative dimension of the invention of new modes of human relationships (and his favoring in this regard of the consideration of homosocial over heterosocial modes of our relating to one another). Juxtaposing the arguments of *HS1* with those of the contemporaneous lectures on race that we now have in English in *SMBD*, however, he argues that Foucault is of considerable help in further clarifying the political and sociocultural dynamics – an intersecting and mutually reinforcing dynamics – of the sexualization of race and the racialization of sex and sexuality evident not merely in the controversy over gay marriage (and integral to them, the controversy over gay adoption) but also in debates over the status of "non-French" immigrants, those subjects who, like so many immigrants elsewhere, are subjects who aren't quite accorded the status of being political or ethical subjects of good or even of any recognizable standing. A critical empiricist, if not in so many words, and broadening Fassin's purview further, Cary Wolfe takes a stand against the metaphysical dissolution of the biopolitical into the zoopolitical in such authors as Giorgio Agamben, at once to reiterate the nuances of Foucault's conception of the biopolitical and to locate the realization of the nomos of the zoopolitical in the realm of the animal slaughterhouse. In doing so, he carries forward a historical and critical ontology of ourselves to subjects beyond the strictly human.

Laurence McFalls and Mariella Pandolfi put Foucault's conception of biopolitics to the service of supplementing Weber's classic

articulation of the modes of legitimate domination. To his triad
of the charismatic, the traditional, and the bureaucratic, they add
a fourth. Drawing on Foucault's insights, they argue persuasively
that biopolitical technologies of power – in neoliberalism, technologies at least as characteristic of humanitarian non-governmental
organizations as of the classic welfare state – rest with and rely
upon "therapeutic domination" to justify their policies and their
interventions into and often at odds with sovereign technologies of
power. They fashion distinctive subjects of domination as they do
so. The "sick," the "damaged," the "vulnerable," the "displaced"
subject is their target. Who could complain? Who could indeed –
but it's because of so little complaint that neoliberalism has its way
with us, promising (in the ultimate analysis) an economic fix for
every structural misfortune that we might find ourselves having to
endure from one apparent crisis to the next. McFalls and Pandolfi
see little light at the end of this tunnel – except the light that might
come from the cultivation of critical ontology as the exercise of an
ethics of the care of the self and others.

Acknowledging the disparities but also pressing the affinities between aspects of Foucault's and aspects of Marx's critical
enterprises, Toby Miller undertakes a (very spirited) analysis of
other dimensions of the justification – one might better call it
the marketing – of biopolitical neoliberalism. He takes up two
pitches: one the hard-sell of neoliberal policies and visions in an
increasingly corporatized university – which almost all of us who
are academics hold near but not at all dear to our hearts; the other
the soft-sell of a kinder, gentler neoliberalism on the reality show
Undercover Boss. He is less inclined than McFalls and Pandolfi to
look to the ethical domain for light. He does not indeed offer
much light, but refuses even so to abandon the critical voice that
Foucault might well have recognized as the voice of the modern
Cynic (for more on which, see very shortly below).

In modulated contrast, Paul Rabinow sees at least some light
in Foucault's later reflections on the cultivation of a critical ethos
that could direct us as thinkers and doers beyond the condition
of *stultitia* – that aimless restlessness that all too many of us (and
perhaps not just those of us who are academics) know very well.
He juxtaposes the understated rhetoric of Foucault's inquiries

into Stoic technologies of the self to Gerhard Richter's parrying at once with his critics and with the recent past. He reads the poetics of Richter's paintings of the Baader-Meinhof group as culminating in metalepsis, a revisionary trope that in some small part at least lessens the stultifying weight that the past imposes on the present. Foucault's critical genealogy of *stultitia* and Richter's metaleptic portraiture of terror and suicide thus prove to share a similar purpose. Both strive to reveal existential possibilities in a near future that would not simply be a repetition of the past. When effective, they can both afford us some glimmer of hope.

My own essay is a complement to Rabinow's. It examines the works and days of Constantine Cafavy in developing Foucault's late suggestion that modern artists are the heirs of ancient Cynicism: as scandalously honest as Diogenes before them, but "after nature" in a double and distinctively modern sense of the term. They aspire to the crafting of an ethos in accord with nature, but also beyond it, an ethos that would be able to know itself in part as a creature of its own making. By his own admission, Cavafy did not and could not succeed in completing the task he undertook. He could only write. With the critical genealogist and the metaleptic portrait-ist, however, he was at least able to fashion the lyrics of an ethos of passion-in-action that, he hoped, would some day be able to emerge full-fledged.

What Is To Be Done? Neither severally nor jointly do the contributors provide any revolutionary response to Lenin's great question. If they have any response in common, it is a resolutely plural response that, in its plurality as in many other respects, is in a recognizably Foucauldean spirit: work, still more work.

Postscript: Suggestions for Further Reading

The themes that we have already visited are still in play: archaeol-ogy (Quadflieg 2006; Vigo de Lima 2010); biopolitics (Blencowe 2012; Morton and Bygrave 2012; Rabinow and Rose 2006); the body and the subject (Bourdin 2008; Bührmann and Ernst 2010; Courtine 2012; P. Miller 2007; Rose 2006); discipline

(Brunon-Ernst 2012; Cicchini and Porret 2007; and see Fassin's, Koopman's and Miller's chapters in this volume); genealogy (Huffer 2010; Lightbody 2010–11; Shoemaker 2008); governmentality (Binkley and Capetillo 2011; Bröckling et al. 2011; Dean 2010; Inda 2006; Larrinaga and Doucet 2010; Miller and Rose 2008). Ethics – whether Foucault's own or as the topic of his later writings – is fast emerging on the analytical horizon (Dupont 2010; Faubion 2011; Heyes 2007; Markula and Pringle 2006; McGushin 2007; Mokaddem 2004; O'Grady 2005; O'Leary 2006; Veyne 2010). We further meet Foucault the theorist of space (West-Pavlov 2009). We meet Foucault the philosopher: all-around (Lightbody and Dalvi 2012); of aesthetics (Tanke 2009); of the archive (Gehring 2004); of art (Tanke 2009); of the political (Kelly 2009). Lexicographers of various sorts are cataloguing Foucault's vocabulary (Ajavon et al. 2004; Revel 2008; Taylor 2011). Theorists of management and organization have been familiar with Foucault for well over a decade (McKinlay and Starkey 1998), feminists for more than two decades (e.g., McNay 1992, 2000; Sawicki 1991). Theorists of education (Peters and Besley 2007; Peters et al. 2009) and nursing (Habermann and Uys 2006) have called on him. At least one kinesiologist has called on him (Andrews 2008). Theologians have begun to call on him as well (Carter 2008; Galston 2010; Hardt 2005; König 2006; Tran 2011). Founded in 2004, *Foucault Studies* is just what its title declares it to be. It's not quite what one would expect – or perhaps it is quite what one would expect – of a thinker whom anthropologist Clifford Geertz once counted among our "all-purpose subversives" (1983, 3).

Part I

Object Lessons

1

The Undefined Work of Freedom: Foucault's Genealogy and the Anthropology of Ethics

James Laidlaw

> It is necessary to free oneself from the sanctification of the social domain as the sole instance of reality and to cease to consider as no more than wind the thing that is essential in human life and in human relations, namely thought.
> – Michel Foucault (*DE4*, 180 [*PPC*, 155]; cited in Veyne 2010, 97)

Until a little over a decade ago, Michel Foucault's writings were most conspicuously influential among anthropologists in attempts to understand the dynamics of domination and resistance under colonial and post-colonial states and political dimensions of modern knowledge practices. Guided by these interests, anthropologists mostly referred to Foucault's early and mid-period writings (especially *OT* and *DP*). More recently, a growing anthropological interest in morality and ethical life has involved more attention being paid to his later "genealogy of ethics." While it would be wrong to say any distinct schools have emerged in the anthropology of ethics, the literature does divide roughly into those who claim morality as a hitherto understudied domain of life, identifying culturally variable "different moralities" as objects of study for a new sub-discipline (e.g., Howell 1997; Barker 2007; Zigon 2008; Heintz 2009; Sykes 2009), and those who go further to argue that ethics is a pervasive aspect of human life that social theory as currently constituted is largely ill-equipped to comprehend (e.g., Mahmood 2005; Evens 2008; Laidlaw 2010; Lambek 2010; Faubion 2011).

The sociologist Zygmunt Bauman (1988, 5) had more of a point than most would wish to acknowledge when he described sociology in particular, and social theory in general, as the "science of unfreedom." Though few of us like or dwell on the fact, social explanation, as it is standardly understood, can be any good only insofar as we can discount the ethical dimension of people's conduct. Invoking "the social" – or "ideological state apparatuses," "the global system," "neo-liberalism," "colonialist discourse," or whatever – can be supposed to explain why people do one thing rather than another only insofar as their experience of freedom of decision is deemed illusory. This is why social scientists have so rarely felt the need actually to deploy any concept of freedom in their analyses. Bauman himself, commissioned to write on freedom as a "concept in the social sciences," explicitly rejects this possibility, as he does various points of view from which freedom might be thought to be an important aspect of the human condition, in favor of the view that what is of sociological significance, and a proper object of sociological attention, is the peculiarly modern and parochially Western ideology that values freedom so highly (1988, 28–9). The anthropology of ethics has at least already achieved enough to "provincialize" that assumption. But the conceptual challenge remains.

John Stuart Mill famously observed that political economy is premised on an abstraction from the complex reality of human motivation and action. It treats of human action, he wrote, only insofar as people act in the pursuit of wealth and "makes entire abstraction of every other passion or motive" (1864, 137). Equipped only with the concepts and standards of explanatory adequacy of "the science of unfreedom," anthropology will remain in a position still more dismal than Mill's economics: able to treat of human conduct only by abstracting from its ethical dimension. It is not then an oversight that anthropology, as many have remarked, has largely and in spite of itself neglected the study of morality. With only these conceptual resources, ethics must remain necessarily outside our purview, and an anthropology *of* ethics must be a contradiction in terms.

Is it necessary to remind ourselves that the remarkably tenacious hope that a "dialectic of structure and agency" that would suffice to make this problem go away (as in Bourdieu 1977, Giddens 1979, and Ortner 2006) remains stubbornly unfulfilled? This way of conceiving the problem accepts from the outset that social explanation must be at the expense of a recognition of agency, since the latter is conceptualized as being in a zero-sum relation with the efficacy of "larger structures." This, I suspect, is why authors writing in this vein have mostly not dared to describe that which they wish to "recuperate" for what they sometimes call "the acting subject" by the name of freedom. In the absence of the promised synthesis, the best we get is a to-ing and fro-ing recognition of the "force" first of one and then of the other end of the polarity.

The reason an anthropology of ethics is more than merely a new sub-discipline, then, is that for it to succeed requires the development of a notion of explanatory adequacy – of what an effective "social explanation" might be – that does not redescribe the conduct of responsible agents as the effects of causal "forces." This, obviously, requires making "freedom" a part of our conceptual vocabulary: not just an object of ideology critique but a concept we think about and also think with. In what follows, I shall try to show that Foucault's later writings provide an ethnographically usable conception of freedom, which the very idea of an anthropological engagement with ethical life requires.

The single most far-reaching – but still largely unappreciated – conceptual innovation in Foucault's later works is his rethinking of the concepts of power and freedom, such that they are not defined negatively in relation to each other, and in which the latter emerges as both a ubiquitous social and historical fact and a central term in the analysis of how subjects have historically been constituted.

The radicalism of the late Foucault in relation to some dominant assumptions of "social theory" is still so little understood that he is routinely invoked, both by admirers and detractors, as if it were logically unproblematic simply to bolt his concepts onto analysis framed largely in loosely Marxist (or, equally implausibly, psychoanalytic) terms. So anthropological journals overflow with assertions about the role of "neo-liberal governmentality" or "the apparatus of disciplinary power" in the functioning of "late capitalism." This is so common that its sheer oddness goes unremarked. It is true that there is almost nothing about which Foucault is unambiguously consistent in all his writings. But antipathy to Marxism (as to psychoanalysis) comes pretty close. We all ought to know the name of the brilliant exegete who achieved a comprehensive synthesis between these apparently antithetical intellectual projects, and to whom so many anthropologists and others routinely refer to justify mingling of their terminologies. But no such figure exists, and that synthesis has never been realized.

It is true that *DP* can plausibly be read, in Marxist terms, as attributing the changes it describes to their functionality for a developing capitalist economy. But *HS1* (published just one year later) explicitly rejects any such argument, and overturns the then-accepted radical consensus, which Foucault labels "the repressive hypothesis," that the demands of the capitalist economy for a pliant workforce had fuelled increasingly severe sexual repression. Foucault countered (1) that the period had seen no such thing, but an increasingly imperative "incitement" to discourse about sexual matters; (2) that the resulting "discursive explosion" saw the constitution of "sexuality," the idea of the subject's defining essence being revealed in its desires; (3) that power had therefore come preponderantly to take not the negative form of repression but positive techniques for the elicitation of desires; and finally (4) that projects aiming at the "liberation" of desire therefore constituted not in any serious sense a challenge to the prevailing configurations of power, but instead their intensification.

This final point was a rejection of a perennial complement to sociological determinism: the ideal of "liberation" as a perfectly unconditioned state achieved by removal of all constraint. This ideal, which no doubt has theological roots, had recently enjoyed a polymorphous efflorescence in French intellectual life, including the diffusely contradictory fantasy of 1968, "it is forbidden to forbid" (Bourg 2007), and the projected insurrection by Deleuze and Guattari's (1983) "desiring machines." While *Anti-Oedipus* was an internal critique of psychoanalysis conducted within a historical-materialist framework, Foucault's historicizing of desire broke the bounds of both Marxist and psychoanalytic thought. As Grace (2009: 53) concisely summarizes, the latter's account of sexuality entailed "a new, non-Marxist ontology of contemporary society." Foucault was later to remark that the importance of 1968 lay in the fact that the new concerns it threw up could not finally be addressed in a Marxist framework, although that is initially what the insurgents of the time sought to do (*EW1*, 115), so that its longer-term effect was the decline of Marxism, and a greater receptivity to his own work (*EW1*, 125; cf. also *EW3*, 268–70). In general, his genealogy of ethics constitutes the most profound repudiation of historical-materialist and determinist social theory, in favour of the irreducible importance of reflective ethical thought. Although he only put things in these terms towards the end of his life, Foucault attributed his coming to see the importance of this to his reading of Nietzsche in the early 1950s, and his consequent break with "the double tradition of phenomenology and Marxism" (*EW1*, 202).

The completion of the first volume of *The History of Sexuality* left Foucault with two compelling questions, which oriented his later writings and shaped the development of his genealogy of ethics. The first was how to complete his reconceptualization of power. He had called for the rejection of the negative "juridical" model of power as external constraint, in favor of recognition of the productivity of power as a constitutive aspect of all social relations. But if there never could be relations from which power would be absent, how then to conceptualize freedom? What is freedom, if not the absence of power? Freedom should be thought, Foucault was now suggesting, not to be in a zero-sum external relation to power, but as an aspect of the configuration of power relations. Aware that this was counter-intuitive, when viewed from within the assumptions he was asking us to abandon, Foucault revelled in the apparent paradox: "power relations are possible only insofar as the subjects are free . . . If there are relations of power throughout every social field, it is because there is freedom everywhere" (*EW1*, 292). This is why Foucault's later interest in freedom was not, as some have supposed, a change in his interests. There could be no question of a *move* in focus from power to freedom, because he had come to see that the latter is not a separate subject matter. Equally, freedom was not to be imagined as a state – the circumstances that will prevail once we have conquered power – that could be secured by any social arrangements, institutions, or laws (*EW3*, 354–5). It will always be something exercised through the medium of relations of power. "This is why I emphasize practices of freedom over processes of liberation" (*EW1*, 283).

The second question bequeathed to Foucault's genealogy of ethics by the analysis in *HS1* was: what are the sources of the kind of subject to whom the repressive hypothesis seemed so intuitively persuasive, the "desiring subject"? How had we come to think that the essence of our being – that which we might imagine "liberating" – lay in our desires? "What had to happen in the history of the West for the question of truth to be posed in regard to sexual pleasure?" (*PK*, 209). The projected further volumes in the *History of Sexuality* series were therefore to describe "how it comes about that people are told that the secret of their truth lies in the region of their sex" (*PK*, 214). The exercise was genealogical, tracing back to find a place and time where the self was not given, in a truth discovered by examining one's desires, but instead was produced by the subject through active self-constitution. To do this, Foucault developed a number of conceptual resources, including a formal analytic for the analysis of techniques of the self (*HS2*, 26–8; *EW1*, 263–6), but the most important for us here are his concept of subjectivation and his distinction between moral codes and ethics.

Foucault used the verb *asujettir* (subjectify) and the noun *asujettissement* (subjectivation) to refer to how subjects are formed in power relations, including how the self acts on and shapes itself, therefore not merely "subjection," as many translations of Foucault have suggested, still less the outcome of mechanical processes of "interpellation" into structures, as in Althusser (1971) and those who, like him, speak of "subject positions" being occupied by a "subjectivity without a subject" (Badiou 2005, 66). Foucault made clear that he did not believe in "a universal form of subject that one could find everywhere" (*FL*, 452), nor therefore in any notion of the subject as sovereign or original, but his thought is equally incompatible with the universalism of Lacanian psychodynamics, or of the sort that Althusser wove into Marxist theorizing.

Processes of subjectivation, including what Foucault called "techniques of the self" and "practices of freedom," which individuals may take up from the rules, styles, and conventions in their cultural milieu, do actually make something real, and the question of the role subjects play in their own constitution is an empirical historical one. The point of his genealogy of ethics was to show how subjects have been made, historically, in radically different ways. So "the subject" is something of which one might have a history, but not a general theory (*HS1*, 82; *PK*, 326).

The distinction, within any historically particular form of moral life, between moral codes and ethics, is central to Foucault's genealogy. *HS2* begins, in a classic Foucault move, with a revision of a commonly accepted narrative, this time the idea that the transition from the pagan world to Christianity was one from a "more relaxed" sexual ethic to greater strictness, caused by the introduction of Christian notions of sin. Moral concern and uneasiness about sexual acts long predated Christianity, as Foucault illustrates with four concerns expressed by authors throughout the period: fear that sexual emission might weaken the body; idealization of fidelity within marriage; perceptions of moral danger in same-sex relations; and the idea that heroic abstinence might give access to wisdom (*HS2*, 15–20). We should resist the reflex whereby uneasiness about sexual acts is "too readily attributed to Christianity (when it is not attributed to capitalism or 'bourgeois morality'!)" (*EW1*, 90; also 179–80; 254). There is a profound change in ethics over this period, but the advent and spread of Christianity did not explain this, and it consisted not merely in greater "strictness" but in ethical concern taking a different form.

Foucault distinguishes between what he calls moral codes – rules and regulations enforced by institutions such as schools, temples, families and so on, and which individuals might variously obey or resist – and ethics, which consists of the ways individuals might take themselves as the object of reflective action, adopting voluntary practices to shape and transform themselves in various ways (*HS2*, 25–32; *EW1*, 253–80). Ethics, including these techniques of the self and projects of self-formation, are diagnostic of the moral domain. Among all the various institutionally sanctioned laws, rules, interdictions, or values, it is those that are associated with

modes of self-formation that we might sensibly regard as "moral"
(*HS2*, 28). But although thus intimately related, moral codes and
ethics must be distinguished analytically, because they may change
independently. Generally, moral codes themselves are more similar
across societies and historical periods than are the forms taken by
ethical practice, and some societies have more elaborate ethical
cultures than others (*HS2*, 30). The transition from pagan to
Christian moralities can only be understood as part of the long
transformation from what Foucault called an "aesthetics of existence" to a "hermeneutics of desire," and in that process moral
codes changed very little: the profound change was in forms of
ethical practice (*HS2*, 30–2; 250; *EW1*, 180; 195–6; 254; 270–1).

Foucault's is by no means the only ethics-morality distinction in
the current literature. At least since Hegel, authors have used the
fact that we have two roughly synonymous words from Greek and
Latin to carve up the general field of moral life analytically, but
the distinctions drawn have not been congruent. The philosopher
Bernard Williams (1985), for instance, draws a distinction that
somewhat crosscuts Foucault's, but from a fundamentally similar
Nietzschean perspective. The anthropologist Arthur Kleinman
(1999), sociologist Zygmunt Bauman (1993), and political philosopher Ronald Dworkin (2000) each draw distinctions which come
close to reversing Foucault's (so for Kleinman the subtle moralities embedded in life-worlds are distinguished from the formalistic
ethics of professional, universalizing discourse) but are part of intellectual projects that are so radically different from Foucault – all
much more overtly prescriptive, for example – that there must be
little risk of confusion. The same is not true, and therefore a little
more needs to be said, of the work of the anthropologist Jarrett
Zigon.

The distinction between morality and ethics Zigon offers as
a framework for the anthropology of moralities (2007; 2008;
2009; 2010) is presented as an elaboration based on Foucault's.
Moreover, Zigon's stated objective of taking morality seriously
as a distinctive aspect of social life is in sympathy with Foucault's
project. But I think Zigon goes crucially wrong in his formulation, so that he ends up undermining that ambition. The resulting
confusion appears to be one of the factors that motivates Faubion

to avoid the term "moral" in his own reformulation of the same Foucauldean distinction (2011). I am less willing to cede the use of the word. Besides, getting clear about how Zigon's formulation differs from Foucault's helps us to appreciate the latter's conceptual originality.

Morality, in Zigon's account, is generated from three sources (2007; 2008, 162–4). Institutions (churches, states, corporations, etc.) all "proclaim the truth or rightness of a particular morality," and do so as if these views were unquestioned internally, although in practice this is generally not so. Secondly, what Zigon calls "the public discourse of morality" consists of "all those public articulations of moral beliefs, conceptions, and hopes that are not *directly* articulated by an institution" – so those found in the media, in political protest, the arts, philosophy, and informal teachings within families. Finally, morality exists as embodied dispositions, the habitual ways in which people act without even noticing what they are doing, that enable them unconsciously to act morally most of the time. This multiplicity of sources of morality is one of the reasons people can unwittingly live with conflicting values. Morality is, then, "a kind of habitus or an unreflective and unreflexive disposition of everyday social life" (2008, 17).

What Zigon calls "ethical moments" occur when all this is disturbed. Something unexpected occurs that makes unreflective everyday life impossible. Situations of this kind, which Zigon, borrowing a term from Heidegger, calls "moral breakdown" (2007, 136), force people to stand back from their normal, ongoing mode of living, and to reflect and make choices. "Thus, it is only occasionally in everyday life that one actually has to stop and consider how to act or be morally appropriate. These moments are what I call ethics" (2009, 260). The choices available are always limited, by prevailing discourse and ideology, but these are nevertheless moments of freedom and creativity in the exercise of choice between a range of possibilities. And when these moments are over, and the subject returns to the "equilibrium" of unconscious embodied practice, his or her morality will have altered, though in most cases only to an imperceptibly small degree.

Zigon claims that "moral breakdown" is "what Foucault called problematization" (2008, 18, 165; at 2007, 138 it is merely "similar to" it), but actually these concepts are very different. For Foucault "problematization" is not the name of distinct episodes or events in the world. It is an aspect of his genealogical method (*HS2*, 11; *EW1*, 117). For any period or milieu, in any text or discourse, one should look for what it is that is problematized, for what is the subject of concern, reflection, and uncertainty, and one should investigate the form which that concern and reflection takes. Something always will be problematized in that sense, and the key to understanding a form of life lies in its precise delineation. So, as Foucault describes in *HS2* and *HS3*, the nature of the marriage bond and a man's management of his household on the one hand, and affective relations between adult men and youths on the other, were problematized throughout antiquity, but the form and content of the concern they elicited changed profoundly (*HS2*, 14–24). Thus for Foucault, ethics and morality are two aspects of one phenomenon, in which ethics may change while moral codes remain constant (and, in principle, vice-versa), so that it makes no sense, as it does in Zigon's terms, to regard ethics and morality as distinct states, or to ask, is this morality now in an ethical moment or not?

So Zigon's ethics-morality distinction has a different structure from Foucault's. To see the consequences, let us follow Foucault in his analysis of the aesthetics of existence in classical Athens. This analysis begins from the distinctive way that pleasure was problematized.

Once again it was not, as some have thought, that, in contrast to a later Christian suspicion of pleasure as a temptation to sin, classical Greeks were relaxed about pleasure. Pleasure was problematical, but the form of concern was distinctive. Skillfully managed, bodily pleasures such as food, alcohol, exercise, and sex were an integral part of a well-lived life, if used in the right proportions and on the right occasions. Danger lay in injudicious use, especially in excess. Foucault contrasts the required attitude of judicious and skillful management of pleasure with the different attitude of suspicion, requiring relentless and searching vigilance, that would characterize later Christian culture (*HS2*, 41). Importantly, the kind of care the Athenian problematization called for did not require imperative rules, or lists of permitted and prohibited acts, but "prudence, reflection, and calculation" (*HS2*, 54).

Sex was distinctive among pleasures only because of its intensity, which added to the challenge in exercising moderation with respect to it. It was a matter of degree. Sexual pleasures gave rise, then, to no distinctive moral problems. Instead, the problematization of sexual pleasure took distinct forms in four broader domains: dietetics, what one ate and drank and related matters to do with the maintenance of bodily health such as exercise and response to weather conditions; economics, or management of a man's household, including his relationship with his wife and others under his care and command, such as children and slaves; erotics, passionate relations with boys; and finally the idea that abstinence might give privileged access to truth. Importantly, the kind of self-mastery that one might aim at in these four domains took different forms. There was not yet a unified area of problematization of "the flesh," the forerunner to "sexuality," as there would be in the early Christian world (*HS2*, 251; *PK*, 460).

Ethical work consisted in establishing a proper relation to one's desires, by establishing domination by the rational and reflective over lower parts of the self: keeping one's desires "under command" (*HS2*, 63–77). This moderation was characterized as freedom (*HS2*, 78): as to be free was to be no one's slave, so a man should control his desires, rather than being a slave to them. To control one's desires, one needed knowledge, but not the knowledge that would be required for the later hermeneutics of desire – of one's own inner state, one's secret thoughts and desires – but knowledge of the world one lived in – of what foods could safely be indulged in during which kind of weather, of the proper recognition of the dignity of a wife's station, of how to punish slaves effectively, and how to approach a beautiful boy without giving offence – and one needed also the experience and judgment to use such knowledge wisely.

So the story Foucault tells of the slow transition from this aesthetics of existence to the hermeneutics of desire is one of change in the form of ethical problematization: from one requiring the active shaping and styling of the self into a skilled and reflective user of one's pleasures, to the relentless inquisition of the self, to seek out and overcome the unacknowledged desires that might lead one into sin. It is in the crystallization of the latter form of problematization that Foucault locates the beginnings of the subject of modern sexuality (*HS2*, 32; also *HS*, 485–7).

Crucial to the way Foucault tells this story is his analysis of affective relations between adult men and male youths in classical Athens. He observes that far from being "tolerated," as some had argued, these relations were subject to "an extraordinarily complex problematization," sometimes assigned the very highest moral value, at others condemned. Why this intense ethical concern? (*HS2*, 187–93; *EW1*, 257).

It was not because both parties were male, nor because there was a gulf of status and power between them. A man's relations with his wife, or for him to have sex with his slaves (male and female), excited no such anxiety. Nor was it a matter simply of difference in age (*HS2*, 193–4). The concern was about relations across the somewhat ritualized divide between a mature adult and a youth who had not formally finished his education (*HS2*, 194–7), and the singularity of these relations lay in the fact that the boy was himself soon to become an adult citizen. Where the ethical question for a man in sexual relations with women or slaves was how to achieve moderation in the exercise of power over others (*HS2*, 82–3; 150–1), with a youth it was the more delicate question of how, in a relation of power, to accommodate the freedom of the other (*HS2*, 199; 203). The first question – moderation in the exercise of power over others – was the analogue of the established theme that a just ruler exercises dominion over his desires. The ruler who is a slave to his desires, subjecting himself to ungoverned appetites, will be arbitrary, cruel, and tyrannical with his subjects (*HS2*, 75). The political analogue of relations between men and boys was not those between rulers and ruled, but the matter, of especially intense concern in a participatory democracy, of the cultivation of responsible citizens.

This discourse entirely presupposed that sexual relations were a scene of assertion and acquiescence in the taking and giving of pleasure, and therefore, among other things though not exclusively, of domination and submission and the enactment of status. The singularity of these "erotic" relations lay in the fact that unlike husband and wife, both were free in relation to each other, so "in a position of reciprocal independence and between whom there was

no institutional constraint, but rather an open game (with preferences, choice, freedom of movement, uncertain outcome)" (*HS2*,
202). It was crucial that the boy's immature status was temporary;
it was not, and crucially ought not to be, a permanent part of his
nature, and so the relation should not simply reproduce and fix the
current disparity between them in active and passive roles. It had to
accommodate the emerging maturity of the boy. Indeed the older
man's role was in part to help that change come about, hence the
figuring of these relations as part of boys' education. Education
always presupposes an initial incapacity in those to be taught, but if
this implied active-dominant and passive-subordinate roles, these
were roles whose proper trajectory was for that difference to be
overcome. So this form of love was always temporary, lasting only
until the boy achieved maturity, when ideally it would become a
life-long intimate friendship (*HS2*, 201; 224–5). Thus the exercise
of moderation in such a relationship consisted of conducting it in
the light of, and aiming towards, that outcome, with both parties
mindful of the honor of the status of adult citizen the boy was
destined to attain.

So the intense problematization of these relations had nothing
to do with "our" morals or politics concerning sexual orientation.
It expressed a set of concerns about conduct in relations between
free citizens. They were sometimes praised, for the cultivation of
brave, loyal, independent, free men; where they were condemned
it was for the corruption of youth, not as the revelation of an
"abnormal" sexual subjectivity but as a case of bad education and
corrupt politics. This then is where the two questions left by *HS1*
coincide: the historical context where subjects were constituted in
terms other than the desiring and confessing self was also where
the problem of freedom was posed and addressed, at the level of
public discourse, not as a matter of liberation but as a question of
how to make oneself into a free subject among others in relations
of power, "the purposeful art of a freedom perceived as a power
game" (*HS2*, 253). Ancient Greek ethics of the arts of existence
were developed only "for the smallest minority of the population"
(*HS2*, 253) and for this and other reasons are structurally not usable
by us; but they could be made a resource that we might think with.
This is the genealogist's task, which is also the anthropologist's: to

describe diverse forms of ethical reflection and practice so as to bring their distinctiveness – together with the contingency of those we take for granted – into focus, in such a way that we might learn not only about but also from them.

To bring out the significance of the conceptual rethinking of freedom, as configuration rather than inverse of power, which Foucault undertakes in his genealogy of ethics, let me return briefly, by way of contrast, to Zigon's superficially similar proposal for the anthropology of moralities. Despite the use of Foucauldean terminology and apparently congruent morality-ethics distinction, Zigon's conception of moral life owes more to Heidegger's phenomenology (authentic being-in-the-world is unreflective, though for Heidegger it was inauthentic) and to Bourdieu (social systems are reproduced through habitus "behind the backs" of their subjects). The result is that Zigon returns, with the "science of unfreedom," to an essentially negative conception of freedom as space for "choice" opened up, in situations of "moral breakdown," by the temporary ineffectiveness of habitus and structured discursive authority. And this means that while for Foucault the ends and objectives of historically variable projects of self-formation have themselves been historically variable, Zigon's commitment to a version of Heideggerian phenomenology leads him to a singular and normative conception of the necessary telos of ethics. "Moral breakdown" puts one in a state of inauthenticity (2010, 9), and "ethical moments" are resolved "so that one can return to the unreflective and unreflexive comfort of the embodied moral habitus or the unquestioned moral discourse" (2008, 18). This normative conception of moral life – "being existentially comfortable in one's world, which is another way of saying living sanely in one's world" (2010, 5) – preempts what should be the empirical questions of what might prompt episodes of especially concerted ethical reflection, and whether the exercise of reflective self-constitution is more vigorous, pervasive, and thoroughgoing in some socio-historical contexts than others.

Foucault's conception of the telos of ethics is markedly different. There is an unmistakeably positive evaluation in his reading of ancient Greek erotic relationships as leading a youth from tutelage to independence, as there is in his reading of Kant on

Enlightenment (*EW1*, 316) as an attainment of reflective maturity through the "undefined work of freedom." Nevertheless,
in accordance with his general thoughts on the relation between
philosophy and politics (e.g., *EW3*, 111–33; 465–73), which could
scarcely be farther from Heidegger's (on which see Faye 2009),
Foucault's genealogy holds back from being ethically or politically prescriptive, and his conceptualization does not commit us
anyway to his evaluations. This is important for an anthropology
of ethics, because if it is part of our calling to correct the parochial
assumption that freedom has only ever been seriously valued or
realized in the modern West, it is equally important that we give an
account of forms of ethical life in which freedom may be at best a
highly qualified value, and where the ideals for which people strive
may be achieved only, in some senses at least, at its expense (e.g.,
Laidlaw 2002; Mahmood 2005; Humphrey 2007). While Foucault
tied ethics conceptually to an *exercise* of freedom, he explicitly recognized that the ideals towards which ethical life has been directed
have been historically and cross-culturally very diverse, and so give
no warrant for supposing that any *pursuit* of freedom is intrinsic to
ethics as such.

2

Déraison

Ian Hacking

40 Years After[1]

I began to read Michel Foucault in 1968, and it gave me a new way to do philosophy. I was working in Uganda, when almost exactly 40 years ago my friend André Gombay handed me, as a gift, *Madness and Civilization*. This was the newly published British edition by Tavistock, 1967, of the abridgment published in the United States by Pantheon in 1965, which was in turn an enlargement of the French abridgement published by Plon in 1964. On the copyright page of the Pantheon edition, we are told that the original French book was "*Histoire de la Folie* © 1961 by Librairie Plon." The original book was indeed published by Plon, under the aegis of Philippe Ariès, after Gallimard had rejected it. But its title was *Folie et Déraison. Histoire de la folie à l'âge classique* (*FD*) (xi + 674 pages long). One fairly literal translation would be *Madness and Unreason: A History of Insanity in the Age of Reason*. Note that this is exactly the title used for the English translation – except with "Unreason" replaced by "Civilization"!

When the book was republished by Gallimard in 1972, it became *Histoire de la folie à l'âge classique* (*HFAC*). *Déraison* had disappeared. Only recently was the entire text translated into English, under the title *History of Madness* (*HM*), but then "Unreason" had never figured in an English title.

My unnecessary foreword to the recent English translation of the full text tells some more of the tale of titles, and how they kept changing (Hacking 2006a). Noting changes in Introductions and other varia, I went so far as to say:

> I suggest that you hold in your hands two distinct books. The main text of each is the same. It is all too easy to compare these two books to the two Don Quixotes invented by Borges (1962), the one written by Cervantes, the other, identical in words, written much later by an imagined Pierre Menard. Despite the words being the same, so much has happened that the meaning is different.

I will not defend that here. I want only to talk about *Déraison*, which gradually but so effectively disappeared from the sequence of titles that it has now gone altogether, even from the French.

"*Déraison*," the Word

A few years ago I was confirming with French colleagues, and also with a Canadian master translator, that the word *Déraison* has little vernacular use. *Le Grand Robert* classifies it, in a by no means admiring way, as "literary." *Déraison* is not quite as uppity as "Unreason," but it does have little role in ordinary speech.

Which is not to say you cannot use it. I was nevertheless taken aback when on April 6, 2006 the front page of *Libération* had the enormous headline "*Déraison d'Etat*" [State unreason]. The occasion was the student rebellion occasioned by the proposed law about the contracts for first-time employees, the *contrat première embauche* or CPE. The sub-headline is: "*Avec Chirac impuissant, la rivalité entre Sarkozy et Villepin paralyse l'exécutif, alors que les syndicats exigent l'abrogation du CPE d'ici dix jours*" [with Chirac powerless, the rivalry between Sarkozy and Villepin paralyzes the executive

branch, at a time when the syndicates are insisting on the abrogation of the CPE ten days from now].

Quite aside from *Déraison*, the headline reminds us of another
fact. An English newspaper would not speak of the "Idiocy of the
State" but of the idiocy of the government. Foucault said that
one of the things he learned when he came to America was the
concept of "government"; he had hitherto thought in terms of the
French category of the state. Hence the notion of governmentality,
which was taken up by many readers, often in a way that I regard
as overblown.

In both the short and long translations of the book on madness,
déraison is translated as "unreason." My attention was drawn to this
word when I was skimming the typescript of the recent translation
of the big book. I was uncomfortable because I thought many of
the sentences in the old translation of the abridgement were much
better than their equivalents in the new translation. I did not read
the book with a view to checking the translation, not at all. But I
did notice a few blatant defects and suggested corrections. In particular, when Michel Foucault wrote *Déraison* with a capital D or
italics or both, the translator had turned the capital into lower case
u, and de-italicized.

The word did not pass unnoticed when the book first appeared
in 1961. Daniel Defert cites Maurice Blanchot: "In this rich book,
unremitting in its necessary repetitions, *presque déraisonable*, we are
present, with much pleasure, at a collision between the University
and *la déraison*" (Defert 2001, 29).

Michel Foucault put *Déraison* up front in his original title,
and often capitalized or italicized the word in his text. Later he
removed it altogether from his title. That is my topic here: What
was that all about? I begin with a confession. I am not sure what
Foucault meant by this unusual word. We find an early trace
of it in the title of an unpublished draft that Daniel Defert says
was written by hand in April 1954 on the back of a duplicated
(cyclostyled) copy of his first book, *Maladie mentale et personnalité*
[mental illness and personality]: "There are three adjacent experiences: dreaming, drunkenness and unreason" (Defert 2001, 23).
In all honesty, I do not well understand what he was trying to
say.

The Timing of *FD*

Foucault showed a first version of *FD* to Jean Hyppolite at the end of 1957. Hyppolite urged Foucault to turn it into a thesis. He did so, and by the end of 1958 showed the result to Georges Canguilhem, who said, "Don't change a word. It's a thesis"! It was examined on May 20, 1961 and published the same month. The French wars of the 1950s in Vietnam and Algeria had been lost, and the Republic put them behind it. The 1960s were the most fertile decade of French intellectual life in the twentieth century. *La Pensée sauvage* [The savage mind] of Lévi-Strauss in 1962. Barthes. Gilles Deleuze published seven of his books during the 1960s, and Jacques Derrida established himself. Foucault's book on madness was one of the first flowerings of this unique decade.

1961 also marks the critical rethinking of madness in the English-speaking world. There was the polemical assault on psychiatry by Thomas Szasz, *The Myth of Mental Illness* (Szasz 1961). Erving Goffman, one of the greatest of sociologists, published *Asylums*, an analysis of what actually happens in institutions for the insane (Goffman 1961). Goffman was also after larger game, for he thought that the insane asylum was just one of many "total" institutions in which a group of people was separated from everyone else, and hence evolved a peculiar locked-up form of social life. He was thinking of boarding schools, merchant ships, nunneries, prisons.

In 1960, R.D. Laing's *The Divided Self: Sanity and Mental Illness* had made radical proposals that schizophrenia was a product of the family situation, not of the demented patient (Laing 1960). None of these authors knew of each other at the time. Laing's collaborator David Cooper coined the name "anti-psychiatry" and later wrote the preface to the British edition of *MC* (Cooper 1967).

The book was, then, launched in France as part of a gigantic wave of new thinking, which coincided with brilliant Anglophone voices challenging established psychiatry. All over the world Foucault was read as a critic of psychiatry. That always happens when an author establishes that something we think of as inevitable is the product of a series of historical events. Foucault's next book was *NC*. That was finished by November 1961, although it was not published until April 1963. The English translation (*BC*) was published in 1973. Foucault thought of it as the remains of, or fallout from, the book on madness – its *chutes*. He tried to assert in the first pages that in writing about madness, and now in writing about medicine, he was not intending to favor one system over the other but to say what made all of them possible at various times.

History of Madness really was, as the first preface says, the beginning of a long series of investigations, and not just a study of madness. That preface was written in Hamburg in February 1960, that is, after the vast book was finished. It was among other things a forecast of what Foucault was planning to do. Innumerable themes found here were to be reworked over the next decade or so, not least among them being that of archaeology, announced at the start. Exclusion. Conditions of possibility. The coming into being of a sense of history. Time, yes, but also the spatial character of all Foucault's analyses is prefigured.

One thought in the 1960 preface was to be decisively dropped. It was the idea of there being some underlying truth about madness. The idea that there is in madness an *inaccessible primitive purity* (*DE1*, 192 [n.a.]). Those words, the original preface, were suppressed in the 1964 abridgement. Perhaps that was a result of Derrida's famous critique, which was launched on March 4, 1963. I believe those deleted words are true to one thought that went into the book. The romantic fantasy lurks here, the purity of the possessed, those who not only speak the truth in paradox, like the fools in Shakespeare, but who are themselves the truth.

Today we all know about Foucault's complete rejection of the idea of an essential self. Hence it is strange to read David Cooper's preface to *MC*, where he argues that anti-psychiatry can do better than psychoanalysis. At great cost to a patient, analysis can at best "achieve a workable conformism – defined as normality, maturity, developedness." Instead, said Cooper, "The truer goal . . . must be in terms of a recognizable synthesis of the field of social practicality with it secret antithesis – the autonomous assertion of pure, spontaneous Self" (Cooper 1967, ix). That capital S "Self" is not, I believe, wholly false to *FD* as originally conceived.

Everybody knows that Foucault withdrew any suggestion that

there might be some pure, ahistorical, madness, but I think it is worth looking again at what he withdrew. I will make a suggestion of the movement in several stages. I suggested we are looking at two books, with identical texts. The title and the preface are changed. Something called unreason – *déraison* – is highlighted in the first book but not the second. Unreason is the voice of art, while madness is not. Foucault's concept of archaeology itself changes its role. All these evolutions may be connected with the way in which Foucault liberated himself from an obsession with madness as inaccessible primitive purity.

Titles

The exact title in 1961 was *Folie et Déraison: Histoire de la folie à l'âge classique* [Madness and unreason: history of madness in the classical age]. Daniel Defert, Foucault's long-time intellectual colleague, companion, and posthumous editor, laid emphasis on the exact title of the original. That first title is a bit like Alice's Cheshire Cat, of which nothing is left but the grin, namely the subtitle. The unabridged book as it now is published in English is called *History of Madness*. Even the classical age, or the age of reason, has disappeared.

A trip through the successive titles is a gradual disappearing act, which points us to the disappearing *déraison*. At the beginning, "Unreason" was right up there alongside "Madness," and it was capitalized in the original French title, as it sometimes is in the book itself. The paperback abridgement of 1964 suppressed half of the first preface. On the cover we see only *Histoire de la folie*. On the title page the full 1961 title appears in block letters, but with *Folie et Déraison* in smaller print than *Histoire de la folie*. Fading, like the cat. This version was translated into many languages, while only an Italian publisher did the unabridged book.

For the 1965 English version, Foucault restored some material that he had cut from the 1964 French abridgement. For a moment, as we shall see, part of the cat's face flickered back. The English slightly less abridged abridgement reinserted a chapter that is all about unreason.

Finally, in 1972, we have the "doubling." The text of 1961 was printed again, untouched. The old preface was now wholly deleted. A new preface was written, that's the one that speaks of doubling, plus some appendices presenting the debate with Derrida. The main title *Folie et Déraison* was dropped. The latest doubling is the complete English translation of everything: text, old preface, new preface, appendices, plus further appendices, plus an introduction by the editor, plus a foreword by me saying there are two books in the reader's hands.

Unreason

Everybody professing to be in the know has long dismissed the English version of 1965/1967 as a callow abridgement. In fact it is highly instructive, for Foucault decided to reinsert into his abridgment the most vivid assertions about Unreason to be found in the big book. They include passages like this:

> All that madness can say of itself, *is merely reason*, though it is the negation of unreason. In short, *a rational hold over madness* is *always possible* and *necessary, to the very degree* that *madness* is *nonreason*.
>
> There is only one word that summarizes this experience: *Unreason*: all that, for reason, is closest and most remote, emptiest and most complete; all that presents itself to reason in familiar structures – authorizing a knowledge, and then a science, which seeks to be positive – and all that is constantly in retreat from reason, in the inaccessible domain of nothingness. (*MC*, 107; italics in original)

Foucault continued immediately by playing on *éblouissement*, dazzlement:

> And if, now, we try to assign a value, in and of itself, outside its relations with the dream and with error, to classical unreason, we must understand it not as reason diseased, or as reason lost or alienated, but quite simply as reason dazzled. (*MC*, 107–8)

What follows is itself deliberately so dazzling that we, or at any rate I, am left in a state of bedazzlement.

> Unreason is in the same relation to reason as dazzlement to the brightness of daylight itself. And this is not a metaphor. (*MC*, 109)

In a footnote (*MC*, 243; *HM*, 619 fn. 75), Foucault says that he is using the word almost exactly as Pierre Nicole did in one of his essays published in the 1670s, where he is wondering about the relation between the heart and all the dazzlements of the mind (*éblouissements de l'esprit*). "Dazzled reason opens its eyes upon the sun and sees nothing; that is, it does not see." A second footnote close on the heels of the first tells us that this is a Cartesian theme often taken up by Malebranche; "to think nothing is not to think; to see nothing is not to see" (*HM*, 619 fn. 76).[2]

In this single paragraph we get an amazing play of "day and night" (italicized), which is

> no longer the fatal time of the planets; it is not yet the lyrical time of the seasons; it is the universal but absolutely divided time of brightness and darkness. A form which thought entirely masters in a mathematical science. (*MC*, 109)

By the end of the paragraph we have been taken from "Cartesian physics, a kind of mathesis of light," through Racine and Georges de La Tour. It is stupendous stuff, to be kept on the back shelf away from sophomores. A display of Foucault's brilliant eye for paint; in the paintings of La Tour, "the page holding the torch reveals under the shadow of the vault the man who was his master – a grave and luminous boy encounters all of human misery; a child brings death to light."[3] Then, in the twinkling of an eye, to the plays of Racine. All interspersed with observations about madness itself: "the madman, conversely, finds in daylight only the inconsistencies of the night's figures; he lets the light be darkened by all the illusions of the dream." Then a pause, a break in the page, and a half-way summary, in two brief paragraphs:

> Madness designates the equinox between the vanity of night's hallucinations and non-being of light's judgments.

And this much, which the archaeology of knowledge has been able
to teach us bit by bit, was already offered to us . . . in the last words of
Andromaque (*MC*, 111–12; yes, *archaeology of knowledge.*)

The tour de force continues:

The curtain that falls on the last scene of *Andromaque* falls on the last
great tragic incarnations of madness. . . .
    This had to be the last scene of the first great classical tragedy; or
if one prefers the first time in which the classical truth of madness
which is the last of the pre-classical theatre. A truth, in any case, that
is instantaneous, since its appearance can only be its disappearance; the
lightning flash is seen only in the advancing night. (*MC*, 112)

After two more pages brilliantly re-enacting tragedies, we return
to unreason:

The movement proper to unreason, which classical learning followed
and pursued, had already accomplished the whole of its trajectory in
the conclusion of tragic language. After which silence could reign, and
madness disappear in the – always withdrawn – presence of unreason.
    What we now know of unreason affords us a better understanding
of what confinement was. (*MC*, 115)

Foucault does not mention dates here, but of course he expected
his readers to know them. The "great confinement" of Chapter 2
was said to be in 1656; *Andromaque* was first produced in 1667. De
La Tour is earlier; his most famous painting in the Louvre is from
1645 (St. Joseph) and he died in 1652.
    One can imagine several explanations for the fact that all this
material was deleted in *FD*, and reinserted in *MC* in English.
The argument with Derrida is the explanation I have most often
encountered, but that does not wholly satisfy me. We read simply
these words in the front matter: "The author has added some
material from the original edition."

Unreason and Art

Unreason was not wholly pruned from *FD*. The whole book is about the play back and forth between madness and unreason.

> In the classical period, the awareness of madness and the awareness of unreason had not separated from one another. The experience of unreason that had guided all the practices of confinement so enveloped the awareness of madness that it very nearly permitted it to disappear, sweeping it along a road of regression where it was close to losing its most specific elements.
>
> But in the anxiety of the second half of the 18th century, the fear of madness grew at the same time as the dread of unreason: and thereby the two forms of obsession, leaning upon each other, continued to reinforce each other. (*MC*, 210–11)

Still later we read that since the end of the eighteenth century "the life of unreason" no longer manifests itself except in the flashes of lightning found in works like those of "Hölderlin, Nerval, Nietzsche and Artaud," which resisted "through their own strength that gigantic moral imprisonment." Standard French history and iconography of psychiatry represents Pinel casting off the chains of madmen soon after the Bastille had fallen. That is a story of liberating the mad. Here we are told instead that the new "moral" treatment of insanity was also the imprisonment of unreason, which had flashed so openly on the canvasses of Hieronymous Bosch.

Casual reference books diagnose Hölderlin as a schizophrenic poet, Nietzsche as a philosopher suffering from dementia caused by terminal syphilis, and Artaud as a bipolar (manic-depressive) playwright. Nerval killed himself: We say suicide is caused by severe depressive illness. It is of course a central thesis of this book that far from these being inevitable ways of conceiving of four very strange men, it requires a specific system (yes, system) of thought to categorize these men – and myriad other people – in terms of mental disorder. But Foucault does not pander to the thought that genius and mental disturbance are of a piece. The art of these men, as he shouts at the end of the book, is the exact opposite of insanity: "Where there is art, there is no madness" (*là où il y a oeuvre, il n'y a pas folie*) (*MC*, 288–9).

Alongside madness there is also unreason. It had much fuller play in the Renaissance, an unreason that Foucault evokes by the ship of fools and the paintings of Bosch, especially the temptation of Saint Anthony. (Foucault is marvelous with paintings: look how much he draws from Goya at the end of the book, and one knows the tour de force on Velasquez that opens *OT*.) He even says that in the early days of confining the mad, the experience of unreason smothered something else, the consciousness of madness.

But then two distinct obsessions emerged, he tells us, madness and unreason. The fear of one and the dread of the other were tamed in the asylum. The life of unreason could break through the resulting silence only in the voices of those who were classified among the mad but who, through their art, rose above madness to act as standards to which the sane and classifying world is unable to answer. There is not a truth in madness, but the voice of unreason shows what neither madness nor reason can express. That is another version of the romantic fantasy of the possessed, those who not only speak the truth in paradox, like the fools in Shakespeare, but who are themselves the truth. The fantasy leaps out at you from the 1961 preface, words suppressed in *FD*: ". . . a madness whose wild state can never be reconstituted" (*DE1*, 192).

Archaeology

I have already quoted that strange passage where we first find the expression "the archaeology of knowledge":

> Madness designates the equinox between the vanity of night's hallucinations and non-being of light's judgements. And this much, which the archaeology of knowledge has been able to teach us bit by bit, was already offered to us in . . . the last words of *Andromaque*. (*MC*, 111–12)

Foucault in fact spoke of archaeology in the part of the preface to the 1961 book that was retained for the 1964 abridgement. There is a moving paragraph stating that there is no longer a common language by means of which madness and reason can communicate:

> the constitution of madness as a mental illness, at the end of the eighteenth century, affords the evidence of a broken dialogue . . . The language of psychiatry, which is a monologue of reason about madness, has been established only on the basis of such a silence.
>
> I have not tried to write the history of that language, but rather the archaeology of that silence. (*MC*, xii–xiii)

An archaeology of silence: neither a history of psychiatry, nor an archaeology of psychiatric discourse. Foucault wanted to understand how a certain absence of discourse became possible. The theme of silence was reiterated in the first sentence of Chapter 2, the famous chapter called "The Great Confinement": "By a strange act of force, the classical age was to reduce to silence the madness whose voices the Renaissance had just liberated, but whose violence it had already tamed" (*MC*, 38). What is absent? The voice of unreason, of which there is a simulacrum on those artworks that were the veritable paradigms of genius in the 1960s, Nerval, Nietzsche, Hölderlin, and above all Artaud.[4]

Déraison at the End

Psychology was inexorably made part of the dialectic of modern man grappling with his truth, which is to say that it will never extinguish what is at the level of known facts. But in these wordy engagements of dialectic, unreason remains mute, and oblivion overtakes these great silent rifts in man.

★

There are others, however, "losing their way, and wanting to lose it forever." This end of unreason, moreover, is transfiguration. (*HFAC*, 549 [*HM*, 530])

The words, deleted in the abridgement, occur right at the end of the last chapter of the book, "The Anthropological Circle." They precede the dazzling discussion of Goya and Sade, which concludes with a passage that was left in the abridgement:

> For Sade, as for Goya, unreason continues to watch by night; but in this vigil it joins with fresh powers. The non-being it once was becomes the power to annihilate. Through Sade and Goya, the Western world received the possibility of transcending its reason in violence, and of recovering tragic experience beyond the promises of dialectic.
>
> *
>
> After Sade and Goya, and since them, unreason has belonged to whatever is decisive, for the modern world, in any work of art: that is, whatever any work of art contains that is both murderous and constraining. (*MC*, 285)

This in turn leads on to the well-remembered statement cited earlier: where there is a work of art, there is no madness.

Deleuze encouraged Foucault to develop this theme, which led to *"La folie, l'absence d'œuvre"* [Madness, the absence of oeuvre] in May 1964 (Foucault *DE*, 440–8). It is an irony that the word *déraison* does not occur in this text, even though it was the idea of *déraison* that prompted it to be written.

Notes

1   This chapter was originally prepared for a conference held in 2008. Hence the "40 years after" in reference to 1968. Its current publication, now a few years later, does not take into account the most recent scholarship stimulated by the reappearance in English of Foucault's original full text.

2   Arnold Davidson observed that Emmanuel Lévinas's thesis of 1959, *Totalité et infini. Essai sur l'extériorité* [Totality and infinity: essay on exteriority] (Lévinas 1961), also makes great play with dazzlement. Tyrus Miller remarked that there is much reference to dazzlement in Hölderlin, and gives as an example the poem *Wie wenn am Feiertage.*

He further notes that Jean Laplanche's thesis of 1959, *Hölderlin et la question du père* (Laplanche 1961), is also attentive to dazzlement.

3   Catherine Soussloff tells me that Caravaggio was another artist deemed to be mad because of his "use of darks and lights" – she refers us to the *Lives* by Giovanni Pietro Bellori (1613–1696), *Le vite de' pittori, scultori et architetti* (1672).

4   For a slightly different interpretation, see Colin Koopman's book on Foucault (Koopman 2012), where the absence is not so much the voice of unreason in itself as it is the dialogue between reason and madness that constituted unreason.

3

Foucault's Evil Genius

Lynne Huffer

The perpetual threat, that is, the shadow of haunting . . . like the
phantom or fiction of an Evil Genius . . .

– Jacques Derrida (1994)

"I have never written anything but fictions," Foucault once said
(*PK*, 193). In *HM*, Foucault rewrites the classical fiction of the
great deceiver introduced by Descartes in his *First Meditation* as the
evil genius. At stake in Foucault's rewriting of this Cartesian fiction
is an ethics of alterity that can be discerned not only in *Madness*
but across Foucault's entire oeuvre. Beginning with the Cartesian
evil genius of the classical age, Foucault will eventually challenge
a modern grid of sexual intelligibility popularized by Freud but
made possible a century earlier by Hegel. Retracing Foucault's
critiques of Freud and Hegel back to Descartes in *History of
Madness*, I show in this chapter how Foucault uses the fiction of
the evil genius to expose unreason as a backdrop for the teleological unfolding of madness-as-sexuality in the modern age. As I will
show, the evil genius is another name for unreason, a term whose
unintelligibility – and thus its difference from madness – exposes
Foucault's ethics of alterity. To be sure, to name unintelligibility
is a paradoxical gesture: if unreason is the evil genius, unreason

also makes nonsense of reason's equations. In its unintelligibility, unreason cannot appear, except in a language whose rational order betrays it. Unable to appear as itself, unreason thus only appears as fiction. In *HM* and *HS1*, one of those fictions is the evil genius.[1]

This chapter will trace the emergence of the evil genius across the pages of *HM* to its final appearance on the last page of *HS1*. My goal is to explain the historical reversal of madness into sexuality Foucault describes at the end of *HS1*: how "we have arrived at the point where we expect our intelligibility to come from what was for many centuries thought of as madness." I will show that the evil genius is crucial to our understanding of modern sexuality in its connection to classical madness; my reading involves a careful parsing of the distinction between madness and unreason in *HM* and an interrogation of the transposition of madness into sexuality at the end of *HS1*. In that process, I will expose the specifically temporal disorientation of unreason: how the evil genius scrambles time and the Hegelian *"possibility of history"* (*HM*, xxxi). As Foucault writes in the 1961 preface to *HM*:

> *The necessity of madness* is linked to that decisive action that extracts a significant language from the background noise and its continuous monotony, a language which is transmitted and culminates in time; it is, in short, linked to *the possibility of history*. (xxxi)

Ultimately, as a time-scrambler, Foucault's evil genius is a double's double: it doubles both the Cartesian original and its double as a new evil genius in Hegel's *Encyclopedia*. As a time-scrambling double, it is a fiction that exposes the temporal dimensions of ethical alterity. In Foucault's hands, the evil genius estranges us from a Hegelian teleological order that finds its completion in us. The evil genius is a "perpetual threat," as Derrida puts it, but its ethical force resides in its capacity to disrupt *our* time. Out of sync with itself, the evil genius reminds us that "discourse is not life: its time is not your time" (*AK*, 211). The evil genius is a fiction whose alterity undoes us.

Some Evil Mind, All Powerful and Cunning

My pursuit of the evil genius across *HM* begins in its ending, in us, on the very last page of *HS1*. There we find a snapshot of the story *HM* tells, about a modern rational moral subject, born in the classical age, who tries to capture as knowledge a guilty sexual nature that haunts him. Importantly, in *HS1*'s penultimate paragraph, Foucault specifies that the *dispositif* [equipment, device, matrix] of sexuality is a sudden Freudian "reversal" (159) of an earlier *Cartesian* matrix. Alluding to Descartes' evil genius hypothesis in his invocation of a Freudian "good" and "bad genius" that grants Freud a "secular" power "worthy of the greatest spiritual fathers and directors of the classical period," Foucault implicates Freud as the direct descendant of a Cartesian father.[2] By linking the good/bad sexual moralism of secular modernity to the good/evil morality of a theistic classical age, Foucault exposes a Manichean moral cosmology at the foundations of the modern *ratio*.

This shift at the end of *HS1* returns sexuality to the famous cogito scene in *HM*, where Foucault's surprising and original claim about the cogito's exclusion of madness generated a debate, begun by Derrida, about philosophy's relation to reason and madness, the problem of language as a rational system, and the historicity of events (Derrida 1978). In shifting the focus of Foucault's "Cartesian moment" away from the cogito to the evil genius, I want to consider how Foucault redeploys the Cartesian fiction as a fiction of his own.[3] Indeed, in a book filled with quasi-fictional characters, the evil genius plays a leading role. I track the evil genius through the byways of *HM* in order to expose a shifting but crucial distinction between madness and unreason. That distinction is crucial not only to the central epistemological question Foucault foregrounds in the book – how can reason know madness? – but also, relatedly, to ethical questions about the exclusions and openings that stem from reason's birth in unreason.

What is the fiction of the evil genius, and how does Foucault rewrite it? As is well known, in the *Meditations*, the evil genius is the most radical form of doubt Descartes introduces in his step-by-step procedure for determining what it is possible to know with certainty. Having systematically sifted certainty from error with regard to the senses and the landscape of dreams, Descartes proposes to go even further by doubting the metaphysical foundations of his sensory and non-sensory knowledge. At the end of the *First Meditation*, he imagines that God is replaced by an evil genius who unravels all the certainties he has just established: "I will suppose that, not God who is the source of truth but some evil mind, who is all powerful and cunning, has devoted all their energies to deceiving me" (1998, 22). With this brain-in-a-vat hypothesis – the *Matrix*-like fiction that we are all controlled by an external device that makes us believe in an illusory reality – Descartes raises the possibility that our conscious experience of our bodies, mathematics, and the world could be a fiction and therefore false. Of course, for Descartes, the metaphysical fiction of the evil genius fails to hold up in the face of its divine counterpart: God. In the *Sixth Meditation*, Descartes rejects the "hyperbolic doubts" introduced by the evil fiction as "ridiculous" (70), ultimately relying on "the immense goodness of God" (69) as the foundation of his belief in reason and its methods for achieving certainty. As Derrida puts it, Descartes "seeks to reassure himself, to certify the Cogito through God, to identify the act of the Cogito with a reasonable reason" (1978, 58). In his reliance on God as a "good" genius whose power is greater than that of a "bad" one, Descartes links goodness with truthfulness, for it is the "good" God's *non-deception* that differentiates it from evil. Thus reason's certainty – its capacity for knowledge that is free from error – is achieved through an explicitly moral decision that chooses good over evil as the path to truth. As Descartes says of the "good" genius: "for from the fact that God is not a deceiver it follows that . . . I am completely free from error" (1985, 70).

Descartes' fiction of the evil genius thus frames *HM* as a story about the cogito's exclusion of madness as an ethical exclusion "in the landscape of a moral universe" (*HM*, 71). In their confinement, the mad, like the poor, are "treated as moral subjects" (*HM*, 60), divided into "good and bad" (60). Explicitly taking up the evil genius theme *after* the drama of the cogito and the great confinement, Foucault exploits it as a fiction: like the Ship of Fools, it is "half-imaginary, half-real" (*HFAC*, 11; *HM*, 22, translation modified), the "space of possibility" (*HM*, 156) out of which is invented "the space of confinement in the imaginary geometry of its morality" (*HM*, 86). In appropriating the evil genius, Foucault both repeats and transforms what Descartes had presented as a hypothetical device in the rhetoric of hyperbole, refashioning it as the limit of our capacity for truth. In Foucault's rendering, the evil genius "designates the peril that beyond man might prevent him in a definitive manner from reaching the truth, a major obstacle threatening . . . reason itself" (*HM*, 157). Contrasting "the brilliant light of the truth of the Cogito" with "the shadow of the evil genius" and its "perpetually threatening power" (*HM*, 157), Foucault's device for doubting the metaphysical ground of all knowledge is not as easily dismissed as Descartes would like: his evil genius "haunts the whole movement of Descartes' *Meditations*" (*HM*, 157).

As a haunting force, Foucault's fiction exposes the "hollowed-out void" (*HM*, xxix) of a disorienting modern world without God. If the evil genius in Descartes is a thought experiment – "a voluntary exercise" (*HM*, 571), as Foucault insisted in his response to Derrida – *Foucault's* evil genius is a ground-shattering force. Deprived of the theological structures on which Descartes depended to distinguish true from false and certainty from error, the modern evil genius "restor[es] to our silent and apparently immobile soil its rifts, its instability, its flaws" (*AK*, xxiv). But *pace* Derrida, this rift-restoring force is *not* "the possibility of a total *madness*" (Derrida 1978, 52); it is, more precisely, "the possibility of unreason" (*HM*, 157): a threat to reason itself.

To be sure, the evil genius might appear at first glance to be roughly the same as Derrida's madness. And indeed, Derrida implicitly equates madness with unreason in his analysis of a logos that splits "reason and madness (unreason)" (1978, 38) in a futile resistance to "the evil genius of non-meaning" (56). But at the moment of the evil genius's first appearance in *HM*, Foucault aligns the evil genius with unreason to insist on its difference from madness: "*madness* could never form the essence of *unreason* for the classical age" (*HM*, 157), he writes, and "no *psychology of madness* could ever claim to tell the truth about any *form of unreason*" (157). Foucault's evil genius – the possibility of unreason – is not bound, like madness, to the expression of truth as certainty. Foucault's fiction of the evil genius turns the structure of certainty and error underlying Cartesian truth into nonsense: as reason's threat it will exceed the bounds of the voluntary exercise introduced by Descartes on the path to certainty. Using a hyperbolic rhetoric of his own, Foucault will out-fiction the Cartesian fiction. In doing so he will also dissolve the borders of a world bounded by the cogito, a *res cogitans* whose excluded madness will be internalized in modernity as the repressed truth of *homo psychologicus*.

Importantly, Foucault's redeployment of the evil genius as a figure of unreason allows him to frame *HM* as a story about a rational exclusion of madness that is also moral. Specifically, against the "backdrop" (156) or "free horizon" (157) of an evil genius that haunts the thinking subject, Foucault retells the story of the cogito as a story about an epistemic, ontological, and institutional exclusion which separates and confines an alterity so threatening that, in Descartes, it could not be entertained except through its containment *within* the opening pages of the *Meditations*. "Descartes speaks so little, and so quickly, of madness" (*HM*, 558), Foucault will write later, reflecting on his disagreement with Derrida. And because Descartes has already established the cogito – I think therefore I am – in his *Discourse on the Method*, the *Meditation* is but a reprise, as an individual exercise, of a proposition that has already been established.[4]

Far from being a faithful repetition of Descartes, Foucault's evil genius doubles Descartes' fiction to expose and critique "an ethical view of unreason" (*HM*, 159) whose exclusionary violence continues to haunt modern rationalism. In his response to Derrida, Foucault points out that Descartes' exclusion of madness signals the juridical disqualification of the mad as subjects, a disqualification that renders them nonexistent in reason's logic and its "merciless language of nonmadness" (*HM*, xxvii). Importantly, as a voluntary exercise, Descartes' evil genius hypothesis buttresses his efforts to "gloss over the *fact* of madness" (*HM*, 158) through his rationalist method of systematic doubt. Foucault, by contrast, exposes the fact of madness Descartes glossed over by uncovering the documented, archival traces of the actual exclusion and confinement of the mad. Further, Descartes depends on God in an "ethical choice" (*HM*, 159) to blot out "the *fact* of madness" (*HM*, 158). Evading madness, he also evades the metaphysical "black spot that threatens all truth" (157), the tear in the fabric of reason "through which unreason might rise up and challenge the sovereignty of higher forms of consciousness" (157) and morality. At the same time, the practice of abstraction and exclusion that allows reason to evade "the *fact* of madness" (158) has a ricochet effect: in excluding madness, the cogito conjures the "possibility of unreason" (158) as a "threat in its most abstract and universal form" (158). That threat is the evil genius. And so, through the practice of exclusion and confinement, Descartes conjures and exorcises an evil genius in a circular attempt to dominate and control the threat behind a *fact* he simultaneously creates and glosses over.

This paradoxical logic generates an evil genius not easily contained as a hypothetical device to be deployed at will by an agential subject. In Foucault's rendering, the evil genius haunts the *Meditations* because it exceeds the already tenuous bounds established by its author, Descartes.[5] As a Foucauldean fiction, the evil genius is "more than the refraction of human finitude" (157); it becomes, rather, "the absolute limit of the incarnation of reason" (158), an external power that threatens "not so much the individual mind as reason itself" (157). Put differently, Foucault uses a *fiction* – the evil genius – to expose the *fact* of a madness that classical rationalism simultaneously evades and produces. Foucault's archivally based insistence on that fact turns Descartes' fiction into a power "half-way between man and God" (157), depriving Descartes of an illusory authorial agency through the character he created to buttress his methodological evasions. Foucault thus reverses the relation between character and author, the evil genius and the cogito: "it is true to say that the Cogito, 'I think therefore I am,' is an absolute beginning, but it should not be forgotten that the evil genius precedes it" (*HM*, 157, translation modified; *HFAC*, 175).

What can it possibly mean to say that the cogito is an absolute beginning *and* that the evil genius precedes it? What are the implications of this seeming contradiction? Both history and metaphysics are at stake in these questions. Contra Derrida, I want to argue that Foucault destabilizes both historical and metaphysical truth claims in his contradictory assertion about the temporal precedence of the evil genius over the cogito as an absolute beginning. In other words, Foucault's evil genius ungrounds the "I think" as both the historical and metaphysical starting point of truth.

First, with regard to history: if history is story in a narrative sense, in the narrative ordering of Foucault's history (the level of the *récit* in narratological terms), it is quite literally true that Foucault's evil genius precedes the cogito. Although it is often asserted that *Madness* "starts" with the Great Confinement and the Cartesian exclusion of madness from the cogito, in fact the Great Confinement does not occur until Chapter Two. On the level of the *récit* [narrative], Foucault's story of madness actually "starts" with an unreason that precedes it. Specifically, in the book's first paragraph we find, in the "large, barren" (3) space outside the city gates where lepers once lived, the "conjuration" (*HM*, 3, translation modified; *HFAC* 13) of their ghosts as a formless haunting. This "new incarnation of evil" (3) is a ghostly background we see only as the shadow cast by the leper's disappearance over history's horizon. This pre-classical "start" in evil's haunting return is the recursive background out of which "the possibility of history" (*HM*, xxxii) and the "necessity of madness" (xxxii) as a "*fact*" (*HM*, 158) is extracted. Importantly, this haunting, recursive, non-originary origin of *Madness* in unreason contradicts Derrida's assertion that Foucault privileges "the singularity of the classical moment" (1978, 42) within a "factual and determined" historicism that fails to interrogate "historicity itself" (42).

But, one might ask, doesn't the narrative precedence of the evil genius still imply a metaphysical anchoring of unreason as the background, *fond*, or substance that gives birth to all that follows? At first glance one can see why Foucault has been read in precisely this way. "fOr the classical age, unreason . . . had a *substantive* function. It was in relation to unreason alone that madness could be understood. Unreason lay beneath it, or rather defined the space of its possibility" (*HM*, 156). But I want to suggest that this seemingly timeless metaphysical structure is in fact a function of a temporal contingency revealed in Foucault's archival method. Foucault shatters metaphysics with the fact of madness, making the present strange in his investigations of a past we can only access through the merciless mediation of reason.

More specifically with regard to time's contingency, Foucault argues that "the necessity of madness" unfolds as language out of a "background noise" that "culminates in time" (*HM*, xxxii). That background noise – the evil genius, the haunted space of the leper that precedes the cogito as absolute beginning – exposes the paradoxical double temporality of *HM* as a story that unfolds in a time that is simultaneously teleological and recursive. By contrast, the I of the cogito as absolute beginning relies on a single, uninterrogated time of history as a telos that culminates in us. By reversing the priority of the cogito and the evil genius, Foucault scrambles that linear conception of progressive time. Destabilizing the cogito, he destabilizes the I whose reason allows him to look back to a before.

Not surprisingly, Foucault links this other conception of time to "the experience of unreason" (*HM*, 363) and explicitly differentiates it from a "knowledge of madness" (363) that he situates "within the direction of nature and history in their development" (363). That "untimely" (363) "time of unreason" (364) is a recursive, murmuring depth: "an unconditional return and an absolute plunge" (364). As madness's "background," unreason makes possible the linear, psychological, man-shaped time of madness "developing along the chronology of a history" (364).

The time of the cogito is the time of madness, which is, as Foucault shows, the time of history. So Derrida is correct in asserting that "the concept of history has always been a rational one" (1978, 36). But Foucault questions precisely the "Hegelian law" (1978, 36) of history Derrida faults Foucault for having failed to question. "History," Foucault writes, "is only possible against the backdrop of an absence of history" (*HM*, xxxi). How are we to read such a sentence if not as a questioning of the concept of history, what Derrida calls "historicity itself" (1978, 42)? And again, that "backdrop" as the "absence of history" makes clear a distinction between the necessity of the cogito's "*fact* of madness" (*HM*, 158) – a fact produced by a moral gesture of exclusion – and the perpetual threat of an untimely unreason that Derrida misses in conflating unreason with madness. Thus, in temporal terms, the evil genius "precedes" the cogito because its nonlinear recursive temporality is the cogito's background, the space of possibility for the "absolute beginning" that is the cogito. The cogito is an absolute "beginning" only from the perspective of the time of madness – that is, "our" time – the rational Hegelian time of history that subordinates "the shadow of unreason" to the light-bringing truth of reason's madness.

What are the consequences of the evil genius's narrative and metaphysical power to unsettle? First, the evil genius gives a name to that which, as madness's untimely condition of possibility, corresponds to the recurrence of past forms in the present: the sodomites of the past who were burned on the scaffold or locked up in hospitals and asylums return, today, as respectable gay men seeking the right to marry. That transfiguration occurs along the "two opposing vectors" (*HM*, 364) of the time of unreason and the time of madness. Simultaneously, the untimeliness of the evil genius threatens the neatness of that first conception because, as a threat to reason and historical time, it challenges the present (and therefore the past) as stable, identifiable anchoring points on a timeline that moves toward its completion in the now. It suggests that we must leave "in suspense anything that might take on the appearance of an ending" (*HM*, xxviii), a "victory" (xxviii), or "a rest in truth" (xxviii). If everything begins with the cogito – I think therefore I am – but that very thinking is preceded by an evil genius which threatens the conditions of possibility of reality itself, that threat hardly goes away in a secular modernity that dismisses such demonic (or divine) fictions with a wave of the hand. Indeed, the ever new incarnations of the evil genius in *HM* and *HS1* haunt the very terms that allow us to make sense of a world. Unlike reason and madness, a pairing that isolates, separates, and speci- fies individuals as certain kinds of subjects and objects (including disqualified, abnormal, and pathologized ones), the evil genius that precedes the cogito makes the transcendental–empirical, subject– object doublet of modern knowledge itself unintelligible. It not only exiles us from the truth of ourselves, as madness does, but it exiles us "from the truth of the world" (*HM*, 350).

To describe this unintelligibility in the language of reason is, of course, to betray it, which is why the evil genius – like all Foucault's histories – can only ever be a fiction, albeit one so powerful it pulls the rug out from under its author's feet. In that fiction, "madness is reason" (*HM*, 184): this too is the "paradox of unreason" (185). And so it is also with the evil genius. If the evil genius is the cogito's "shadow," to speak about it at all in its "substantive function" is to enlist it in a game of truth whose rules are set by reason. To speak is to betray it: to name unreason as if we could know it is, like Descartes, ultimately to dismiss it in an ethical decision disguised as truth. When we play with unreason we engage, like Descartes, in an exercise whose rules are bound to an illusion: the illusion of the cogito whose "victory" (*HM*, xxviii) as history is a Phyrric one.

To speak about the evil genius as if we could know it is, as Foucault puts it, "doubly impossible" (*HM*, xxxii): it is narratively and metaphysically impossible. Which is why Derrida is right to say, as Foucault himself admitted, that *HM* is an impossible book. But it is not speaking madness, as Derrida claims, that is impossible; in Foucault, there is no binary opposition between reason and unreason or, synonymously, between reason and madness but, rather a logic of the fracture that produces a tripartite structure: reason, its madness, and an unreason that haunts them. In that structure, it is unreason that cannot speak.

But if unreason cannot speak, this does not mean it is silent: it is not an inaccessible, metaphysical ground or substance outside of history, as many of Foucault's readers have claimed. Indeed, the opposing temporal vectors of madness and unreason collapse the distinction that would erect an inside or an outside of history. Unreason persists not as silence but as a murmur, as the "space of possibility" (*HM*, 156) for madness and history. That murmur is a function of the double temporality of unreason and madness: not an essence, as Derrida claims, embedded in "the metaphysics of presence" (1978, 60) of transcendental phenomenology, but the residue of contingency, the trace of disappearances, the leper's ghost, the shadow cast in the shape of the past as it falls.

Foucault articulates this concrete, non-metaphysical conception of unreason through the example of language. If unreason is the temporally shifting background out of which language is extracted, we can hear its murmur through the alterations of grammar. As a legible mark that registers change, grammar signals the epistemic shifts that track the contingency of the here and now out of which we speak: the point of reference for a *before* that leaves its mark, as grammar, in the *now*. Foucault asserts that "for the classical age unreason had the value of a noun, and had a substantive function" (*HM*, 156). And so, Foucault writes, "we have lost the ability to understand unreason other than in its adjectival form" (156). What was once a noun is now an adjective: what was once a substance is now an attribute: a modifier, inessential, contingent.

What does it mean to recall a "substantive function" that is no longer: to reveal substance as contingent? Giorgio Agamben reminds us that Foucault once described his investigations of the past as "the shadow cast by his theoretical interrogation of the present" (2009, 54). In its substantive function as a noun, unreason is unintelligible to us: we see it only as a clever device in our own Cartesian game, as the shadow of unreason, as the adjectival trace of that which we repudiate as *unreasonable* in our own investigations of ourselves. We, Victorians, "see the negativity of the madman in the unreasonable" (*HM*, 185), in the adjectival form of an untimely noun we cannot access or apprehend. So doing, we denounce "all that is unreasonable" (185), and turn it into an object of our knowledge. That knowledge of an object is, of course, only an empirical reflection of ourselves as transcendental knowing subjects. Thus the cogito creates a vicious circle where to know unreason is to know ourselves. That knowing (the cogito) casts a shadow, and we turn that shadow into a "dark secret" within us. Thus in our knowledge we are trapped by ourselves, chasing our own inner shadow.

It is in this context that Foucault introduces, in Part Three of *HM*, a "new evil genius" (350). This new evil genius is knowledge repackaged through dialectical reversal and sublation: a science of mind that "brings mystification and clarity at the same time" (350), and which "enchants to the point of extreme disenchantment the truth about the self that man has entrusted to his hand, his face, and his language" (350). As the shadow-borrowing new form of what was once unreason, this "new evil genius" is a Hegelianized Descartes: "an evil genius who operates not when man wishes to accede to the truth, but when he wishes to give back to the world his own truth" (350). This Hegelian "genius," introduced in the crucial pages about *Rameau's Nephew* that open Part Three, will culminate in the Freudian talking cure, where "the possibility of the evil genius no longer lodges in *perception*, but in *expression*" (350). This new evil genius is garrulous and sexy.

A Sexy Evil Genius

From *HM* to *HS1*, Foucault presents the emergence of Freud's *homo psychologicus* as a doubling of the Cartesian moment that gave birth to the cogito. As we have seen, we find a trace of that doubling in the penultimate paragraph of *HS1*, where Freud appears as a "good" or "bad genius" (159) who makes us love sex. In "To Do Justice to Freud," Derrida critiques Foucault's presentation of this Descartes–Freud convergence in reason as not doing justice to Freudian psychoanalysis. If Foucault writes that "psychoanalysis cannot and will never be able to hear the voices of unreason" (*HM*, 511), Derrida argues, contra Foucault, that psychoanalysis "breaks with psychology by speaking with the Unreason that speaks within madness" (1994, 237).

At stake for me here in Foucault's Freudian doubling of Descartes is *not* the question of psychoanalysis per se, but rather the role of sex in a scientific project that produces *homo psychologicus* as a modern cogito. I will therefore focus in this section on what is missed in the snapshot of the Descartes–Freud doubling at the end of *HS1*: namely, the mediating role of Hegel. In "Cogito and History of Madness," Derrida had already complained about "the absence of any precise reference to Hegel" (1978, 36) despite what he saw as Foucault's Hegelianism. In his Freudian return to Foucault in 1991, Derrida revises his view slightly, albeit with a caveat. Noting one reference to Hegel's *Encyclopedia* at the end of *History of Madness*, Derrida writes: "one should . . . pause a bit longer than Foucault did on [the] passage" (1994, 250).

The passage in question is crucial to my story because it is there that the "new evil genius" appears (*HM*, 350). But first, it is worth remarking that the explicit Hegelian reference Derrida notes is announced much earlier, at the beginning of Part Three, in the pages dedicated to *Rameau's Nephew*. Recalling Descartes and "the evil genius hypothesis" (*HM*, 343), Foucault contrasts the Cartesian cogito with Rameau's Nephew, who "knows very well . . . that he is mad" (343). This "evil genius" moment in *Madness* is a Hegelian moment, for it is Hegel who borrows from Diderot the fictional character named Rameau's Nephew as Spirit's dialectical pivot (see

Huffer 2010, ch. 4). Indeed, in *The Phenomenology of Spirit* (1807), Hegel's Nephew functions much like Descartes' evil genius, as "the perversion of every Notion and reality, the universal deception of itself and others" (Hegel 1977, 317). Derrida does not mention this explicit doubling of Descartes in Hegel, nor its connection to the later Hegelian passage from the *Encyclopedia* which Derrida claims, with regret, he has no time to consider. Derrida simply notes that, in Remark 408 in the *Encyclopedia*, Hegel situates insanity as the manifestation of the contradiction within the subject between the particularities of self-feeling and the universalizing unfolding of consciousness guided by reason. Derrida regrets the abbreviated, elliptical nature of Foucault's reference to "these few extraordinary pages of Hegel" (1994, 250) where "a certain Evil Genius (*der böse Genius*)" (250) appears, wishing Foucault had done more to link them "to the great dramaturgy of the Evil Genius that concerns us here" (250). "One should," he writes, "and I myself would have liked to have done this given more time, pause a bit longer than Foucault did on a passage from Hegel's *Encyclopedia*" (250).

Unlike Derrida, I read Foucault's Hegelian ellipses as strategic: a way to use Hegel in order to undo him, recognizing as Foucault did that "we have to determine the extent to which our anti-Hegelianism is possibly one of [Hegel's] tricks directed against us, at the end of which he stands motionless, waiting for us" (*AK*, 23). I take these ellipses as an invitation to draw out the links Foucault himself never made explicit. With regard to the evil genius trajectory I've been tracing, Hegel functions as a pivot between the age of Descartes and the Freudian period. More important, with the dialectical "perversion of every Notion and reality" (1977, 317), it is Hegel who, ironically, makes it possible in modernity to think something other than chronological time: the perversion of historical time in the nonlinear time of unreason. In doing so, Hegel introduces the mechanism of *reversal* that interrupts and complicates the progressive temporality that would link Descartes to Freud in an unbroken line of influence.

To be sure, in the journey of Spirit, the Nephew's perversion of chronological time gives way to its rational sublation in the teleological drive of history. Hegelian time is time-as-we-know-it, time that finds its completion in the present. But Foucault's repeated if ambiguous evocations of an other-than-Hegelian, dedialectized conception of time become less ambiguous if we imagine that conception as the arrest and fracture of the dialectic in the moment of reversal or perversion.[6] Again, that moment is marked in *History of Madness* by the return of the Cartesian evil genius in the time of the Nephew who says "I am mad." That Cartesian return makes possible the "new evil genius" (*HM*, 350) of the *Encyclopedia*, or the doubling of Descartes' evil genius in Hegel. And it is in Foucault's *Hegelian* hands, as "the perversion of every Notion and reality, the universal deception of itself and others" (1977, 317), that the evil genius comes to name a metaphysical ungrounding that Descartes' voluntary exercise could not allow.

Rameau's Nephew thus establishes a Hegelian context for the final appearance of the evil genius in the last chapter of *HM*, "The Anthropological Circle." Describing the four antinomies that disperse the threat of unreason in modern "reflective thought" (519), Foucault hones in on the objectification of madness in modern scientific perception as an organic "disturbance of the cerebral functions" (520). "But," he writes, "madness differs from sicknesses of the body in that it manifests a truth not found in the latter: it reveals an inner world of bad instincts, perversity, suffering and violence, which until then had lain sleeping" (520). The modern "reappearance of madness" (517) reveals "an essential relation to the truth" (517); as such, it reveals more than a simple organic disturbance but rather the old world of unreason: all that had "lain sleeping" as madness was learning to speak "an anthropological language" (516). This "depth" of unreason reemerges in Hegel as another evil genius. Foucault cites Hegel in the *Encyclopedia*:

> Evil is implicitly present within the heart, because the heart, being immediate, is natural and selfish. *It is the evil genius of man that becomes dominant in derangement.*[7]

This moment in *Madness* is crucial not only for its exposure of a *modern* madness that speaks against the "sleeping" background of a persistent unreason, but also for its framing of the dialectical reversal where the classical age's external power of disorder and deception is interiorized as "the evil genius of man" (*HM*, 520).

Let me focus here on the explicitly *moral* terminology we find in Hegel. For it is an ethical perception that differentiates judgments about madness as an organic disturbance from other kinds of bodily sickness, judgments that make possible what Foucault calls "the infamous 'moral treatment'" (522) which, with Joseph Guislain and François Leuret in the early nineteenth century, "used confinement as the major means of submission and repression" (522). Here we find, in Hegel, the doubling of Descartes and the Great Confinement in a new moral treatment of madness.

Foucault's insistence on that part of the *Encyclopedia* where Hegel considers madness in moral terms pinpoints the shift from madness to sexuality that *HS1* makes explicit. Specifically, Foucault describes Hegel's evil genius as an evil *nature* that inserts "guilt in the form of a *sexual* fault" (*HM*, 522) into the natural knowledge that forms the horizon of modern science. The horizon appears, once again, against a background of unreason: unreason as the alterity of nature becomes reason's nature, the nature in which we find our truth. Importantly, Hegel's evil genius is a *guilty* nature internalized in man as "the self-seeking determinations of the heart, vanity, pride, and the subject's other passions and imaginings, hopes, love and hatred" (Hegel 2010, 115). This passage in Hegel reverses the exteriority of Descartes' evil genius, thereby forming a link to Freudian sexuality and the reappearance of the evil genius on the final page of *HS1*. The moral terms of that reversal are important. Foucault describes the "evil genius of man" (520) that "becomes dominant in derangement" (2010, 115) as "wickedness in its wild state" (*HM*, 520), citing Hegel's lines about "this evil implicitly present within the heart, because the heart, being immediate, is natural and selfish" (Hegel 2010, 115; cited in *HM*, 520). So doing, Foucault exposes reason's moral perception of the particularities of nature.

In the *Encyclopedia*, Hegel uses the evil genius to link a morally negative conception of madness with the negativity of a mind "set free into its natural state" (2010, 115). As Berthold-Bond explains in *Hegel's Theory of Madness*, Hegel's ontology of madness is an ontology of origins: "like Freud," Berthold-Bond writes, "Hegel saw madness as a reversion to and recovery of psychic origins: in madness, the mind 'sinks back' into the earliest phases of the development of the soul, the domain of the unconscious play of instincts, or what he calls 'the life of feeling'" (1995, 3). In the dialectic, this life of feeling is "retained and integrated within the rational self" (Berthold-Bond 1995, 3). As Hegel puts it, a conscious subject, "sober and healthy," is able to subsume "each particular content of sensation, idea, desire, inclination" into "its intelligible place in the system" (2010, 115). As "the *dominant genius* over these particularities" (115), the rational subject is guided by the power of "self-possession and of universal, theoretical or moral principles" (115). It is thus the triumph of the universal over the particular that keeps a morally charged madness at bay. But when those principles "lose their power over the natural forces that they usually suppress and keep concealed" (115), then the "earthly throng gets free" (115). Hegel describes those natural forces as an "evil . . . implicitly present within the heart, because the heart, being immediate, is natural and selfish" (115). And thus "it is the evil genius of man that becomes dominant in derangement" (115).

One can see here how the Hegelian logic of the evil genius both repeats and reverses the Cartesian system, where a demonic external force that threatens to deceive us becomes a demonic nature we carry within. In each instance, madness unfolds against a background of unreason. In Descartes, the cogito's instability is exposed by an order whose divinity might easily be demonic.[8] In Hegel, the mind's dialectical journey toward universal knowledge depends on the sublation of a nature whose freedom can just as easily lead us into madness. In the more sweeping terms of *HM* as a whole, the Cartesian theological moral system that pits the good genius of God against an evil genius becomes, after Hegel and the Nietzschean death of God, objectified as the truth of nature.

That process of objectification takes the evil of nature, internalized in man as the evil genius, and transposes it into sexuality. In so doing, the theological inheritance of "guilt in the form of a sexual fault" (*HM*, 522) is neutralized by science. The guilty Hegelian reversion to nature becomes, over time, a "more rigorously objectified" (523) illness, "circumscribed inside the space of a body and invested in a purely organic process" (523). Thus medicine learns to hide "its moral accusations behind the objectivity of observation" (523). Through "serene, distant observation" (523), those rational doctors who diagnose madness in their patients are able to distance themselves from "this evil, this fault" (523) and "the dark power of attraction" (523) that their knowledge implies with the "worrying ambiguity of recognition" (523).

That power of attraction is the power of the evil genius whose shadow our knowledge implies. The power of unreason derives then, not from its metaphysical status outside of history but as a function of our modern, historical knowledge. As Ian Hacking puts it, unreason is the Cheshire Cat that has faded, leaving only the grin of madness to remind us it was there: that grin is the adjectival form of a substantive function we can only perceive as the shadow we cast looking back from a present whose seeming stability is an illusory ideal (Hacking 2006a, ix).

Let me conclude by highlighting the present-day biopolitical and ethical stakes of this fictional destabilization of subjectivity and truth. What does it cost to tell the truth? "At what price can subjects speak the truth about themselves?" (Foucault 1994a, 120). In Foucault's view, the cost of our truth-telling is the idealist violence of a rationalist history that ends in us: the violence of splitting ourselves from an other we repudiate and reabsorb as a secret nature tucked "deep within us" (*HS1*, 157): "a sort of mirage in which we think we see ourselves reflected – the dark shimmer of sex" (157). That self-recognition denies the evil genius and the "worrying ambiguity" of erotic lives – from sodomites to fetishists – rationalized into biopower's life-ordering matrix. A new evil genius has replaced the old one: the matrix has replaced the cosmos. Unless, of course, opening ourselves to the *unreasonable* time that makes nonsense of new and old, we plunge ourselves into a fiction that undoes us, embracing the ambiguity of that other recognition: the persistence of an immanence – call it unreason, evil genius, eros – that cannot be sublated into a sexy reason.

Notes

1   For an analysis of the specifically fictional aspect of the Cartesian evil genius in the Foucault–Derrida debate, see Judovitz (1989).

2 *HS1*, 159. The omission of key words in the process of translation most likely accounts for the fact that Anglophone Foucault scholars have missed this clear allusion to Descartes at the end of *HS1*. Hurley's English translation of Foucault's text renders the French term "*mauvais génie*" simply as "genius" (*HS1*, 159), thus erasing the traces of the Cartesian "*malin génie*" or "evil genius" present in the original. For the French original, see *HFAC*, 210. The French original also makes clear the collapse of Cartesian "genius" into a fabular "genie" exemplified by the figure of Cucufa in Diderot's fable, *Les Bijoux indiscrets* [*The Indiscreet Jewels*], which Foucault discusses at the beginning of Part Four of *HS1*.

3 In his 1981–2 lecture course, Foucault uses the term "Cartesian moment" to frame his analysis of "the problem of truth and the history of truth." See *HS*, 14.

4 Descartes establishes the cogito in Part Four of his *Discourse on the Method*: "And observing that this truth 'I am thinking, therefore I exist' was so firm and sure that all the most extravagant suppositions of the skeptics were incapable of shaking it, I decided that I could accept it without scruple as the first principle of the philosophy I was seeking" (Descartes 1985, 127).

5 Dalia Judovitz makes a similar claim in relation to Derrida's reading of Descartes by focusing on hyperbole as a rhetorical gesture that exceeds subjectivity, although her reading of Foucault's role in this fictional play differs from mine.

6 On dedialectizing thought, see especially *EW2*, 69–89 and 147–70.

7 Hegel (2010, 115). This translation from the original German differs slightly from the Hegel translation cited in the new English version of *HM*. For the sake of consistency, all of Foucault's subsequent citations of Hegel will refer to the English translation cited here.

8 On this point, see Lee (2012, 151).

4
Toward an Ethics of Subjectivation: French Resistances to Psychoanalysis in the 1970s

Didier Eribon

There is no doubt that among the major intellectual concerns of the 1970s, the question of the place of psychoanalysis within the field of knowledge, the question of the social functions of psychoanalysis, was at the heart of things. And so, in my eyes, the radically critical gesture performed by a certain number of theoreticians in those years in the face of psychoanalysis constitutes one of the most important legacies, one of the aspects of the intellectual ferment of that time that today most urgently needs to be rediscovered.

I focus on two authors, or rather on two books, that are emblematic – stylistically very different, yet in the end quite close in terms of their projects. They seem to me emblematic precisely of this will to escape from the dominance of psychoanalysis, emblematic even of the battle waged against it. These two books can be taken as reactions to the Freudo-Marxism that reigned in France at the outset of the 1970s, reactions to the way psychoanalysis had invaded the social body, reactions to what one author called the "psychoanalysm." More generally and more profoundly, these two books represent a resistance to psychoanalysis itself. One is Roland Barthes' *A Lover's Discourse: Fragments*. The other is Foucault's *HS1*. The two books are nearly exactly contemporaneous, the former published in early 1977, the latter in late

1976. Both authors were professors at the Collège de France at the moment the books appeared.

Barthes' book presents itself explicitly as an attempt to rehabilitate perhaps not love itself (which needs no rehabilitation), but discourse on love, speech about love, in a moment when both those things had come to seem ridiculous – at least among leftist intellectuals. To speak of love or of jealousy or of things of that nature was, at that moment, to run the risk of being labeled a backwards petit bourgeois, mired in conventional and reactionary forms of conjugality, of couplehood, of sentimentality. If one wanted to live and think as a subversive or a revolutionary, one had to dismiss this kind of sentimentality while imagining subverting society through the liberation of one's own desires. One's pleasures, one's orgasms, needed to be unfettered or unchained, as the slogan from May 1968 had it. Certainly the books of Wilhelm Reich and Herbert Marcuse were two of the key references in this type of discourse, a discourse that proliferated at the end of the 1960s and in the early 1970s. The extraordinary extent of Reich's influence, in particular, needs to be emphasized. Almost all of his books were published or republished in France in the space of the few years following 1968 and his *Sexual Revolution* is undoubtedly one of the books that had the most marked influence on French cultural life of that time. The Freudo-Marxist ideology of sexual liberation became a kind of sexual and political received wisdom, a common parlance. (Today it has been so completely replaced by its opposite, a kind of retrograde and normative psychoanalytic common parlance, that it can be hard to imagine how potent the injunction to be subversive was in those years. Or, perhaps we should say, the opposing kind of received wisdom is so powerful nowadays that it is easy to imagine how widespread what a reaction to it must have been.) In this ideology of sexual liberation, love had become something truly "obscene," as Barthes puts it. In the chapter entitled "Obscenity," somewhere in the middle of *Fragments*, he comments on the fact that it is acceptable for people to have problems with their sexuality, yet ridiculous to have problems with one's sentimentality: "Historical reversal: it is no longer the sexual which is indecent, it is the *sentimental* – censured in the name of what is in fact only *another morality*" (1978, 177). To this

Barthes adds: "Amorous obscenity is extreme: nothing can redeem it, bestow upon it the positive value of a transgression; the subject's solitude is timid, stripped of any *décor*: no Bataille will give a style [*écriture*] to that obscenity" (178).

Barthes' goal is to react against the discredit cast upon amorous discourse by the prevailing Freudo-Marxist jargon. I am not doing any interpreting here. He says as much himself, quite clearly, at the outset of his book. Here are its opening lines:

> The necessity for this book is to be found in the following consideration: that the lover's discourse is today *of an extreme solitude*. This discourse is spoken, perhaps, by thousands of subjects (who knows?), but warranted by no one; it is completely forsaken by the surrounding languages: ignored, disparaged, or derided by them, severed not only from authority but also from the mechanisms of authority (sciences, techniques, arts). Once a discourse is thus driven by its own momentum into the backwater of the "unreal," exiled from all gregariousness, it has no recourse but to become the site, however exiguous, of an *affirmation*. That affirmation is, in short, the subject of the book [that] begins here. (1; emphasis in original)

Barthes thus offers us a set of considerations that are intentionally *out of date*. This untimely, inappropriate gesture is offered as an *affirmation*: an affirmation of love, of amorous sentiment, of the discourse of love, in the face of and in opposition to all of the discourses that find such things ridiculous. It is a gesture of resistance to the spirit of the times, the *doxa* of the moment, to the historical present: "The lover's sentiment is old-fashioned, but this antiquation cannot even be recuperated as a spectacle: love falls outside of *interesting* time; no historical, polemical meaning can be given to it" (178–9; emphasis in original). Given that the spirit of the times also includes what circulates as "knowledge," Barthes' gesture is not only one of opposition to Freudo-Marxism. What he is claiming, it turns out, is not only the right to compose a kind of discourse that is no longer acceptable, that has been marginalized and scoffed at by those who claim that sexual liberation is the path to political liberation. He is also claiming the right to oppose psychoanalysis itself.

And if Barthes would still from time to time make recourse to statements or remarks of a psychoanalytic inspiration (I might go so far as to say, if he would sometimes allow himself to slip into speaking the jargon belonging to the received wisdom of a certain psychoanalysis, and while doing so allowing himself to display a surprising degree of naivety, so much so that it sometimes almost comes to feel as if it were a parody, slightly ridiculous – a fact of which he admits to having been aware), it is also because, as he explains it, the protagonist of his book, the character who says "I," a kind of novelistic "I" (even though he asserts that the book is not a novel), in any case the "I of writing,"[1] is a cultivated individual (a kind of double for Barthes himself) who has in his head the psychoanalytic culture of his time – which also counts as a chic way of speaking. (Barthes always liked to be chic in his way of speaking. He admits it himself.) It nonetheless remains the case that his book can be read as a kind of evasive maneuver vis-à-vis psychoanalysis, an effort to escape from its clutches.

Of course there are many texts by Freud and Lacan – especially those Barthes mentions – that can be cited to prove that psychoanalysis has never stopped thinking about love. Nonetheless, for Freud or Lacan love is always the symptom of something else (see Le Brun 2002, 289–340). For the psychoanalyst, love never exists in itself, or for itself. It must have a relation to what is already given, already produced in a subjectivity, to the past history of the subject, to that subject's childhood (with its figures of the father and the mother, with its obsession with reducing everything to the Oedipal – an obsession of which there are so many contemporary examples, and of which Deleuze and Guattari had already, in their 1972 *Anti-Oedipus*, performed such a devastating critique – a critique that was of immense importance in French intellectual life at the time, especially for people like Barthes and Foucault).

Barthes wants to deny any claim to knowledge about love, for at the end of his preface or short foreword, titled "How this book is constructed," he pointedly insists on the existence of what he calls the "innocence of [the lover's] imaginary," and further specifies that that imaginary is "indifferent to the proprieties of knowledge" (9; translation modified). He means that the imaginary has a spontaneity that cannot be reduced to the conceptual schemas of psychoanalysis (it's the machine-like unconscious of Deleuze and Guattari: it produces things); he means that the imaginary exceeds those schemas, overflows their boundaries, fails to correspond to them in any exact way. But if I am particularly fond of this remark, it is because it shows us Barthes making use of a Lacanian notion all the while knowing that his way of using it is highly unorthodox. The lover's discourse doesn't give a fig for orthodoxy. I find it quite interesting that of the Lacanian triad of the Real, the Symbolic, and the Imaginary, Barthes only keeps the Imaginary. He seems unconcerned with the logical relations between the three terms, with their interrelations, for his goal is to subvert the hierarchy in which the imaginary is subordinated to the symbolic. In one interview, Barthes is asked, "Is there a relation between the theme of the imaginary, central to your work, and the Lacanian imaginary?" He replies:

> Yes, it's the same thing, but doubtless I deform the theme, because I isolate it. I have the impression that the Imaginary is the poor relation within the psychoanalytic family. Stuck between the Real and the Symbolic, it seems undervalued at least in the common parlance of psychoanalysis. My book, on the other hand, involves an affirmation of the Imaginary. (2002b, 378)

An imaginary that has no links with a "symbolic"! There's an idea that threatens the normative edifice of psychoanalysis: the imaginary is given free rein, it is pure creation, it is joined to nothing but itself. It produces discursive figures, feelings, relations (and thus signs, language, and reality – all of which need no explaining, but simply to be affirmed). One need look no further. The Law, the Father, the Phallus are all sent packing. Here there is no paternal lack, no mother acting as lawmaker, no Oedipus, no Castration. The whole ideological and political Lacanian mess (and how political it is!) has been swept away, including all those notions intended to give an order to amorous bonds, to tie them down to a form of truth that could be revealed through analytic interpretation with its particular conceptual arsenal. Barthes understood very well that that "truth" as well as the conceptual arsenal intended to produce it as truth was always backed up by the traditional family order that it both defended and promoted. I don't have the space here to present the analysis of Lacan's texts that I offered in *Une morale du minoritaire* [A morality of the minoritarian] (2001); I can only summarize it briefly. Lacan's intellectual project in the 1930s – closely allied with the psychiatry of that moment – consisted in an attempt to rescue what he called "sexual polarization," which was threatened by feminism, by what he called the "virile protest of woman." These were responsible in his eyes for a general – and for him a dangerous – devirilization of men and of society at large, and for a proliferation of male homosexuality. His structuralist turn in the 1950s amounted to placing in a symbolic order – a transcendent one, one that precedes culture and that is itself the only access point to culture and to language – what he had in the 1930s situated in a political and social order that he was trying to defend against all those "struggles" that were unsettling it. The deep conservatism of Lacan and the Lacanians is not linked to structuralism; rather structuralism was a means by which Lacan intended to place out of reach everything that he had set out to protect in the 1930s. It was a means of hoisting social structures up to the level of symbolic structures so that they could then be presented as inaccessible to transformation. From now on would be a question of nothing other than language itself, of the unconscious structured as a language, in which, as he would say in 1972, "the Other is always the other sex."

It is against this transcendence of the symbolic order that Barthes rebels. Part of his rebellion involves his rehabilitation of the imaginary as a space of free production, or in any case production that is not constrained by the laws of sexual difference, of the signifying order, of Oedipus, of castration. There is no transcendence of the Phallus (only, one might say, its immanence). We might think of the battle between Lacan on the one hand, and Deleuze, Guattari, Foucault, and Barthes on the other as a confrontation between a theory of transcendence and theories of immanence. Lacan is a thinker of transcendence. (This is why in France today's Lacanians are so close to Christian personalists in their intense hostility to gay marriage, same-sex parenting, and so on. Both groups consistently refer to the "symbolic order" in which sexual difference is purportedly constituted as a structuring principle for the human subject.)

Foucault, as well as Deleuze and Guattari, are on the side of immanence. Their work is constructed in opposition to transcendence,
notably to the transcendence found in psychoanalysis (and also
against various representatives of philosophical transcendence, or
against political transcendence and its various unifying concepts, its
programs, and so on). It is obvious that Barthes was not a systematic
thinker like Deleuze, nor did he develop historical analyses like
Foucault, yet in his own way he affirms the immanence of love in
opposition to the laws of transcendence that govern psychoanalytic
interpretation.

In opposition to what he calls in *Le Neutre* [The neuter] "the
arrogance of the concept" (and therefore in opposition to the
bodies of knowledge that manifested this arrogance most flagrantly,
Marxism and psychoanalysis: 2002a, 200), Barthes turns to what I
might call Greek thought. I cannot quite say Greek *philosophy*, for
in his eyes skepticism is not really a philosophy to the extent that
it suspends the totalizing character of philosophy. In *Le Neutre* he
refers to Pyrrhus as his principal source of inspiration. Such skepticism is not a philosophy, a new dogmatism, a principle, but simply
the desire for a suspension of knowledge, the desire to keep it at a
distance, even if only for a moment.

Love is thus a creation, and therefore a creation of oneself as
a subject (and not only an amorous subject). By way of love, by
way of an amorous relation or relations, I create myself, even if I
do so by always returning to the same discourses and figures. And
just because it is almost never a question in this book of the body
or bodies or of sexuality, that does not mean that the body is not
important for Barthes – quite the contrary. In *Roland Barthes by
Roland Barthes* (1977), he writes that every author has his or her
word of predilection, what he calls, using a term from Lévi-Strauss,
a mana-word. His own, he says, is "body." And so it is that the
evasion of psychoanalysis, the resistance to its ways of taking hold
of things, can be produced just as well in an economy of pleasures
as in amorous creation – or in friendship.

At the same moment that he publishes *A Lover's Discourse*, Barthes
is in fact giving his very first year of courses at the Collège de France,
on "How to Live Together." Barthes is no precursor of the neo-
Christian, neo-conservative politics that characterizes a large section

of the intellectual left in France today. That so-called left, to justify its opposition to any social movement and especially to any minority social movement, invokes a jargon it imagines to be inspired by Arendt ("the common world," "living together"), paying no attention to the fact that Arendt in fact said the opposite of what they take her to say. For her it was not a question of advocating the dissolution of all particular points of view on the world into some undifferentiated soup. Those particularized points of view were to be preserved and multiplied. In Barthes' case, the question of "living together" arises in a reflection on friendship, on the possibility of forming small communities within which one can live out the full intensity of an amical relationship while everyone keeps his or her own personal freedom. His thoughts center on the notion of *idiorhythmia* [private rhythm] that he finds in certain monasteries on Mount Athos, in which each monk could attend liturgies at the hours that suited him. To live together according to idiorhythmic principles means each person living according to his or her own rhythm. These relational groups and this communitarian ethic on which Barthes is elaborating can only be thought of in connection with quite small groups: fewer than ten, maybe eight. It hardly seems to resemble the experiences of living in communes that developed in the 1970s, where very little idiorhythmia seems to have occurred.

Thus we can see that Barthes' thinking, in order to set psychoanalysis aside, depends on what we might call an affirmation of love and a politics of friendship. (Not that those two things are mutually exclusive, given that someone can be involved in an amorous relationship all the while also pursuing relationships of friendship as well.) Barthes says that the relationality characteristic of friendship is established as a way of life, a kind of life with its own rules and rhythms, through which individuals invent themselves by inventing their relations with others, whereas amorous relationality sets itself up as a space in which a subject gives free rein to the non-codified innocence of her or his imaginary. It is here clearly a question of affirmation, of creation, of production. This is ascesis, and we are in the multiform space of an aesthetics of existence.

★

Now the point of departure for *HS1* is also a rejection of Freudo-Marxism. We see in Foucault's way of proceeding something analogous to what we have seen in Barthes. He moves from a critique of Freudo-Marxism and of the ideology of sexual liberation that was omnipresent in the early 1970s in leftist French intellectual culture to a more general critique of psychoanalysis. From this critique of psychoanalysis he will move later to a theory of subjectivation in terms of self-creation, ascesis, and an aesthetics of existence. I have given a long analysis of Foucault's texts in my book *Insult and the Making of the Gay Self* (2004, 235–348). I won't repeat those analyses here in detail. It will suffice to recall that for Foucault it is not love that is the operative factor in the creation of the self. It is in part, as he says at the end of *HS1*, on the "body" and "pleasures" that the counter-attack which he longs for against the "apparatus of sexuality" could be based. (Psychoanalysis is intrinsically linked to this apparatus, and indeed makes up a large part of its machinery, and so the attack against the apparatus is necessarily an attack against psychoanalysis itself, as Foucault made clear at the end – the very last page – of his book, and in several interviews). In later years, notably in the thinking that would accompany, in the courses given at the Collège de France, the writing of the later volumes of his *History of Sexuality*, it turns out that the idea of friendship as a locus of relationality also permits one to escape from the will to knowledge of psychoanalysis, and from the naturalism of desire. For in the practice of friendship one is able to think about self-invention by way of relational practices that create new and unexpected things instead of simply attempting to discover the truth about what one already is. *Se déprendre de soi-même* [to shake oneself loose from oneself] is obviously an anti-psychoanalytical project.

At the beginning of the 1980s, notably in *HS*, Foucault focuses on the idea of the aesthetics of existence, on philosophy as a practice of the self, an exercise. This resonates for him with important contemporary preoccupations, linked to his encounter with gay communities in the United States, in New York and San Francisco. His work on "self-governance" in antiquity resonates with his way of looking at the invention of new ways of life in which he is participating, and which it is part of his project to think about. Whether it be in his historical work on Greece or his political reflections on the gay movement and gay lifestyles, it is the question of friendship that takes center stage. Friendship becomes the anchor for subjectivation, becomes the locus for the creation of new bonds between subjects, and thereby becomes a politics of self-transformation and of the transformation of others.

Certain psychoanalysts have taken the liberty of making fun of Foucault's progression from the body and its pleasures to the problematic of subjectivation in ancient Greece. Jacques-Alain Miller (Lacan's son-in-law) imagined it would be possible to invalidate Foucault's counterattack against Lacan's discourse, to disqualify his radical critique of psychoanalytic normativity on behalf of "bodies and pleasures," by labeling it a "perverse" discourse that had reached such a degree of madness that it was willing to contest the scientific rationality of the analytic order:

> Is it not clear that his counterattack against the apparatus of sexuality that has psychoanalysis at its heart was based on no solid disciplinary ground, no practice, except for the utopia of a body outside sex whose multiple pleasures would no longer be drawn together under the iron rule of castration? The ground was hardly sufficient, *nothing more than a fragment of perversion* to which, in [*HS1*], Foucault gives no other consistency than that of a utopian point without which one cannot think outside the limits of psychoanalysis. (Miller 1989, 82, my emphasis)

Yet surely this response is nothing other than a magnificent confirmation of Foucault's diagnosis of the functions of psychoanalysis as an arena in which the sexual order becomes fixed around the unifying concept of castration (that is to say, sexual difference). There is a history to be written of the methods deployed in psychoanalysis's resistance to the gay resistance to psychoanalysis – the main one being to dismiss critics of psychoanalysis by consigning them to madness or perversion.

As for all those who, like me, prefer Foucault's idea of "multiple pleasures" to the cure with which Miller's father-in-law threatened them, it certainly seems that Foucault makes a solid case, whether regarding the eroticized body or friendship as an art of the self, or both together, and he builds that case on solid ground – ground that, from the end of the nineteenth century to the end of the twentieth (from Pater and Symonds to Foucault and Wittig, by way of Wilde, Gide and so many others) allowed certain people to resist the never-ending efforts of psychiatrists and psychoanalysts (along with priests, police, and judges) to force back onto the straight and narrow the deviants and "perverts" that they have always been and continue to be.[2]

And in fact Miller seems to have understood this, because, after having affirmed that "it is precisely the absence of this solid ground that sent all of the archeology slipping down rapidly in a retrograde movement that could not be stopped and had no limits" (and this is evidently a bad thing for a psychoanalyst who likes nothing better than to put on the brakes and to impose limits), he wonders if Foucault did not find in Greece, in the idea of an aesthetic of existence, "the firm ground he was looking for." Miller is a good reader; he has a very good intellectual grasp of Foucault's project, even of what actually happened in Foucault's work, what happened there that was perhaps not even part of Foucault's explicit project. Yet his excellent understanding is only used to condescend, to offer a severe judgment, to condemn. He speaks as if from on high, thanks to his theory based on Castration and a few other words written with capital letters, relying on what Eve Sedgwick (1990) has helpfully named "epistemological privilege." Heterosexual and heteronormative knowledge (and psychoanalysis is never anything other than a heteronormed knowledge) reaffirms its superiority by high-handedly and condescendingly judging, with the tone of a medical diagnosis, the discourse that seeks to resist it. In Miller's text we find ourselves not too far from the psychiatrists of the early twentieth century described by George Chauncey in *Gay New York* (1995), who were dismayed to observe that the deviants they were trying to cure were capable of claiming to be proud to be what they were . . . which only made them sicker in the eyes of their judges. In the 1930s, Lacan was a homophobic psychiatrist, and then he became a homophobic psychoanalyst: surely one of the most homophobic ideologists in twentieth-century France. And, as one sees, his heirs are faithful to his tradition.

It is quite striking to me that at the moment Foucault was beginning *HS1* and pondering the cultural creation of self, at the moment Barthes was writing *A Lover's Discourse* and pondering the art of living together, both of them were also thinking about figures who suspend gender binarisms and sexual difference (Barthes 2002a; Foucault *HB*).

There are many other authors, male and female, from the late nineteenth century through today, who could take their place in this tradition. This is why I wonder if it is really possible – or even desirable – to pursue the project of reconciling queer theory (or, more generally, radical thought, whatever name one gives it – and is there really any good reason to give it a name, to use labels to fix it, producing conformity and close-mindedness rather than an openness to new kinds of questions?) and psychoanalysis. Isn't there rather, between the two of them, a fundamental incompatibility – this notwithstanding all that major authors of queer theory such as Eve Kosofsky Sedgwick, Judith Butler, Teresa de Lauretis, Michael Warner, or Lee Edelman (or even someone like Leo Bersani, who positions himself outside queer theory and yet works to elaborate a new kind of critical thinking) owe to psychoanalysis? Wouldn't the urgent task, for critical, radical thinking, rather be to resolutely turn its back on psychoanalysis? To pay it no attention? Or even to combat it?

I feel a deep intellectual and political and even emotional affinity with Judith Butler. We all know how important an interest she has taken, for example, in questions of drag or of transsexualism while interrogating the essentialism of identities or the way individuals are assigned to gendered identities or sexual identities. We might even say that she belongs to the tradition of thinkers I have been invoking here, so great is her effort to escape from the violence of gender binaries. Yet I have no choice but to disagree with her when she sets out to reconcile Foucault and psychoanalysis, or, more precisely, as she puts it in *The Psychic Life of Power*, to provide, by way of Freud, what she sees as lacking in Foucault's theory of power: a theory of the way in which power functions within the individual psyche (1997, 83–105).

A number of Butler's works have in common a double gesture that consists in conducting a merciless critique of the heterosexism of psychoanalysis, notable of Lacanian psychoanalysis, while also striving to reformulate analytic concepts, notably those of Lacan, in order to make them more amenable to a diversity of morphologies, sexualities, desires, and identifications, or to take the "structures" defined by Lacan as eternal and intangible and make them accessible to social transformation. Examples of this would be her project to rework the notion of the Phallus, opening it out onto what she calls "the lesbian Phallus," or the notion of the Oedipus complex in order to think through the way triangular desire operates in families with same-sex parents (1993, 57–91; 2000; 2004, 102–30). Her analyses are always powerful, and their richness and fecundity extend well beyond the limits of her dialogue with psychoanalysis. Yet it often seems to me that, instead of spending so much energy and intellectual sophistication in an effort to reformulate the key notions of analytic doctrine in order to make them compatible with the multifarious reality of desires, fantasies, identities, affective, sexual, and familial arrangements – in sum, with the lives that individuals live in all of their inalienable diversity – it would probably be simpler, more effective, and more productive, theoretically and politically, purely and simply to refuse the pertinence of those notions. It would be more productive to rid oneself of the sense of self-evidence that these notions have for us, for that sense has been inscribed in our minds through a process of acculturation focused on these very notions. More productive would be simply to reject them, along with the regime of thought that they define, delimit, and impose, and in which we remain trapped so long as we accept the terms and, along with them, the conception of mind with which they are intrinsically linked: all this rigmarole of ancient mythology which was built up precisely on the exclusion of very multifarious realities, and which works to perpetuate that exclusion by insisting on its inevitability. It is not possible to free these notions from their heterosexist content, because they are heterosexist constructions, built up on heterosexist social and cognitive structures. So we should take the opposite road: once you have decided to take as your point of departure an innovative reflection on the mind, gender, affectivity, love, friendship, sexuality, the family, kinship, and so on, which is to say all the forms and all the lives that have been excluded or pathologized by analytic theory (which was precisely the theorization of their exclusion and their pathologization), the goal should be to get rid of the very theory that excluded and pathologized them.

In much the same way, I have a great admiration for both the

brio and the motivation behind Leo Bersani's recent writings, in
which he works to bring Freud and Foucault together (after having
expressed a clear preference for Freud over Foucault in *Homos*
[1995], then for Foucault over Freud in *Caravaggio's Secrets* [with
Dutoit 1998] or in "Sociality and Sexuality" [2000]). Still, it is
hard for me to follow him when he claims to wish to rescue *Three
Essays on the Theory of Sexuality* because of its final sentence, in
which Freud admits that our knowledge is too fragmentary for us
to be able "to construct . . . a theory adequate to the understanding alike of normal and of pathological conditions." For as Bersani
himself makes clear, Freud's project throughout the entire volume
has been to construct precisely such a theory (2004).

Indeed, I cannot help asking myself, not the question Bersani
poses to himself – "Why return to Freud via Foucault, if it is only
to reread Foucault as if he were Freud?" – but rather why Foucault
should be reread via Freud if the end result is only to entangle
Foucault's thought in those nets of psychoanalytic thinking from
which he was working to free himself throughout his whole body
of work. Bersani proposes to connect Foucault's project of studying the question of the invention of a new relational culture with
Freud's interrogation of the psychic mechanisms that resist the very
possibility of any such invention, which is to say the death wish,
destructive impulses. If every social group is riven with power
conflicts, these conflicts, Bersani says, find their most satisfactory
description in psychoanalysis. Consequently, if today's psychoanalysis has need of Foucault's utopia, in which novel relations
between individuals can be created, Foucault's thought needs to
be able to take into account a kind of psychic density that it has
neglected and that psychoanalysis could give back to it.

This amounts to imagining that Foucault and Freud might
complement and complete each other, whereas both Foucault's
conception of relationality and his theory of power were worked
out in the course of an uncompromising effort to call into question
the analytic theory of drives, of "sexuality," and of the associated
structure of mind. Bersani is perfectly aware of this opposition.
Indeed, he highlights it, but only in order to later relativize or
even dismiss it, in a gesture that is in many ways close to that of
Judith Butler. This is the case despite the fact that he presents

what he is doing as a challenge to queer theory – suggesting a "harmony" (although he sensibly offers the qualification "temporary") between Freud and Foucault, a "to-and-fro" between their thought, as if the theory of an economy of drives put forth by Freud and the theory of power elaborated by Foucault were nothing but two approaches or two partial and complementary perspectives whose joining together was long overdue.

In the two cases I've just been discussing (Butler and Bersani), the attempted reconciliations in the end serve to blunt the radical force of Foucault's thought by seeking out a compromise between what he was trying to do – to produce a different way of thinking about subjectivation and relationality – and what he was trying to undo – the psychoanalytic conception of desire and of the subject of desire.

In any case, I think it is necessary to make a choice: Freud (Lacan) or Foucault. Foucault or psychoanalysis. This is because the greatness of Foucault's project resides precisely in the fact that his aim was to scuttle the psychoanalytic theory of the individual psyche and oppose to it a theory of individuation as the effect of a subjected body, a disciplined body. (That, for him, is the "psychic life of power," and from it comes his idea that the "soul," produced by disciplinary effects of individuation, is the "prison of the body.") Psychological, psychiatric, and psychoanalytic discourses and institutions are not the only products of a disciplinary society; so is the psychological individual and even the very notion of psychic "interiority." Psychological (psychiatric) knowledge proceeds by digging through people's childhoods in order to find there the origin of their "anomalies" and in order, by means of some kind of interrogation, to discover their hidden truth. It creates their psychological truth at the same time that it creates them as individuals possessing a psychology that has its own truth, linked to the past, to the family, and to an axis of sexual and psychic normality on which all people find themselves situated, fixed, judged. Psychoanalysis is simply the heir of this "psy-function" that was put into place as an effect and corollary of the "discipline" that was exercised over bodies. The psyche in which psychoanalysis is interested is a product of a disciplinary society, and psychoanalysis is a cog within the larger disciplinary technology (see Foucault, *PP*).

Foucault develops his theory of subjectivation as a form of self-reinvention (a form that is both non-psychological and non-psychoanalytic) in tandem with his theory of the mechanisms of power that impose discipline on a body and control over a psyche as part of the implementation of the individuation of the subjugated subject. On the one hand, he insists on the creation of new relations between individuals, new modes of life (what we might define as a "politics of friendship") and, on the other, he insists on the intensification of pleasures. (He calls this "desexualization," meaning an erotic polymorphism, a body that has become a surface on which pleasures – which cannot be reduced to genitality – proliferate. Sadomasochism would be one example of this. It could also be called the "depsychologization" of sex and of sexuality. Bersani seems to me to be unquestionably closer to Foucault when he develops his reflections on the dissolution of the psychological subject in considering what goes on in gay cruising or in the "impersonal intimacies" that operate in more or less anonymous encounters.)

In any case, we can see both in Barthes and in Foucault ways of reflecting on love and on friendship – and on sexuality – that lay the groundwork for thinking through what subjectivation is (or what resubjectivation is, since it is more a question of reinventing oneself, of freeing ourselves from what history has made of us) in a way that does not have recourse to psychoanalysis. Rather, it bypasses it, or dismisses it, since what is at stake is to escape from the "scientific" nets of this cultural and political ideology, from its conceptual frameworks, and especially from its interpretative logic, which seems always to reduce everything to the binary structure of sexual difference and to subsume everything under the rule of a transcendentally constitutive and unavoidable "symbolic order." However modest it may seem, the politics proposed by Barthes and by Foucault makes an effort rather to open new perspectives for the historical invention of our selves, for experimentation and innovation. It is a politics that has no other program than that of wanting to allow differences to proliferate, and, along with them, freedoms and possibilities. What is implied is an ethics of subjectivation that would quite deliberately break with the manner in which psychoanalysis conceives of psychic life and would, in doing so, open an undefined space of generosity that welcomes a multiplicity of individual and collective choices, to a plurality of aspirations and of ways of life.

Notes

1 See the interview given by Barthes to *Art-Press* in May 1977, reprinted in 2002b, 401: "The person who says 'I' in this book is the *I* of writing . . . It is me and not me. It is no more me, if I can be allowed a comparison that is also a kind of infatuation, than when Stendhal calls forth a character." On his hesitations regarding novels, which he assimilates to "habitual forms of social recuperation," and on the care he took to make sure his book would not be a "love story," see the September 1977 interview from *Playboy* in the same volume (417).

2 On Lacan's constantly restated and reaffirmed desire to "cure" homosexuals of their homosexuality, see e.g. Lacan (1998, 207–12).

5

Michel Foucault's Critical Empiricism Today: Concepts and Analytics in the Critique of Biopower and Infopower

Colin Koopman

Putting Foucault to Work Today

Michel Foucault is one of our most widely read theorists today. He is also one of the most widely used. Foucault has been productively deployed and redeployed for all manner of pursuits that he himself could not have dreamt of. This suggests a tremendous fecundity in Foucault's writings. But where exactly do we locate that fecundity? In the totality of his work? Is every last blessed bit of Foucault valuable for us today? Or should we be more selective? Is it the case that Foucault's richness for us today has more to do with only a part of the many moving pieces exhibited in his writings? The argument I develop here rests on the claim that in pushing with Foucault beyond Foucault we expose ourselves to dangers as well as opportunities. If not sufficiently self-reflective, our uses of Foucault may run counter to his own work or, more problematically, counter to our own intentions and efforts as these motivate our inquiries.

In what follows, I encourage such self-reflectiveness in an explicitly methodological vein that should be of use for both critical philosophy and critical social science. I begin by offering a distinction between *analytics* (or *methods*) and *concepts*. I argue that this distinction helps sort out different elements in Foucault's work, different insofar as they are differently productive. Following this, I turn to a consideration of how this distinction features in Foucault's own work on biopower, focusing here on *HS1*. This prompts a contrast between two contemporary uses of Foucault that intersect in different ways with the analyses of biopower in *HS1*. I discuss these with an eye toward what comes to the fore when different elements of Foucauldean inquiry, analytics and concepts, gain priority over one another. On the basis of this distinction, I then offer an outline of an emerging field of inquiry that could make use of Focuault's work on biopower whilst also needing to go beyond it. My suggestion shall concern a *concept* of infopower that Foucault's genealogical *analysis* of biopower invites but does not itself fully develop. If biopower in its first functioning made heavy use of technologies of statistics and recordkeeping, then those very technologies have in the century since developed a gravity of their own in part due to the contributions of electrification, digitization, and other processes at the heart of our contemporary information societies. The interrogation of infopower after biopower thus offers an exemplary case for scrutinizing the utility of Foucauldean *analytics* beyond their original *conceptual* employments. Making some sense of the infopolitical developments of our present, I shall suggest, is up to us, beyond and after, but still possibly very much through, Foucault.

Analytics and Concepts in Foucault

I begin with a distinction between two different elements in Foucault's work which might be put to use by inquirers pursuing their own lines of research which are not necessarily to be found in Foucault's thought: analytics and concepts. *Analytics* refer to strategies, techniques, and forms for inquiry: the ways in which inquiry is conducted. *Concepts* refer to the ideational material that is the yield of inquiry: that which inquiry works to produce. Analytics function as grids or lenses that make possible a coherent practice of inquiry, whilst concepts function as the materials which inquiry works with in drawing objects of inquiry through the analytical grid. There are, of course, other elements featured in Foucault's work that vary independently of analytics and concepts – a fuller taxonomy would attempt to take all of these into account (see Koopman and Matza 2013).

Concepts form a major aspect of Foucault's historical-philosophical work and they are that which lend much of his work its vividness. Some of the most memorable examples of concepts in Foucault's corpus include discipline, biopower, security, and care of the self. These concepts might be better described as conceptual networks or conceptual assemblages insofar as they invoke a complex plurality of notions. Certainly it is true that none of Foucault's most important concepts is simple. Their complexity is a condition of their transformability. Biopower in the nineteenth century was, according to Foucault, a complex amalgam of efforts in public health, nationalism, medicine, psychiatry, demography, information sciences (e.g., statistics), emerging sciences of sexuality, and the tentacles of public policing efforts. Today, biopower in the early twenty-first century is an assemblage that includes genetic technologies, biological weapons, dense global communication assemblages, and other newly emergent objects of analysis. This easy-to-see shift underscores an inherent danger in "applications" of Foucault's conceptualizations to fields where his thought did not range. Foucault's concepts were often precisely tailored for the fields into which he was inquiring. Thus, it may well prove fruitless to inject these concepts in unrevised fashion into wholly different fields. Certainly, extending Foucault's concepts beyond the sites of inquiry for which he developed them would require putting those concepts to the test of the new realities which they are proposed to cover.

Analytics refer to the methodological constraints in virtue of which Foucault is able to operationalize the concepts central to his work. I conceive of Foucault's analytics as broadly referring to the various research strategies and tactics that Foucault employed to guide (that is, to modalize) his own inquiries. As one of several possible modes of inquiry, Foucault's analytics can be contrasted with other analytic strategies: structuralist analysis, hermeneutic interpretation, and systematic theorization. The most familiar examples of analytics in Foucault's works are archaeology and genealogy, both of which involve, and in complementary ways, the history of present practices. Another analytical device that is properly central to all of Foucault's work concerns the focus of inquiry around problems or problematizations – Foucault's much discussed emphasis on contingency is always focused on the contingencies by which the most fraught and fragile problems of our presents were constructed.

Recognizing archaeology, genealogy, and problematization as analytical devices helps establish the specificity of their critical effectiveness. An analytic is a tool for inquiry (for instance, an analytics of power, or of knowledge, or of power/knowledge). Foucault's analytics should not be understood as if they were designed as answers to philosophical conundrums and so should not be read as mounting arguments for certain philosophical theses (for instance, nominalism or constructivism). At the same time, however, Foucault clearly does not only offer analyses of the various sites of inquiry on which his work was trained (though he clearly does that as well). Foucault wrote histories, to be sure, and in the course of doing so he developed historical methods that function as analytical grids for inquiry. Neither looking to establish a general theory nor looking to assert only a string of particular points, Foucault's work productively and reflexively traffics at the level of critical analytics, methods, and designs. The analytical aspect of Foucault's work is a provocation to prevailing modalities of critique. This was noted by Hubert Dreyfus and Paul Rabinow in their justly influential early book on Foucault's method, claiming that Foucault's "practice of historical writing is cast in unorthodox terms" (1982, 118). They settle on a characterization of this practice as an "interpretive analytics" that "enables [Foucault] to go beyond theory and hermeneutics" in the sense just described (1982, 124). This work, they show, is properly a "diagnosis of the current situation" (1982, 119). Foucault's work was always diagnostic, always oriented around the work of problematization, which is the work of undertaking inquiry for the sake of gaining conceptual grip on a complex problematic field.[1] Foucault's analytics are, as such, diagnostic analytics.[2]

In his late "What Is Enlightenment?", Foucault wrote of the modern tradition of self-critique as not "a theory, a doctrine, nor even as a permanent body of knowledge that is accumulating" but rather as "an attitude, an ethos, a philosophical life" (*EW1*, 319). This attitude, he continued, must take the form of "diverse inquiries" which would require three forms of coherence. First, "methodological [or analytical] coherence" as gained through "the at once archaeological and genealogical study of practices." Second, "theoretical coherence" in the specification of "historically unique forms" as sites where generalities get "problematized." And third, "practical coherence" in the work of "putting historico-critical reflection to the test of concrete practices" (*EW1*, 319). I will say more later about this third, practical aspect of Foucault's critical practice, namely its empirical aspect. For now, however, I want to draw attention to the first two aspects in their emphasis on geneal-ogy and archaeology as analytical (or methodological) approaches performing a diagnostic (or problematizing) work, for this offers evidence on behalf of the general line of interpretation proffered by Dreyfus and Rabinow.

It is on the basis of analytics that Foucault's work gains its rigor whereas concepts are what lend his work its vividness – analyt-ics provide guidance to motion and concepts afford friction for inquiry. These two together form the fantastic combination, highly readable and yet profoundly precise, that are Foucault's books. Distinguishing these two aspects of elements within Foucault's work helps us see that they are non-co-determinative. This is a deceptively simple point that many contemporary uses of Foucault nevertheless neglect, for example in attempted efforts at "genealogies" of "biopower" that consist in arguing that (but not genealogically investigating how) the concept of biopower helps make sense of some contemporary political practice. That analytics and concepts are non-co-determinative means that one can, for example, use a given set of analytics (e.g., Foucault's genealogy) without employing any particular set of concepts (e.g., discipline). Thus one could just as well write a genealogy of sovereign power as a genealogy of some insidious new exercise of disciplinary power. Or, to state again what should be obvious but which is overlooked with surprising frequency in the literature, to employ a given set of concepts (e.g., Foucault's discipline or biopower) is not by itself determinative of any given analytic (e.g., genealogy). Thus one could (and many do) write of the nefarious effects of contemporary forms of disciplinary power and biopower without detailing these effects on the basis of a patient methodology for critical inquiry such as genealogy. Such accounts often suffer from a lack of methodological and theoretical coherence, and in part as a result of this further suffer from a debilitating lack of practical-empirical coherence. In other words, accounts such as these are too often exercises in mere speculation.

How do analytics and concepts function in Foucault's work and the work to which we might put Foucault's thought? One way to answer this question is by way of a brief review of *HS1* in terms of the distinction just offered. According to this approach, *HS1* offers a critical analysis of the complex congeries of concepts congregating around sexuality beginning in the nineteenth century. *HS1* involves the use of an *analytic* procedure (namely, genealogy) for inquiring into a particular *field* or site of inquiry (namely, sexuality) in such a way as to yield a family of *concepts* (namely, biopower, amongst others) that help make sense of this object.

To begin with the *analytic* procedure, I shall summarize the methodology guiding Foucault's project here as possessing (at least) three qualities that taken together are distinctive of a genealogical analytic for diagnostic problematization. Genealogy, as I shall be summarizing it, is a form of critical inquiry that emphasizes *complexity*, *contingency*, and the idea of *conditioning*. In a phrase, genealogy is critical inquiry into the complexity and contingency of the conditions of our present.

First, genealogy involves a form of historical inquiry meant to facilitate an analysis of the full-scale complexity of its objects of inquiry. Thus, *HS1* can be read as a history of a wide range of practices that intersected across the eighteenth and nineteenth centuries to form a deep problematization that sits at the center of who we are today. The knotty problem at the center of it all is naughty sex, such that the book tells the history of how sex itself contingently came into being, and not all that long ago. The story therein digests a remarkable diversity of practices. Chief among these are the bio-, medico-, and psycho-sciences, insofar as these particularly inform our conceptions of the meaning, function, and (limited) possibilities of sexuality today. These sciences of sex formed through a complex mesh of instruments and practices involving a long back-history of confessional rituals whose technologies of truth were later operationalized in a variety of nineteenth-century domains including psychiatric examinations, familial surveillance, pedagogical inculcation, and grandiose efforts in public health, all of which invoked increasingly meticulous forms of power, knowledge, and subjectivation.[3] Foucault casts a wide survey over the nineteenth century in order to gain some grip on the sexuality with which it still haunts us.

A second notable feature of Foucault's methodology is its emphasis on historical contingency in place of rational necessity in history. Foucault, of course, was not the first to emphasize contingency in history. Foucault's crucial analytical breakthrough was to make use of contingency as an analytic modality for demonstrating how certain practices have come to seem necessary. The major insight, then, is not contingency so much as the excavation of contingency at the heart of necessity. What could be closer to us, what could hold us in greater thrall, than our sexuality? And yet Foucault's primary point in *HS1* is that the thrall we are in has no nature or necessity behind it. All it has is a complex history. It is no less enthralling for it, no less an object of obsession, but at least it is not a necessary obsession that puts us in touch with something supposedly deeper in ourselves than our own contingent self-fashioning.

I understand the orientation toward complexity and contingency as twain aspects of a historicized form of Kantian inquiry into the conditions of possibility that enframe subjects capable of acting and objects capable of being acted upon. This brings me to the third of my three aspects of Foucault's analytics, namely conditioning. Foucault is not merely describing the contingency and complexity of the present, but rather the way in which the present is contingently and complexly conditioned. It is in virtue of this focus on conditions that Foucault can be said to be a kind of Kantian. There is, of course, much in Kant that Foucault felt free to leave behind. That is probably for the better. But the idea of conditions of possibility was a powerful Kantian insight. It is the best insight of the critical philosophy. Foucault recognized this and so appropriated the labor of critique for his own purposes. Thus, we can recognize Foucault's critical analytics as orienting inquiry around the work of conceptualizing the conditioning limits (i.e., the conditions of possibility) that simultaneously enable and constrain the practices under investigation. If for Kant these conditioning limits had been transcendental, for Foucault the empirical is historically conditioned by the empirical.

The *concepts* that result from Foucault's analysis of the contingency and complexity of that which conditions the present were harnessed in *HS1* for a specification of a particular functioning of power that Foucault famously names biopower. Biopower, for Foucault, is a form of power in which politics and life directly and deeply impact one another, such that political technologies can no longer afford to ignore questions concerning the regulation of life itself and the biological and human sciences can no longer leave aside as secondary, questions concerning the political valences of their yield: "For the first time in history, no doubt, biological existence was reflected in political existence . . . One would have to speak of *bio-power* to designate what brought life and its mechanisms into the realm of explicit calculations and made knowledge-power an agent of transformation of human life" (*HS1*, 142–3). Biopower for Foucault has to do with an assemblage of historical intersections that are central to contemporary organizations of regimes of knowledge, power, and self hood. These intersections are complex, they are the product of contingencies, and they continue to condition who we are in the present. There is much more that can be said about biopower, of course, but for the purpose of distinguishing biopower as a conceptual product of Foucault's inquiry and the methodological apparatus that helped produce that concept, the minimal characterization above is safest for now, so that we can turn in a moment to different ways in which that concept has been taken up since Foucault.

What, then, can we say about the relationship between concepts and analytics in Foucault? While there is clearly an elective affinity between Foucault's analytics and concepts, these are nonetheless distinct aspects of the project outlined in *HS1*. This noted, we can locate the attraction and power of Foucault's work in his dual deployment of these differentiable kinds of elements. While so many theorists in the humanities are content to make transcendental (non-genealogical, non-empirical) pronouncements about biopower, technology, writing, history, and everything else, and so many laborers in the social sciences are content to offer astute empirical analyses of highly circumscribed objects of inquiry that often seem to have little bearing outside of a scholarly domain, Foucault's work expresses a powerful interdigitation of analytic and concept working together at decisive edges "beyond theory and hermeneutics" (Dreyfus and Rabinow 1982, 124). Therein lies a good share of Foucault's fecundity for us today.

Biopower after Foucault

The distinction I have been drawing matters because it matters to how we use Foucault today. We find ourselves facing today two diverging theoretical tendencies, each of which exerts tremendous influence at the same time that they negotiate a complex relationship with the thought of Foucault. These tendencies can be usefully framed in terms of two divergent uses of Foucault's genealogy of biopower, as he presented it in *HS1* and elsewhere. On the one hand, there are those critical-transcendental appropriations of Foucault's concept of biopower that would inflate this concept to something that simply could not be made sense of by way of a genealogical or archaeological analysis. On the other hand, are those critical-empirical usages of genealogy that confidently leave the specifics of his conceptual apparatus to the side in order to develop inquiries into other aspects of our present over which we do not already have good grip. Each tendency exhibits different kinds of theoretical relay with Foucault's genealogies of biopower.[4] Both aspects of Foucault are valuable for us today. But insofar as the present in which we find ourselves is one that is constantly transforming, we gain more from Foucault if we make use of his analytics to analyze emergent transformations than if we stick to concepts that were fashioned for situations that have already been transformed.

In offering cautions about contemporary transcendental invoca-
tions of biopower, I have in mind work that collects a diverse range
of theorists. Certainly it is not the case that all of these theorists are
of one mind about biopower. Yet they all might be said to be of
a shared mindset about how biopower should be positioned as a
theoretical object. Perhaps the most prominent instance of work in
this vein is that of Italian philosopher Giorgio Agamben. Agamben,
in *Homo Sacer*, positions biopower as one of "the keys to the his-
torico-political destiny of the West" (1998, 182). In *The Open*,
Agamben is similarly preoccupied with something that he takes to
be more originary than the contours of biopower as described by
Foucault: "In its origin Western politics is also biopolitics" (2004,
80). Insofar as he spreads biopower as a thin film over the entirety
of Western history, Agamben is able to gather together a remarkably diverse array under the auspices of this concept. It is on this
basis that he provocatively suggests that there is a "biopolitics of
both modern totalitarianism and the society of mass hedonism and
consumerism" (1998, 11). Roberto Esposito in *Bios* forwards a
similar style of methodological inflation: "the politics of life that
Nazism tried in vain to export outside Germany . . . [has] been
generalized to the entire world" (2008, 147). The indictment
lurking behind both Agamben and Esposito rests on their unquiet
attempts to dedifferentiate fascist totalitarianisms and liberal capital-
isms. Toward the aim of issuing stark political judgments, Esposito
and Agamben cannot resist finally ontologizing what Foucault
rigorously preserved as fully historical.[5]

Caution about this work is needed insofar as the current theoretical moment is witness to the enormous influence of this style
of theorizing biopower. Transcendental philosophy, alas, is still a
sexy kind of thing for those inhabiting an academic culture per-
vaded by theory envy. Though all this may be a sufficient cause
for thinking there is deep insight in the transcendental analysis of
biopower, it is not to my mind a good reason for that thought.
This is because the deployment of Foucault's concepts without the
guidance of Foucault's analytics risks losing a grip on the specificities for which those analytics give our analyses traction. I regard
such usage as generally, though certainly not always, against the
grain of the better insights of Foucault's work. If the prevailing

norm in contemporary uses of Foucault involves adoption and elaboration of his conceptual material without corollary attention to the analytical elements of his wider methodological repertoire, then caution is warranted.

Caution is also warranted by Foucault himself, at least insofar as he offers explicit cautions against precisely these kinds of "inflationary" use of concepts in *BB*. Whereas *HS1* concentrates explicitly on biopower's many scientific, especially social-scientific, dimensions, the *BB* lectures should be read as a companion genealogy of the specifically governmental dimensions of biopower. According to Foucault's methodological claims in *BB* concerning the study of biopower, an inflationary style of critique makes it "possible not only to use different analyses to support each other, but also to refer them back to each other and so deprive them of their specificity" so as to result in "an increasing interchangeability of analyses" (*BB*, 187, 188).[6] Foucault in fact had in mind precisely the sort of equivocations through which Agamben and Esposito propose to gain force for their arguments: "the welfare state has neither the same form, of course, nor, it seems to me, the same root or origin as the totalitarian state, as the Nazi, fascist, or Stalinist state" (*BB*, 190). Now Foucault, of course, does not get to be the sole authority on how we can and should make use of his work. But the concern he raises with respect to a lack of specificity is surely something that any reader of Agamben, or Esposito, can recognize as a potential problem.[7] This is, however, not the place to offer a complete criticism of these appropriations of Foucault.[8] It is better to light a candle than to curse the darkness – rather than dwelling on what I find wrong with transcendental Foucauldeanisms, let me turn instead to empirical Foucauldean critiques that I find more productive.

An empirical deployment of Foucault's analytics might be useful precisely where we find ourselves in changed, or changing, circumstances. The use of Foucauldean analytics in contexts where inquiry requires substantial variation of his concepts, or perhaps even detachment from his concepts, represents a productive path forward today for Foucauldean inquiry after Foucault.[9]

Consider as an exemplar of such uses of Foucault beyond Foucault the elaboration of biopower developed in Ian Hacking's histories. Hacking's histories of the overlay between the biological and the political feature two interwoven processes. The one he calls "the avalanche of numbers" and the other he places under the banner of what he calls "making up people." Hacking's "avalanche of numbers" refers to the solidification and explosion in the nineteenth century of "statistical information developed for purposes of social control" (2006c, 6; cf. 1990). This period was witness to the emergence of all manner of demographic data in public health, the rise of census bureaus, education statistics, crime statistics, and all other manner of numbers for very large sets of things. The all-seeing avalanche that brought life under the auspices of power in seemingly innocent books of tables, numbers, and other such data had a corollary that has to do with the categorizations of the kinds of persons counted in that data. Hacking explains: "Enumeration demands *kinds* of things or people to count. Counting is hungry for categories" (1982, 280; cf. 1981, 194). Thus, "statistics has consequences for the ways in which we conceive of others and think of our own possibilities and potentialities" (2006c, 6). The solidification of racial categories on census forms is a familiar case in point. In our times, a more recent wave of intersections of statistical enumeration and human categorization has been spawned by genetics.[10]

Now, one might ask, particularly if one is accustomed to thinking about biopower under the sway of Agamben's influential inflations, what does all this obsession with numbers and numeracy, and counting and classifying, have to do with Foucault's provocative critiques of the politics of modern sexuality? Where we find ourselves at bureaus of numbers we are quite a distance from the politics of the death camps that Agamben proposes as a paradigm for biopower. We know why the death camps should matter so much to us. But why should Hacking's institutions of enumeration matter too? Indeed why, as I am suggesting, should *histories* of statistics matter just as much as, if not more than, *ontologies* of the camps?[11]

In favor of Agamben's approach, or at least the initial plausibility of that approach, is the observation that biopower need not, as it were, automatically implicate statistics. That Agamben himself offers a theory of biopower without reference to its supposed statistical aspects indicates the sure conceptual difference between sciences of numbers and the regulation of life. Agamben shows that it is quite possible to take life as an object of politics without even a minimal understanding of life as an informational object. In further support of Agamben's approach is recognition that practices of counting are only obliquely featured in Foucault's own illumination of the implementation of biopower, at least as he charts its histories in his major published works, most notably *HS1*. Though this book certainly makes occasional reference to statistical notions as integral to biopower, Foucault's concentration on the increasing "interference" (*HS1*, 64) of the political and the biological in that book never makes fully explicit how this entwinement makes use of statistical-informational techniques as a crucial third relay in this assemblage.[12] Thus, contemporary theorists forming their conceptions of biopower by way of engagement with Agamben's work may find themselves puzzled at claims that Hacking's efforts represent crucially important work on biopower.

Although it may not be downright nonsensical to claim that political arithmetic could be only a very minor episode in a politics of life, it would in fact be quite senseless to assert this about the *actual history* of the operations of modern biopower. Granted that Foucault's *concept* of biopower does not necessarily entail statistical techniques, the *analytical* procedures through which he conceptualized biopower positively invite further genealogical inquiry into the functional role played by statistics (and much else, too, of course) in biopower. In other words, that Foucault's account of biopower is a conceptual product of a genealogical investigation already suggests the need for exactly the kind of history of statistical information undertaken in Hacking's work (and the work of others). If Foucault's account does not already include histories of these matters at the same level of detail as found in the work of Hacking and others, I would suggest that this is only because in the work of history not everything can be kept in place – selection is inevitable. Further, if we allow our range to extend beyond Foucault's major publications, we can in fact note compelling engagements with questions of statisticalization and informationalization in his work, perhaps most fully in his discussions of "normation" and "normalization" in *STP*.[13] These lectures help show how Hacking cannot be far off the mark, an impression which some readers unfortunately may have if they take too much of their Foucault from Agamben.

That a study of the history of statistics is motivated by Foucault's genealogies of biopower does not, of course, entail that Foucault's genealogies develop that history in sufficient detail. Indeed they do not. This is why it is up to us, after Foucault, to take up Foucault's concepts and keep them in genealogical motion. My argument is that the connection between statistics and biopower is best seen not as purely conceptual, but rather as an emergent historical connection whose conceptual contours deserve to be illuminated historically, for instance, genealogically. Hence the importance of being able to specify the kind of work that Foucault's analytics expressly facilitate.

Infopower after Foucault

I have suggested that Foucault's genealogies of biopower lead quite naturally to Hacking's genealogies of statistics. In this section I develop that claim with an eye toward the conclusion that the history of statistical biopower can be read as an early chapter in the history of what we might be prepared to call today "infopower." My suggestion is that in attending carefully to the contours of Foucault's work, we can see how there is already an incipient idea of powers of information present in his work on biopower. If part of the orbit of the historical moment of biopower can be shown to be a politics of statistics, then the next moment in that history may very well have been the emergence of an infopower whereby statistics and other manner of informational phenomena begin to gain a gravity of power all their own. There is a history of the present (I mean our present today, not Foucault's in 1976, nor even Hacking's in 1990) that moves from, say, the politics of health in the eighteenth century, to the politics of the census and social regulation in the nineteenth century, to the politics of, say, electronic communications surveillance in the twentieth century. All of this forms a background out of which there emerge some of the bravest new objects of our twenty-first century: for example, the immanent ubiquity of eyewear that informationalizes everyone's immediate environment (including facial recognition of passers-by on the street, keyed indirectly to online data profiles containing such information as phone numbers, places of employment, and home address) or the promise of a government surveillance enterprise that would amass a yottabyte of data (a yottabyte being 10^{24} bytes, which is an amount that if stored on current hardware would occupy the entire surface of Delaware and Rhode Island combined). The infopolitical problematics therein may seem a long way from biopolitics indeed. But my claim will be that such infopolitical practices are part of a present, our present, whose history is best seen as emerging out of a biopolitical past. To see how the history of infopower can be seen as an extension upon Foucault's history of biopower, consider first that Foucault contrasted biopower as "the right to make live and let die" from the classical right of sovereign power "to take life or let live" (*SMBD*, 241; cf. *HS1*, 138). In coming to terms with the very idea of biopower, it is crucial to note two things about it. First, the idea of making live only makes sense at the level of the population. Second, population is a concept that can be elaborated only through statistical, and therefore informational, techniques.

How is biopolitics a politics of the population? Foucault himself explicitly counted it as such: "power [with respect to biological existence] is situated and exercised at the level of life, the species, the race, and the large-scale phenomena of population" (*HS1*, 137; cf. *SMBD*, 245). But what does he mean here? Were it situated *only* at the level of the individual, the techniques of biopower would be incoherent at best and intolerable at worst. In the political rationality Foucault was seeking to understand, making a single individual to live could only be a sovereign intervention. Beyond the familiar sovereign-legal bans on assisted suicides, the idea of making an individual live is for us unthinkable. Try to imagine the impossible levels of control implicit in directing a single individual life to increase its life span or decrease its proneness to major disease and illness. But if exercised at the level of the population, this power to make live is something easy to both imagine and endorse. It thus imperceptibly became something that almost all of us today are always in favor of. Public health and hygiene, inoculations, nutritional labeling, and school exercise are only a sliver of the ways in which we pursue the biopolitical project of "making live" at the level of populations. There may, of course, be disciplinary implementations at work in many of the most familiar exercises of biopower. For example, public health is biopolitical in orientation though quite often disciplinary in its techniques of execution ("wash your hands," "get your shots," "eat your vegetables"). Thus, though biopolitics may often involve extensive and thorough uses of disciplinary implementation, the specificity of biopolitical regulation cannot be wholly comprehended in terms of disciplinary dressage. The techniques involved in training children to eat their vegetables are not sufficient to invest the idea of tracking correlations between vegetable consumption and physical health across populations of schoolchildren nationally. This is why the biopolitics of the school lunch are *more* than just disciplinary matters, and also *more* than just sovereign matters, too. After all, biopower can, even if rarely, function wholly outside of the scope of discipline. One example would be atomic warfare, mentioned by Foucault himself as exemplary of this mode of power (*HS1*, 137). Another would be urban water management systems in highly developed nations, where it is difficult to discern visible disciplinary correlates. These examples help show how biopower is *primarily* about the regulation of populations and thus only incidentally, even if quite often, implicated in the disciplinary training of individuals. The important point is just that these are all distinct modes of power – which is exactly why inquiries into their relation can be so productive.

A second important facet of biopower begins to take us out of Foucault's texts and into those of historians of nineteenth-century statistics such as Hacking. Here the crucial point is that a politics of population is an inherently informational politics. Populations are not natural kinds, though they are not therefore unreal. Populations are the real correlate of certain informational technologies, most obviously those of statistics and of counting. Before one has techniques in place for counting a population, there just is no population in a meaningful sense, and certainly not as an object of biopolitical intervention. Sometimes counting is easy enough, and involves only a clipboard, pen, and paper, but often counting is much more complex than that, especially where the objects one is counting are disparate and diffuse such that counting takes much time. Consider an edict issued in France by the radical National Convention upon having replaced the Legislative Assembly toward the end of 1792 – the Convention's Committee of Public Works sent a circular instructing agents "to obtain an exact knowledge of the population of the French territory," therein justifying the instructions by claiming that "all means of public prosperity are on the agenda and we can no longer neglect to know one of its most essential elements, the population. An enumeration of free men! Can one conceive of the idea without carrying it out?" (quoted in Headrick 2000, 72–3). As it turned out, this particular instruction proved enormously difficult to implement – something seemingly so simple as counting is a technical art and requires all kind of supporting apparatus to gain stability.[14] Once one has mechanisms in place for enumerating countable members of populations, there are further technical matters at stake in observing and transforming these numeral correlates of masses of living human beings. Statistical techniques help facilitate these observations and transformations. These techniques of counting and statistics represent a specifically informational engagement with populations, or a work on populations as informational phenomena.

These twin aspects of biopower, the concept of a population as a correlate of statistical techniques, are sometimes explicit in Foucault's discussions, but as noted above, are not developed there in full detail. Here is where Hacking picks up on a crucial theme in Foucault and develops it further according to the genealogical manner of Foucault's own investigations.[15] Hacking's genealogy focuses on utilitarian reformers such as Adolphe Quetelet in Belgium and William Farr in England. These were statisticians who sought to deploy enumeration for beneficial social control. Their goal was not to use numbers to wield repressive sovereign power over populations. Statistics would rather be the crux of the productive improvement of the lives of the laboring masses. These functionaries, says Hacking, "created the infrastructure of one of the kinds of power by which our society operates" (1990, 119). One of Hacking's favorite phrases throughout this book is "information and control" (cf. 3, 5, 94, 115, 141).

In virtue of the history of info-control, largely only implicit in Foucault, and far more explicit in Hacking, we can risk today to speak of an infopolitics that constituted one vector in the emergence of the more general problematization of biopolitics: *an infopower operative within and alongside of biopower*. And what happened to these powers of information after their emergence? Has infopower remained within the orbit of biopower? Or are we prepared to think of an infopower that, despite emerging from within the context of biopower, is today a form of power in its own right?

A critical investigation of *the possibility of infopower's detachment from biopower* such that it has assumed gravity in its own right would be one way of taking Foucault beyond Foucault, and of taking our selves into our present today (it would also, presumably, involve taking Hacking beyond Hacking). And why might this matter? A critical investigation of the history of our present infopolitics seems much needed today insofar as we find ourselves in the midst of increasingly complex, confusing, and critical informational problematics.

I have already mentioned a few humble technologies (e.g., Google Glass) and hubristic enterprises (e.g., the National Security Agency) now yielding a potentiality for bewilderingly massive informational surveillance. Consider also the recent spate of headline-level conflicts over infopower between such illustrious agents as the Pentagon and WikiLeaks or the Recording Industry Association of America, the Department of Justice, and MegaUpload, or the not unrelated anxieties over privacy and identity in digitally networked social media contexts.[16] Or consider the quite different, but surely resonant, debates over genetic enhancements and cloning, which are surely debates about life and the body, but also just as surely debates about the politics of information insofar as the concept of the gene is, at bottom, an informational concept as it gets operationalized in molecular biology.[17] These examples, it might be objected, can all be seen as fitting neatly within the mold of biopower, and perhaps also disciplinary power and sovereign power, too. But my argument is only that biopower (and other familiar forms) cannot fully exhaust the new modes of information surveillance, aggregation, and distribution in our midst – a history of infopower is useful not because we have left biopower behind but rather because something new is emergent too.

One of the brightest examples of this for us today is financialization. While the statistical techniques and property codes at the heart of finance capitalism obviously emerged through biopolitical and sovereign crafting long ago, the middle decades of the twentieth century were witness to whole new orders of informational possibility that simply cannot be boiled down to biopolitical and sovereign techniques. Informational forms emerged in those decades having very little to do with the management of populations and explicit legal controls. And yet they possess a remarkable impact in terms of facilitating new ways of conducting our conduct. It should be unsurprising that these are among our shiniest new objects of cultural perplexity. We, as yet, little understand the problematics out of which they arose. And it would be a mistake to reduce those problematics to all-too familiar terms. For we would thereby miss most of what is novel in, say, the securitization of risky mortgage debt or institutional shifts from pit floors to speculative screen trading. These perplexities are part of a thread that weaves from stable conduct at the Chicago Options Board to hyper-unstable objects such as all-digital peer-to-peer encrypted currencies like BitCoin – my claim is just that this thread is not wholly spun out of biopolitical material.

The broader powers of information in which we are enmeshed are today so ubiquitous as to sometimes seem necessary (rather than contingent), simple (rather than complex), and obligatory (rather than entrenched but ultimately optional) – this is why we find it difficult to even think of life outside of the constraints of our contemporary problematics of information. And yet human cultures and societies were, obviously, not always deeply penetrated by processes of informationalization. It is only within the last two decades that conditions emerged such that your personal information might be vulnerable to appropriation and theft on a global scale due to its accessibility over the internet, and it is only within the last two centuries that conditions emerged such that it even makes sense to speak of there being information that is personal. It is only in the last two decades that we have begun to dream about real-time networked statistical aggregation (of, say, financial data), and only in the last two centuries that it has even made sense to speak of a politics of a stable statistical object like a gross national product.

There is a history of making information stable, usable, and powerful. Foucault directs us to that history, but he himself did not write all of it. Nor have I here mounted a complete argument for the coherence of infopower. Such a project would clearly be beyond the scope of anything less than a book. Rather, I have sought to attend to the need for this project, or some other project quite like it, as an instructive exemplar of how we might make further use of Foucault today. *I have sought to exemplify how Foucault's analytical strategies demand of us that we move beyond the conceptual territory already illuminated by those very strategies.* This, I have argued, is a decidedly different direction from more familiar efforts in inflating Foucault's conceptual apparatus to the effect of what we might call the bloating of biopower. If we today work to further develop certain strands of the massive history of biopower beyond Foucault's own histories, we put ourselves in a position to learn something that Foucault himself did not teach us, and indeed could not have taught us, given that his present which is now in the past simply could not have prophesied our present today. What is therefore at stake here is an attempt to attend to the specificities and advantages of Foucault's own critical analytics.

Foucault's Critical Empiricism

What Paul Patton calls "Foucault's relentlessly empirical approach" (2011, 41, cf. Veyne 2010) can best be discerned in the mobilization of Foucauldean analytics for the purposes of inquiry into such emergent phenomena in the present as infopolitics, rather than in a generalization of Foucauldean concepts that forces them to colonize domains that demand different conceptualizations. Thus, if the work of transcendental Heideggerean-Foucauldeans from Agamben to Esposito and beyond would seek to disinter concepts from the historical weight that would always condition them, then this would require a transcendental philosophical perspective that a

careful Foucauldean empiricism would eschew. Foucault's empiricism, of course, is not just any empiricism. While it is certainly the
empiricism of the smallest differences and the most momentary
shifts, it is also the empiricism of explosive and momentous intersections.

Foucault offers us what should be called a *critical empiricism*. This
is a form of critique whereby we can engage how we are conditioned today, in all our complexity and contingency. This is a
critique that would attend to all the little differences that separate
us from who we could otherwise be and all the unobvious relations
that are welded together to form our very selves. Foucault's critical
empiricism offers us, among other things, methodological analytics
for bringing into view these constitutive features of our presents
and indeed our very selves. These analytics are the truest source of
the ongoing fecundity of his work for us today, at least insofar as
we might aim to make use of Foucault to go beyond Foucault.[18]

Notes

1 I take Foucault at his word when he states, in a 1984 interview, that
   "the notion common to all the work that I have done since *History
   of Madness* is that of problematization" (*PPC*, 257). This notion
   is central in my interpretation of genealogy and archaeology in
   Koopman (2012), where I show in detail that Foucault's retroactive
   self-interpretation here is most insightful.

2 James D. Faubion rightly notes that Foucault's methodology is one
   that does "not seem appropriately construed as pursuing the necessary conditions that make ancient philosophical discourse on the
   carnal pleasures possible, much less the necessary conditions of any
   possible practice or discourse that could be called ethics" (2011, 44).
   Thus for Faubion, "analytic" is an imprecise term, given the stark
   contrast between its classical valences and Foucault's own work.
   Unlike Faubion, I am content with Foucault's own usage of "analytic" as a description of his detranscendentalized procedures (cf. 43).
   Faubion prefers the label of "diagnostic" for Foucault's procedures
   (and his own, too) because he takes an analytic in its classical sense

as a "methodology specifically designed to identify the necessary conditions of any possible experience" (43). Though this interpretation of the term "analytic" is true to the philosophical tradition, I am content with the existing terminology even if it is not always technically precise.

3   See Part III, and Part IV, Chapter IV of *HS1*.

4   For a review of the literature on biopolitics, see Thomas Lemke's *Biopolitics: An Advanced Introduction* (2007b). On what is missing from Lemke's account, see Morar and Koopman (2012).

5   Other influential examples of this style of transcendentalizing, ontologizing, and even metaphysicalizing Foucault can be found in the collaborations of Michael Hardt and Antonio Negri in *Empire* (2000) and *Multitude* (2004), and more recently the work of Esposito's translator Timothy Campbell in *Improper Life* (2011).

6   Foucault details four problems with conceptually "inflationary" critique. Having already named the first above, the other three are that inflationary critique: (2) facilitates a generalized and nonspecific form of polemical denunciation or "a general disqualification by the worst," (3) "enables one to avoid paying the price of reality and actuality," and (4) too often fails to develop critical reflexivity (*BB*, 187–8).

7   See Connolly (2005), Lemke (2007a), Oksala (2010), and especially Patton (2007) for criticisms to this effect.

8   See Koopman (forthcoming) for an elaboration of these criticisms.

9   Examples of such work include Ian Hacking's *The Emergence of Probability* (1975), *The Taming of Chance* (1990), *Rewriting the Soul* (1995), and *Mad Travelers* (1998), some of which are discussed below, as well as works such as Ladelle McWhorter's *Racism and Sexual Oppression in Anglo-America* (2009), Arnold Davidson's *The Emergence of Sexuality* (2001), Paul Rabinow's *French Modern* (1989) and *French DNA* (1999), Nikolas Rose's *The Politics of Life Itself* (2006), Jenny Reardon's *Race to the Finish* (2005), Mary Beth Mader's *Sleights of Reason* (2011), James D. Faubion's *An Anthropology of Ethics* (2011), James Ferguson's *The Anti-Politics Machine* (1994), and Saba Mahmood's *The Politics of Piety* (2005).

10 In a discussion of what he calls, following a widely read article by Paul Rabinow (1992), "biosocial identity," Hacking notes that "knowledge of genetic 'identities' will forge social ones, creating

new communities of shared recognition based on partial science . . .
new kinds of people will come into being, people characterized by
a certain risk factor, who band together to create a social group that
evolves its own collective characteristics" (2006b, 88).

11 The emphasis here is exclusively on the difference between "histories" and "ontologies." There is no implication whatsoever that the
camps do not matter or should not matter – clearly they do and for
reasons quite obvious to all. Indeed it is that obviousness that helps
specify the delicate difference between totalitarianism and statistics as
objects of philosophical critique. My contention, to state it simply,
is that today we do not need philosophers to tell us that something
went terribly wrong at the camps – we all know this. By contrast,
philosophy can make itself quite useful by explicating what is problematic (in Foucault's sense of that term) about statistical thinking
– given especially that so many take it as obvious that there is nothing
at all problematic here.

12 Foucault indeed mentions, but only mentions, statistical notions as
part of the technical workings of biopower (cf. *HS1*, 25, 144, 146).
My point is just that he does not there develop these notions in detail
such that nobody should read this book as a major contribution to the
history of statistics. A different interpretation of the relation between
Foucault's concept of biopower and informatics is developed from a
media-and-information theory perspective in Galloway and Thacker
(2007, 70–7). In my view, Galloway and Thacker needlessly over-
state the extent to which Foucault's work itself actually functions as
a guide to, rather than a pointer toward, all manner of informatics.
Such overstatement is unfortunate because it blocks paths of inquiry
where we need to press beyond Foucault himself and precisely for
Foucauldean reasons.

13 *See STP(E)*, 29–86 (Lecture 2 and especially Lecture 3), Foucault *BB*,
and *EW3*, 134–56. It is worth noting that in the late 1970s Foucault
was in extensive communication with a number of scholars who
were working on these informational aspects of modern politics –
some of this work was collected in *The Foucault Effect* (Burchell et
al., 1991). See also Foucault's own editorial efforts in this area in
Foucault (1976b).

14 An easy exercise will make this vivid, at least for we academics:
try counting all the books in your library. Though it seems at first

blush that this should be remarkably easy, it will not be long before you come across items that will require you to make decisions. What about manuscripts? And digital copies? Books on loan from the library? How to count multi-volume works? If you count your books in one way, and I count mine in another, difficulties may ensue. Thus it was that counting all the people in France, under the administration of different local officials with different sensibilities for how to count, proved a resilient problem in the late eighteenth century.

15 For explicit statements of his project's debts to Foucault, see Hacking (1982, 279; 1990, 21).

16 For one helpful introduction to some of the issues involved here that I would read as amenable to a Foucauldean analytic (even if explicit in the departures from Foucauldean concepts that may be required here), see Chun (2006, 2011).

17 For a source of these ideas with which Foucault himself was surely conversant, see the work of François Jacob, winner of the 1965 Nobel Prize in Medicine: "Heredity is described today in terms of information, messages and code . . . What are transmitted from generation to generation are the 'instructions' specifying the molecular structures" (1970, 1). Foucauldeans interested in the connections between contemporary bioscientific information and contemporary biopower would do well to consider the leads of Rabinow (1992, 1999) and Rabinow and Rose (2006).

18 For comments on previous versions of this material, I would like to thank Tomas Matza, Nicolae Morar, and audiences at the Northwestern University Philosophy Department, the Pacific Association for Continental Theory, the Society for Phenomenology and Existential Philosophy, the Critical Genealogies Collaboratory and a Foucault Circle session at the American Philosophical Association. Special thanks also to James D. Faubion for characteristically thoughtful suggestions that facilitated important improvements.

6

Foucault's Face:
The Personal is the Theoretical

John Forrester

"*Pas de publication posthume*" [no posthumous publication]. So states Michel Foucault's will. And he would, it is said, admonish his friends: "Don't pull the Max Brod Kafka-trick on me." I would not have liked to be in Max Brod's shoes. Nor in Daniel Defert's. But I wasn't. And I'm grateful that they found a way to publish what Kafka and Foucault forbade them to publish. But that doesn't mean to say I think they were right. They did right by me and by many, very many, others. But I can't see how they obeyed the legal injunction placed on them. Let's have a look at what was involved. Before I do so, I must preface my remarks with a disclaimer. I am not an expert on copyright or the law governing last wills and testaments and I will not enter into a quasi-legal consideration of the issues. I wish solely to see how the works of Michel Foucault, many more of them now in print than when he died, are refracted, reflected and transformed by the wriggles that allowed this work to appear, despite his pithy and ultra-clear command: "*Pas de publication posthume.*"

His editors have struggled successfully – to their own satisfaction – with the letter of this law, so that there has been a continuous flow of Foucault's posthumous works, rising to a crescendo in 2004, the twentieth anniversary of his death, with the publication of three more transcriptions of the courses he offered at the Collège de France in the 1970s and 1980s. The most striking rationale offered is that, because these were public lectures, they had already been placed in the public domain "*dans son vivant*," as the French language says, in his lifetime. Their transcription and editing therefore is not the production of posthumous texts, but the transformation from one already published medium – for instance, the tape-recorder – to another, the book.

Daniel Defert, long-time companion and literary executor: "I remember Marguerite Yourcenar saying she wrote for posterity, even if it wasn't published; this made Foucault laugh, since he cared little for posterity if he was no longer there to continue the conversation" (Bellon 2007).

A little reflection on the specific content of Foucault's writings yields a plausible account of why Foucault forbade these posthumous works. If we turn to one of his most influential texts, *AK*, the drive for ephemeral anonymity is explicitly stated:

> I am no doubt not the only one who writes in order to have no face. Do not ask who I am and do not ask me to remain the same: leave it to our bureaucrats and our police to see that our papers are in order. (17)

Yet the next sentence gives an interesting twist to the project of anonymity: "At least spare us their morality when we write." Which turns the sphere of writing into a projected ideal space free of the police, of the morality of the bureaucrats, where anonymity becomes the condition of possibility of writing beyond morality. And thus beyond the given.

Anonymity is a strategy, a strategy of the present. In an interview in 1967, he said: "In the past, the problem for the person who wrote was to pull himself out of the anonymity of the all; in our time, it is to manage to obliterate one's proper name and to lodge one's voice in that great din of discourses which are pronounced" (*EW2*, 291). In 1984, in a more moderate tone, he said the following:

> the only law on the press, the only law on books, that I would like to see brought in, would be a prohibition on using an author's name

twice, together with a right to anonymity and to pseudonyms so that each book might be read for itself. (*PPC*, 53)

If we turn to a well-known essay of Foucault's in which he explored the notion of authorship, "What is an Author?" of 1969, we get an even clearer idea of some of the roots of his antipathy to being a named, monumental author.

That text attempts to give a historical sketch of the author function. The idea of the unity of authorship, an equivalent to the unity of the personality, is neatly dispatched there through examination of the structure of a mathematical paper, in which there are at least three authors at work: there is the author of the preface, describing the circumstances of the work's composition, uniquely placed and non-substitutable; the author who speaks in the course of the demonstration, saying "I conclude" or "I assume"; thirdly, the author who comments on this demonstration, discussing its importance and its implications – who "is situated in the field of already existing or yet-to-appear mathematical discourses" (*EW2*, 217).

This division of author functions is found in all texts, although the division will operate differently in Poe's "The Purloined Letter," in Gödel's paper on the incompleteness of arithmetic, and in an anonymous eighteenth-century text on masturbation collating the testimony of innumerable sufferers from the habit. Foucault's principal interest lay in the historical development of different modalities of attribution of authorship. The first function of the author, he argues, was simply as potential subjects of punishment, in the case of the written discourse being transgressive (*EW2*, 212). Authorship subsequently acquired its function as an economic stake in the ownership of texts. Yet Foucault notes how this seemingly comfortable world of commerce also engendered its own dangers: the possibility of transgression as an imperative peculiar to literature, restoring danger to writing.

The third function is that of the complex relation of the author to an individual, who may acquire the status of "creator," "genius," "designer" – but even these "are only a projection, in more or less psychologizing terms, of the operations we force texts to undergo" (*EW2*, 213).

Let us take it as given that Foucault wished to detach himself, as far as possible, from these author functions. But did he wish to give up the transgressive function of writing? Not at all: he wanted to put into question the law governing transgression, patrolling the illicit and the blasphemous. Being an author was declaring oneself to be complicit with this law, to be complicit with the categories of blasphemy and moral responsibility. "Do not ask me to remain the same": the aim of the law, and especially the law governing writing, is the obligation to remain the same. Being free of the author function would allow Foucault to move even faster through the archives, through the systems of thought that he took as his object and framed for his own and others' illumination. Anonymity was, then, an attempt at freedom. In the Preface to *HS2*, written in the weeks before his death, he responded to the question as to his motivation in writing:

> It was curiosity – the only kind of curiosity, in any case, that is worth acting upon with a degree of obstinacy: not the curiosity that seeks to assimilate what it is proper for one to know, but that which enables one to get free of oneself. After all, what would be the value of the passion for knowledge if it resulted only in a certain amount of knowledgeableness and not, in one way or another and to the extent possible, in the knower's straying afield of himself? (8)

Before I leave the question of "what is an author?" and the disappearance of Michel Foucault, I do need to add the most obvious of all the reasons to be derived from his analysis for Foucault's prohibition on posthumous publication. In the essay, he delineated a special type of author-function, which he called the "transdiscursive" author – author of a theory, tradition or discipline, such as Homer, Aristotle, the Church Fathers and Hippocrates. And, very much closer home, he names Marx and Freud as authors who gave rise to the rules for the formation of other texts. One has the feeling, as Foucault attempts to unpack this category of transdiscursive author, that the intuition of the peculiar specialness of Marx and Freud is an important one, but his capacity for delineating what exactly the transdiscursive authors achieve or how they do so is less than clear. I suspect Foucault had in mind a certain sort of relationship that political activists and psychoanalysts have to the texts of Marx and Freud. Be that as it may, fifteen years later, it was becoming clear that Foucault himself might be in danger of becoming such a transdiscursive author. In the well-known and enlightening – for Stone – exchange between Lawrence Stone and Foucault in the *New York Review of Books* in 1983, Stone could write, "Today [Foucault] enjoys an almost unparalleled position of intellectual dominance over the interpretation of many key aspects of the evolution of Western civilization since the seventeenth century" (Foucault and Stone 1983). If you have an inclination towards anonymity, these words would sear your flesh! Imagine how much hangs on the word "almost"!

So far I have connected the theme of Foucault's elected anonymity with his account of the linguistic and historical conditions for the author function. Authors are not given in nature, nor are they given in culture; they are historical formations. There are two other objects that Foucault was well known for putting into question in a similar way: firstly, the concept of "man" and the concept of the "individual." The final paragraphs of *OT* announced the imminence of the death of man: One can certainly wager that man will be effaced, like a face drawn in sand at the edge of the sea (*OT*, 387). Again that figure of the "effaced face" – "*s'effacerait*" and "*visage*" in the French. The death of man was simply a claim about the conditions of possibility of the concept of "man," conditions met, Foucault argued, with the inception of the modern episteme as inaugurated and given its foundation in the Kantian transcendental doublet: the transcendental and empirical egos. "Man" is the name for the object of those sciences made possible by the restructuration of knowledge around this doublet. It is not the author "Kant" who makes this possible, but the "Kantian transcendental doublet" – a conceptual formation, in the same way as one might isolate the conceptual formation of structural-functionalism as the foundation of a certain sociology and anthropology. The Kantian structure that Foucault accurately deploys, however, entails a notion of anonymity far profounder than the desire to be without name. The Kantian structure postulates a transcendental subject which is inherently unknowable, just as the "*Ding an sich*" [thing in itself] is not a possible object of knowledge – only the empirical ego or subject is a possible object of knowledge. Thus "man" emerges as a possible object of knowledge on condition that one give up, as Kant required of "pure reason," the project of knowing the subject. Canguilhem caught this aspect of Foucault's analysis in a breathtakingly premonitory image in his review of the book in 1966:

> The Kantian *I think*, a vehicle for the concepts of understanding, is a light that opens experience to its intelligibility. But this light comes from behind us, and we cannot turn around to face it. The transcendental subject of thoughts, like the transcendental object of experience, is an unknown. (1994, 86)

The light that comes from behind us is the light that reveals our objects to us and simultaneously casts our faces into shadow: a face that therefore becomes like the dark side of the moon, always turned away from the sovereign gaze of the scientific observer. This subject without a face reappears in another passage made famous by Foucault: the Kantian subject with the light streaming from behind him towards his object is also the supervisor at the heart of the Panopticon, who sees without being seen, who is the principle of meticulous and constant vision without being embodied in any definite form or person. But the light is not streaming from behind the supervisor: it is streaming from behind the subjects of panoptical discipline, who are thereby turned into objects of knowledge: "By the effect of backlighting, one can observe from the tower, standing out precisely against the light, the small captive shadows in the cells of the periphery" (*DP*, 200). As Foucault underlines, the function of the gaze does not have to be embodied. The regular disposition of the cells of the Panopticon must simply be "given to be seen," "*donné-à-être-vu*," not actually seen. One does not expect Jeremy Bentham to be on duty night and day at the centre of the Panopticon: it is "a machine for creating and sustaining a power independent of the person who exercises it" (*DP*, 201). The function of the observer is strictly and necessarily faceless: "the inmate must never know whether he is being looked at any one moment; but he must be sure that he may always be so" (*DP*, 201). The supervisor and the inmate thus enact

the transcendental-empirical doublet of the Kantian ego. Hand in
hand there is the production of a twin figure of the faceless, anonymous, unverifiably existent supervisor on the one hand; on the
other, there is the "inmate" – the object of empirical knowledge,
the object of the panoptical apparatus and the disciplinary sciences
of man.

In the move from *OT* to the panoptical structure of power, we
have shifted from an account of subject-free systems of knowledge
to a subject-free structuration of power. The critical response to
these two accounts was also parallel: systems of knowledge or
regimes of power are made by real people, real scientists and philosophers, real doctors and architects, who propose knowledge,
whose conditions of work and thought are material and institutional, who are self-interested agents. So the real subjects of history
must be restored. Then we will see, so this reading goes, that
Foucault's account, particularly in relation to power, is equivalent
to saying the new system of power is a mobilization by doctors,
bureaucrats, architects and others of their own self-interest. It is a
conspiracy of the professionals. As Lawrence Stone put it: "Was
[the Great Confinement] merely the result of a conspiracy of
professionals to seize power for themselves to lock people up and
determine their treatment?" (1983). Or take a more recent formulation of Foucault's supposed argument, from Thomas Laqueur's
recent history of masturbation. One senses Laqueur's unease at
his own inability to understand Foucault's argument when he says
"the argument goes roughly as follows":

> the West witnessed a major shift away from the play of the sovereign's
> power over the body of the subject to what Foucault called "bio-
> power," the control by professionals of aspects of the inner being of
> men and women, boys and girls that these professionals had themselves
> helped to create as arenas for the exercise of power. (Laqueur 2003,
> 270)

Laqueur sums up Foucault's view as being that "modern society
is a creature of dominated subjectivities" (276) and contests this
theory since Laqueur ascribes the fundamental transformations as
not taking place in knowledge or power but in "the self."[1]

Stone, Laqueur and many others – principally historians – insist on reading Foucault as advancing a conspiracy theory of the introduction of disciplinary power. The notion of "conspiracy" responds to the invisibility – the anonymity – of the agency that exerts power. The invisibility of the supervisor has become displaced onto the agents "behind" the system itself. The common characterization of paranoia finds its place here as well. The notion of conspiracy is, as a principle of historical causation, a disreputable one; one would not argue that the construction of the railways and the transformation of transportation of goods and services was a conspiracy of the engineers, or that the deployment of the internet was a Pentagon conspiracy. Why would one want to argue that the building of asylums, hospitals, and prisons was a conspiracy of the doctors and legislators? Yet it is a peculiarly tenacious reading of Foucault. Part of the problem may stem from a slippage: the introduction of paranoia-inducing disciplinary systems must have had a cause from the same stable. And there is nothing more paranoid than conspiracy.

Yet there is another reason, a more philosophical reason why Foucault's conception of disciplinary power is systematically misread. To explore why this is a misleading interpretation of Foucault, I will turn to another philosopher, Jean-Paul Sartre. In the section on "The Gaze" in *Being and Nothingness*, Sartre writes:

> Let us imagine that moved by jealousy, curiosity, or vice I have just glued my ear to the door and looked through a keyhole . . . But all of a sudden I hear footsteps in the hall. Someone is looking at me! (1958, 347–9)

When I hear the footsteps, I become aware that I am most exposed to the gaze of the other precisely at the moment when I gaze on the unaware other. In that moment, Sartre writes, "the self comes to haunt the unreflective consciousness":

> all of a sudden I am conscious of myself as escaping myself, not in that I am the foundation of my own nothingness, but in that I have my foundation outside myself. I am for myself only as I am a pure reference to the Other. (1958, 349)

There is no need for a real other to be present. A crackle of leaves is sufficient for the structure of the gaze to somersault over.

Sartre's account of the gaze is not historical, nor is it intended to evoke historical structures. What he demonstrates is the experience of the gaze of the other as inherent to the structuring of reflective consciousness. Under the gaze of the other, I acquire a self. What Foucault is advancing is a historical placement of the structures that reproduce, deploy, and utilize the structuration of my relationship to myself in the field of the gaze. There is nothing new about the structure of being for others in the field of the gaze. What is new is elaborating a technology to make use of this fundamental human experience and finding enthusiastic allies to renew its promise and efficacy under changing historical and geographical conditions.

In "The Eye of Power," Foucault recounted how he first became aware of the panoptical technology in exploring the architecture of hospitals in the late eighteenth century, when it was a question of ordering bodies, circulating air, regulating contagion and physical proximity, "ensuring a surveillance which would be both global and individualizing while at the same time carefully separating the individuals under observation." Bentham's *Panopticon* turned up as the incessant reference in the slightly later projects for the reorganization of the prisons:

> The back lighting enables one to pick out from the central tower the little captive silhouettes in the ring of cells. In short, the principle of the dungeon is reversed; daylight and the overseer's gaze capture the inmate more effectively than darkness, which afforded after all a sort of protection. (*PK*, 146)

This extension of the clinical gaze only receives its truly panoptical twist once one adds in the Sartrean dialectic of being under the gaze of the other even when the overseer is absent or asleep. Another formulation is to recognize that the principles of moral treatment of madness – the moral reform of the individual through the example and under the authoritative gaze of the master, the asylum director – have been turned into a building-technology, which was always the original aim of the first asylum builders. Retroactively, we can say that the doctor–patient relationship

Foucault described as the true innovation of alienism, of psychiatry, is always already panoptical in spirit. Or we can inverse the
relation: the apparatus of surveillance is always already imbued
with the dialectic of moral mastery and cure promised by the
therapeutic optimism of the early psychiatrists and alienists.

Foucault developed his critique of power as sovereignty for a
number of reasons, but one of them was to reject the notion that
power is always one thing and that history is simply a sequence
of revolutionary moments in which one interest group replaces
another. The panoptical gaze may always have the Sartrean structure of producing a self that is the object of shame, pride, or other
motivating states, but inventing a structure for its reproduction and
intensification changes not only power relations but also the very
objects on which that power is exercised. Panoptical power works
through producing a self with certain characteristics: one learns
to look at oneself through the eye of power. It is this dynamic to
which Foucault attributes the production of "individuals."

In the classical age, before the splitting summarized in the
expression "empirico-transcendental doublet," there was one
subject, the Sovereign. But then the light begins to fall from
behind this subject, its face falls into shadow, and a new kind of
subject is generated: the modern individual, the ordinary individual. From the Greeks to the classical age, individuality had been,
Foucault implied, a matter of fame. With the new disciplinary
procedures, the threshold of visibility of the individual is lowered:
the examination can create individuals out of the little people, the
ordinary people, you and me. Shame not fame. The sciences of
criminology and of psychiatry, the practices of military regulation
and surveillance, of educational institutions and training: these
create individuals in their specificity with a view to using and controlling them, not with a view to commemorating and celebrating
them. In *DP*, the individual emerges in the modern administrative
technology of power as an individual who is coerced, the product
of a "tactic" of "coercive individualization" (*DP*, 239).

However, Foucault was clearly not entirely satisfied with this
account of the origins of modern individuality. His dissatisfac-
tion in part related to the fact that he had not addressed the
relation of the individual to traditional political theory; he had

allowed traditional political theory to retain its quasi-legal subject, with which to found contractarian visions of society. One of his attempts to address this problem still passed over the central problem: he attempted to extend the vocabulary of mechanism, strategy, and tactics he had employed to describe power by raising the question of war (*EW1*, 59). A later model, however, was to confront the problem of the relation of power to the "individual" more directly: the "pastoral."

The term "pastoral" complemented the theory of micro-power covered in his earlier account of the eighteenth and nineteenth centuries, allowing a new view from a different perspective. It permitted a more comprehensive exploration of earlier power structures, before the absolutist state, before the medieval period: it allowed Foucault to jump back 2,000 years to spend his last years studying the Greeks and Romans. He now proposed that the principal distinguishing feature of expansionist Western societies is the introduction of the shepherd and his flock. The classical Greek model of city and its citizens provided no model for the care of individuals by the state; it was an innovation introduced from the Orient (from Egypt, Sumeria, Judea – and later the Hebrews). The shepherd-God watches over his flock rather than his land, bringing together dispersed individuals, guarding over them at every moment in a devoted spirit. Hence there are two forms of power: one political, one pastoral. Political power, the Greek model, provides the legal framework of unity; the role of pastoral power is to "constantly ensure, sustain, and improve the lives of each and every one" (*PPC*, 67). The contrast between the two forms of power meshes well with Foucault's depiction of the development of biopower and the disciplinary society from the eighteenth century on. But bear in mind that pastoral power is now a political theory in its own right, a transcendent (although historically specific) and ancient principle:

> This form of power is salvation oriented (as opposed to political power). It is oblative (as opposed to the principle of sovereignty); it is individualizing (as opposed to legal power); it is coextensive and continuous with life; it is linked with a production of truth – the truth of the individual himself. (*EW3*, 333)

Not surprisingly, Foucault also points to the Church as the distinctive institution that embodied this pastoral power (*EW3*, 333). And it is the Christian development of the "oriental" theme of the pastoral, not the original Hebrew version, that is the long-term historical embodiment of pastoral power (*PPC*, 71).

However, Foucault takes some pains to explain why pastoral power as he had described it in *DP* and *HS1* as an essentially modern phenomenon does not appear fully formed until the eighteenth century. He specifies that the distinctive pastorate of souls is an urban phenomenon, requiring a level of culture that Europe did not possess until the modern era; what is more, the bonds of master and serf characteristic of feudal society, a non-urban, agricultural society, were not conducive to the development of pastoral power. Nonetheless, in its development of the monastery and monastic orders, the medieval Church did nurture the seed that would be released with the Reformation. Here again, Foucault is setting his face against classical controversial historical theories. It is not the turn away of Reformation theology from the Church to the individualistic relationship with God centred on conscience and guilt; hence it is not the Weberian nexus of individualized Protestantism and capitalistic individualism that gives rise to the modern individual. Nor is it the advance of the merchant class, with its ideology of private property and the individualized money transactions of a proto-market economy, from which the modern individual arises. It arises instead from the dissemination of the pastoral practices associated with religious and monastic orders. The Reformation and its aftermath is simply an occasion for the dissemination in secular form, not the invention, of these practices. They are associated with secular institutions: "those of the family, medicine, psychiatry, education, and employers" (*EW3*, 333–5).

The modern individual is thus associated with the development of "closed" institutions to which most of Foucault's work had been devoted, from his first book on the asylum, via the hospital to the prison and the psychoanalytic consultation. Think of the target here as a Popperian thesis of the distinctive blend of economic liberalism, critical individualism, and the open society. The open institutions of European society and its precursors are classic images and prototypes – the agora or marketplace; the law courts and the parliament. Every citizen has the right to participate in the market, the law court and the parliament. In contrast, Foucault sees the closed rather than open institution as the distinctive modern institution, the monastery rather than the market. Closed institutions exclude and include in the same gesture: schools exclude parents; hospitals exclude the healthy; prisons exclude normal life, the non-criminals, as well as incarcerating criminals; the asylum is a retreat, a site of segregation and, most tellingly, a technology for the therapeutic *isolation* of those rendered mad by their families, by the everyday social milieu.

We might, then, contrast two different sorts of modern individuals: open individuals, participants in civic society, atomized property holders, voters and taxpayers; and closed individuals, with private lives, secrets of the soul, inner sensibilities and thoughts. Liberal political theory defends the public, open individual, convinced that the sacred heart of this individual, its private, secret self, is a kind of extension towards the interior, a hinterland, of the open individual, as if the private individual with his complex interiority is simply a consequence of a Great Trek undertaken by the public individual of civic society. Foucault, on the other hand, sees the closed individual as having a genealogy entirely separate from the atomized individual of political theory and economics: his individual has a genealogy in the closed institution. Foucault's list of these closed individuals is familiar – the child, the pervert, the hysterical woman, the madman, the Romantic genius, the dandy, and the most private and quintessentially modern individual of all, the fantasizing masturbator. None of these would, he points out, seem to be a likely prototype or a likely derivative of the public, democratic, laboring man, a figure without content or interiority. This is not to deny that the open and the closed individuals interact in complex ways. Foucault's, and our, epoch has been crucial for this linkage, when the language of civic rights has become linked with the figures of closed individuality: we have the era of "identity politics," in which the experience of the private – religion, sexual identity – become the defining characteristic of the public individual. And, as Foucault noted, the modern welfare state is "one of the extremely numerous reappearances of the tricky adjustment between political power wielded over legal subjects and pastoral power wielded over live individuals" (*PPC*, 67).

Modern psychoanalysts would claim that caring and nurturing is the earliest and most deep-rooted form of power experienced by the individual: it is the power of the mother. The pastoral power evoked by Foucault does have an almost maternal ring at times. Juridical power is paternal, patriarchal power, and it is also negative in two different senses: it says no, and it is legitimized and exercised through the self-sacrifice of the citizens or subjects. Pastoral power is nurturing and caring, has the welfare of individuals as its initial and final goal; it is positive power, in the sense that caring altruistically for another is positive: it involves a gift. It was perhaps precisely the benign face, the caring aspect, that made it even more imperative for Foucault to scrutinize this power; he characterized it as a struggle "against that which ties the individual to himself and submits him to others" (*EW3*, 331). Foucault thought that our era, like the Reformation, is, in this respect, principally a time of struggle in the attempt to create a new subjectivity.

How curious that Foucault came all this way, from posing the question of the treatment and understanding of the mad individual in insane asylums, to addressing the question of the distinctive features of the country and the city, of church and state in early modern Christian Europe! Yet the trajectory becomes more explicable if we see how tenaciously Foucault was addressing, particularly throughout the 1970s, the question of the origin of the modern individual. To answer this question, he found himself obliged to retrace the history of political thought, of the founding institutions of modern Europe – closed and open, ecclesiastical and secular. And, having located in the Christian pastoral tradition the roots of that Western violence which he implied gave rise both to imperialism and to the private self, he now addressed full frontal the possibility of finding an alternative way of being a modern individual. This alternative way had, of necessity, to be non-Christian; it had to escape from the hermeneutics of the self, from the pastoral injunction to singularize. It had to be not only a genealogy of power but also of ethics.

Superficially, Foucault's last books on Greek and Roman ethics are a different kind of project from the question of the production

of the modern individual through the modern matrix of individualization. He seems to be seeking the outside to his own thought
– he succeeded in "straying afield of himself": a pre-pastoral, pre-
individualizing set of ethical practices, in which a self is constructed
that is not first and foremost a self for the state or for God – as it
will become with the transformation of confessional practices in the
modern world. Foucault analyzes the technologies of the self that
"permit individuals to effect by their own means or with the help of
others a certain number of operations on their own bodies and souls,
thoughts, conduct, and way of being, so as to transform themselves
in order to attain a certain state of happiness, purity, wisdom, per-
fection, or immortality" (*EW1*, 225). This is a benign as opposed
to panoptical form of, a facilitating rather than coercive, individualism. Certainly when it came to morality, Foucault was resolutely
anti-universalistic. "The search for a form of morality acceptable
by everyone in the sense that everyone would have to submit to it,
seems catastrophic to me" (1984, 37; cited in Dreyfus and Rabinow
1986, 119). The refusal of the Kantian moral tradition, the tradition of the categorical imperative with its claim that the morality of
the subject must be a universal morality if it is to be worthy of the
name, this refusal is unequivocal. Rorty defends Foucault against
the charge of moral relativism with the simple observation that he
can always reply to the universalist injunctions: "What has universal
validity to do with me?" (1991, 198). There is nothing illogical in
such a reply, nor in the moral discussion that might well ensue:
"What if everyone felt like you?" Met by Yossarian's impeccably
universalistic riposte: "'Then I'd certainly be a damned fool to feel
any other way. Wouldn't I?'" (Heller 1962, 445).

The bridge that my argument attempts to cross passes from the
erasure of death to the desire to have no face, to the origins of
the author function and then to the account of the origins of the
modern "individual." In the course of *A*, Foucault criticized the
concept of repression he had himself employed in earlier work by
introducing a fundamental contrast between two modes of exercise of power: on the one hand, the exclusion of lepers in order to
purify the community, on the other hand, the inclusion of plague
victims.[2] But the response to plague was itself twofold. On the one
hand:

the plague appears as the moment of panic and confusion in which individuals, threatened by visitation of death, abandon their identities, throw off their masks, forget their status, and abandon themselves to the great debauchery of those who know they are going to die. There is a literature of plague that is a literature of the decomposition of individuality; a kind of orgiastic dream in which plague is the moment when individuals come apart and when the law is forgotten. (*A*, 47)

Foucault then evokes another dream of plague: "Plague is the moment when the spatial partitioning and subdivision of a population is taken to its extreme point . . . an exhaustive sectioning of the population by political power, the capillary ramifications of which constantly reach the grain of individuals themselves" (*A*, 47). The means for this sectioning involves dividing every part of the city into quarters, which are then isolated. Sentries watch over every door; inspectors armed with registers of names make an inspection of every street twice a day and summon the occupants of every house, who are required to show themselves at a window. If they fail to appear at the window, it must be because they are in bed, and if they are in bed they must be ill or dead. Action is then called for.

This monitoring of the plague was one of the many models Foucault elaborated for the understanding of the structure and genealogy of modern power. It is historical, it is literary, it fires the imagination. And it is uncanny: side by side, the evocation of the dissolution of the individual in the orgy of the dying; and the routine call of the inspector at a window where a face fails to appear.

And the use of this thematic of the absent and anonymous face at the window? In bridging comments about the posthumous Foucault, the anonymous Foucault, the inevitably dispersed author function, the different genealogies of the modern individual, we have arrived at a surprising conclusion: that if there is a personal dimension to Foucault's legacy (and there is – "Don't pull the Max Brod Kafka-trick on me"), it shows us how the personal and the theoretical are intertwined. "Do not ask who I am and do not ask me to remain the same": the absent "Foucault" shows us again how to make our theories out of all the resources that each of us has to hand.

Notes

1 "This new sexuality (the exigent relation between the self and solitary sex) is thus primarily made, to put it in Foucault's terms, in relation not to knowledge or to power but to the self" (Laqueur 2003, 276).
2 This contrast between the exclusion of the leper and the ordering of the plague-town also introduced the section on "Panopticism" in *DP*, 195 *et seq*. Foucault did not discuss the "orgiastic dream" and the "great debauchery" in that book.

Part II

Cases in Point

7

Biopower, Sexual Democracy, and the Racialization of Sex

Eric Fassin

Foucault's Laughter – or his Yawn?

Were he alive, Foucault would have a good laugh. In France at the end of the 1990s, thus spoke the opponents of (so-called) "gay marriage," or rather its light version voted into law in 1999: the *Pacte civil de solidarité* (or *PaCS*, i.e. civil pact of solidarity) – a domestic union for both same-sex and different-sex couples that preceded the opening of marriage to all in various countries, starting with the Netherlands in 2001. This sardonic comment could seem to express the tension between the radical and the liberal politics of homosexuality (see Fassin 2001). In the United States, it had been voiced earlier, starting in 1989, in the intracommunity debate: were not liberals accused of siding, usually unwittingly (like Thomas Stoddard), but sometimes willingly (like William Eskridge), with conservatives like Andrew Sullivan whose explicit aim was to "civilize" (other) gays through the institution of marriage? In response, feminists (like Paula Ettelbrick) and queers (like Michael Warner) advocated a radical critique of norms – starting with matrimony.

However, the ghost of a sarcastic Foucault was not mobilized in France by radicals but instead, somewhat surprisingly, by a group of (straight) "conservative progressives": their defense of a queer counterculture only served to justify, among left-of-center intellectuals, their ostensibly conservative defense of an ahistorical "symbolic order" premised on the joint authority of Lacanian psychoanalysis and structuralist anthropology. Marriage was not the issue – and in this they diverged from right-wing conservatives; but from their point of view, access to adoption and reproductive technologies should be reserved to straight couples – naturally. The sacralization of filiation through its naturalization implied its protection from democratic demands. Of course, this rather unexpected opposition to gay rights on the part of liberals had nothing to do with homophobia, or so they argued; it had everything to do with preserving the foundations of (our) culture. They thus joined or even anticipated Vatican theologians in denouncing a denaturalization of sexual difference involved in the politics of gender and same-sex marriage that allegedly threatens the order of things. Indeed, had he been alive, Foucault would have had a good laugh.

All the more so since it was the author of *VS* that these conservative progressives tried to enroll as a standard-bearer of sexual liberation against social norms – despite his resounding critique of the "repressive hypothesis." In fact, Foucault never wrote one word against the legal recognition of same-sex unions.[1] On the contrary: while his real interest (both intellectual and political) did reside in the invention of relations ("creating a new cultural life under the cover of our sexual choices"), he made clear that for him the politics of homosexuality also included civil rights – "an aspect that must be supported": as he pointed out in the early 1980s, "we should not consider that these problems have been resolved today" (*DE4*, 736 [*EW1*, 157]; throughout, translations from the French are my own).[2] His position was to go beyond, not against, liberal politics: "In my opinion, we should consider the battle for gay rights as an episode which cannot represent the final stage." It is "but a first step. If you require people to reproduce the bonds of marriage for their personal relation to be recognized, then indeed you have accomplished little progress." For "we live in a legal, social, institutional world in which the only relationships that are possible are extremely rare, rigid, and poor." Hence the need for inventiveness: "We must fight against this impoverishment of the relational fabric."

However, it is true that once Foucault started exploring "invention," he never discussed marriage. His investigation went in a different direction: "Let's take the example of relations of friendship." Actually, when he did mention conjugality and filiation, friendship among males became his model: "we have to gain the recognition of relations such as temporary cohabitation, adoption" – and when asked: "of children?" he significantly responded: "Or – why not? – that of an adult by another adult. Why could I not adopt a friend who is ten years younger than I? Or even ten years older?" (*DE4*, 308–14 [*EW1*, 158]). The point is to defamiliarize the family, thus estranged from any naturalist temptation: why should adoption law follow the rules of biological reproduction? The distinction between kinship and friendship simultaneously vanishes, as if this were the condition for viewing marriage or family as potential sites of invention: kin *as* kith, so to speak. This homosocial model was soon to find a mirror image in the context of the epidemic of AIDS: while families of origin often rejected their own blood, in Kath Weston's anthropological study, "families we choose" (including not only lovers but also former lovers as well as friends of both sexes) assume the everyday care of the sick and dying: in other words, kith *as* kin (Weston 1991).

So, while there is no reason to believe that, were he alive in the age of same-sex marriage, Foucault would not have a good laugh, perhaps he might yawn. Since, for him, invention occurs, if anywhere, outside marriage and family, it is not unwarranted to suspect that he could very well be bored by today's politics, rather than caustic. Nevertheless, instead of using the philosopher's name to legitimize a radical position (or, ironically, a conservative progressive one) in current debates, it seems more useful to wonder what makes marriage uninteresting, along with liberal politics, to him. This lack of interest has to do with the status of law in Foucault's thought: "if what you want to do is create a new way of life, then the question of the individual's rights is irrelevant" (*EW1*, 158). At best, legal recognition serves a negative purpose, with "a new relational law that enables the existence of all kinds of possible relationships, instead of being prevented, blocked, or erased by the relational impoverishment of institutions" (*EW1*, 158). Paradoxically, the philosopher of discipline thus seems to endorse a liberal view of the State – as if the law only served to forbid, or at best forbade forbidding. This seems to be the price for thinking, beyond the law, about the politics of norms.

The Politics of Laws and Norms

What if, though, one were to take seriously Foucault's own definition of power? Not only does it forbid (or conversely allow); it also facilitates, activates, creates. It cannot be reduced to repression or prevention; it is at least as much about production. Formulating is shaping: the power of the law thus contributes to the advent of that which it enunciates. This shift from a negative to a positive definition of what power *does* is of course central to the philosopher's argument about discipline. But why not apply this theoretical reformulation to the power of the law – and beyond, of debates about the law? Thinking beyond a political model defined until now by sovereignty, as advocated in *VS*, need not entail forsaking the state, no more than the politics of norms are bound to be exclusive of a politics of rights. In fact, Foucault's work could be used today to move beyond the limits of an opposition between liberal and radical politics: changing rights can reshape norms, just as evolving norms can redraw rights.

Let us consider marriage – precisely because it is an issue that usually divides liberals and radicals. Surely, opening this venerable institution to same-sex couples could have an impact on its significance, as its conservative opponents understand all too well, though one need not share their gloomy vision: the revision of norms in no way implies their disappearance. But it would simultaneously transform the relationships it is supposed to merely "recognize": for better or for worse (a *caveat* which makes all the difference both from liberals, who would only acknowledge the former, and from radicals, who tend to worry solely about the latter), that which is recognized is altered by such recognition (though not, admittedly, beyond recognition). Homosexuality does not carry the same meaning, either for society or for the social subjects at stake, when relegated to the margins of a counterculture or since "gay marriage" has entered public debate, if not law. From one anthropologist to another, from Kath Weston's "chosen families" to Ellen Lewin's "lesbian mothers" and "gay fatherhood" (Lewin 1993, 1998, 2000), the transformation of the ethnographic data indicates a shift in the cultural norms organizing the lives of lesbians and gays that parallels the evolution of public debates about queer families and same-sex marriage.

This is why it is important to question what Foucault presented as a clear-cut distinction between cultural invention and innovation in terms of law: if State power contributes to shaping and reshaping norms, then renewed forms of subjectivation can arise precisely within these new logics of subjection. Normative invention may very well invest legal innovations. Therefore, the recognition of same-sex unions does not necessarily imply normalization, no more than queer politics must obtain at the expense of civil rights. The ceremony of marriage here serves as a case in point. The meaning of the ritual is not (and cannot be) equivalent for same-sex and different-sex couples: for the latter, it is traditionally about *being* normal; for the former, it is today about *becoming* normal. This distinction is partly lost in the term "normalization": becoming normal is a reminder that one was not before, and thus that one will never quite be normal. This is why the marriage of two men or two women cannot *not* be political. Different-sex couples may engage in this institutional framework without any consideration of its cultural implications, as if marriage were a purely private adventure; by contrast, same-sex couples can never ignore the social resonance of their intimate choice: indeed, whether they want it or not, their personal is political.

In getting married, gays and lesbians do something to marriage just as much as marriage does something to the definition of homosexuality. So, while some would consider that lesbian and gay couples only imitate what is essentially a heterosexual ritual, and thus conform to a preexisting norm, it can also be argued that this imitation is a kind of mimicry that questions its very meaning. On the one hand, the emergence of "gay marriage" as an issue has revealed, if not "outed," the straightness of the ceremony. This

Eric Fassin

has been manifested in the last decades by the success of a renewed
ritual of marriage proposals, at least in the United States: men pub-
licly proposing to women compose a straight performance that is
also a performance of heterosexuality. On the other hand, gays and
lesbians have resignified marriage as the ultimate form of coming
out: publishing the banns makes intimacy public – not only the
bond that unites the couple, but also their (alleged) sexual orientation: a same-sex couple is publicized as a homosexual couple.
Instead of desexualizing homosexuality, the recognition of gay
and lesbian unions thus becomes a way of sexualizing marriage
– it homosexualizes same-sex couples just as it heterosexualizes
different-sex ones.

The relationship between laws and norms has to be understood
in political terms. According to conservatives, laws must contain
the decadence of norms. For example, legalizing abortion only
encourages this practice. In the view of liberals, laws should simply
confirm the progress of norms. For instance, legalizing divorce just
takes into account a transformation already under way. In France,
during the controversy surrounding same-sex marriage and the
law on *PaCS* at the end of the 1990s, while conservatives only
had to update their rhetoric for this new battle, the liberal model
appeared strangely outdated: as the public conversation focused on
"filiation," namely adoption and reproductive technologies, this
only revealed that there was no prior awareness of "queer families." Of course, so-called "homoparental" families (a term coined
in French precisely at that time) existed earlier – before they had a
name. But they had neither statistical reality nor public visibility.
In particular, in the French social sciences, neither the sociology
of the family nor the anthropology of kinship had ever taken into
account these social arrangements. The debate thus seemed to pre-
date the reality it purported to address.

Radicals themselves were sometimes at a loss: had not the
critique of normalization been preempted by conservative progressives? However, this trap could also turn out today to be an
opportunity to move beyond the formulations available when
Foucault was alive. When discussing (homo)sexual politics in the
early 1980s, the French philosopher did not seriously examine
the relationship between laws and norms: while his unambiguous

support for gay rights arose no profound interest on his part, he simultaneously started exploring cultural invention with his usual acuteness – as if the two were necessarily unrelated. However, in the 2000s, a new intellectual and political agenda arises that helps bypass the alternative of liberal and radical legacies: how can we prolong Foucault's redefinition of power, in positive instead of negative terms (that which creates, rather than prevents), and think how the politics of law redesign the politics of norms in democratic societies?

Sexual Democracy and the Public Sphere

The chronological distinction between sovereignty and discipline was not, on the part of Foucault, a purely historical argument; it was also an attempt to dispel the illusions of liberal democracy. While political philosophy focused on the shifts *in* sovereignty inherent in the advent of democratic regimes, the author of *DP* insisted on the shift *from* sovereignty, with the advent of a new form of power relying on disciplinary coercion; hence his theoretical move – away from laws, towards norms. The point was to reduce the gap between liberal and illiberal regimes by emphasizing what they had in common: totalitarian regimes only exacerbated, in his view, logics that were equally at work in Western societies. The difference between the former and the latter was thus a matter of degree, not of nature: biopower applies to both. As a consequence, Foucault was not in a position to examine the specificity of democratic societies. Along with most radical critics of "the West," he eschewed any such discussion – perhaps for fear that it should lead, once more, to a self-congratulatory celebration.

However, to approach today's sexual politics, including the public debates surrounding marriage for same-sex couples, it may be worth taking seriously the singularity of democracy, not so much as a regime, but rather as a type of society. In order to do so, there is a need for a concept that shuns self-righteousness, which is what I have tried to develop under the name of "sexual democracy."[3] My definition of a democratic society relies on its self-definition: a society will be called democratic if it claims to determine its own laws and norms. The rules of the game are not inherited; they are not posed *ex ante*, but composed *ex post*. While this proposition may seem tautological, in fact, its premise is legitimacy: what is deemed legitimate, and thus carries authority, in a given society at a given time. In a democratic world, no prior authority (such as God, Tradition, Nature, Science, etc.) is assumed to impose the order of things – as would be the case in what Max Weber called "traditional" legitimacy: its justification is supposed to be internal, not external – allegedly immanent, rather than transcendent.

A second element follows from this first defining feature: the starting point is not the essence of societies, whether democratic or not, but how they represent themselves. In order to apprehend this representation, we can borrow the notion of the public sphere, first developed from a liberal perspective by Jürgen Habermas, but later appropriated critically for more radical purposes – from Nancy Fraser to Michael Warner. If the politics of laws and norms have to be apprehended simultaneously rather than separately, then the public sphere is the mediating term that is missing from Foucault's theoretical framework. It is not outside, but inside us; not above, but within: it permeates us. On the one hand, then, the public sphere defines us; but on the other, it is also defined as "us." *As* rather than *by*: this distinction helps understand the difference between critics and apologists of democracy – but more importantly for our purpose here, between the self-representation of these societies and the actual logic that presides over their organization.

Who has access to the public sphere in allegedly democratic societies? While this question can be answered in a critical mode, by insisting on those who are excluded or marginalized, silenced or relegated to counter-publics, supporters of democracy usually answer: "we do, since that is what we are." And indeed, while critics can rightly point out that we do not all have access to the public sphere, conversely, one should bear in mind that the public sphere has access to all of us: today, no less than anyone else, radical queers are bound to define themselves in relation, even if in opposition, to the debates on so-called "gay marriage." Even racial minorities that are (in France and throughout Europe) more often an object than a subject of public discourse (spoken of, rather than speaking) cannot be ignorant of the stories told about them: while young women have to situate their sexuality in relation to expectations of repression, young men cannot but identify themselves in reaction to clichés of sexual violence – either to confirm or deny, to endorse or dispel the stereotypes (from virginity for women to rape for men) that are supposed to define them and thus contribute, if only in reaction, to their subjectivation.

A third element derives from the other two: liberty and equality are key values in democratic societies. Not that these principles actually organize them, of course – as liberals would have it with an optimism that is unfortunately belied by experience. The point is that these words have some currency in democratic societies: they are valued, which means that they can be used as tools, even weapons, to make claims for the transformation (or, for that matter, conservation) of the social order. At the same time, liberty and equality are not transcendent exceptions in a world of immanence: appearances notwithstanding, they cannot replace, say, God or Tradition. These values are not so much the foundation of democratic societies as what these are about, that is, what is at stake in the political struggles of democracy. What they signify does not preexist their usage: they are invested with meaning by the political logics that literally instrumentalize them to different, sometimes conflicting ends.

Let us take two examples that have to do with sexual politics: the parallel debates on prostitution, on the one hand, and the Islamic "veil" (or "headscarf," or any other term), on the other (although the two have sometimes, paradoxically though significantly, overlapped). In the former, abolitionists have maintained that their campaign against exploitation and domination is waged in the name of equality between the sexes and the liberty of women. But so have their opponents, who insist on not reducing the claims of sex workers to mere alienation, and on refusing to consider that women have to be protected against men. The same tension prevails in the latter debate: those who would ban the *niqab* and even the *hijab* speak in the name of women, of their freedom and demand for equality – just as much as those who reject this interference with their free choice as women and equal standing in a racialized society. Liberty and equality only take on meanings within such controversies: their definition is the very issue that animates these political battles.

All the examples above have to do with what I propose to call "sexual democracy." If democracy is defined in terms of immanence, not transcendence, through a self-representation of society that presupposes the importance of a public sphere in which liberty and equality carry political value, then, a question surfaces: is there any limit to democratization? In societies that claim to be democratic, does anything escape this process? Conservatives insist that sex does and should remain outside of history and politics – whether talking about gender identity or family structure, heterosexuality or reproduction. However, more and more voices now respond by suggesting that sex cannot be reduced to some ahistorical, apolitical "nature" of things – whether biological or not. Moreover, there is a historical reason why the current political battle about the boundaries of democracy focuses on sex (in its dual meaning of gender and sexuality): sexual politics was supposed to be an oxymoron, at least according to the liberal definition of democracy, which is based on the distinction between the two spheres, private and public. Today's redefinition in terms of sexual democracy questions such a partition. Why should any private realm elude democratization? On what grounds would sex (and only sex!) exist outside of politics? What is so special about sex?

Sexual Democracy and Biopower

Indeed, there is something special about sex – and that is where the concept of sexual democracy overlaps with that of biopower. Foucault famously introduced this notion at the end of *VS* (188, 191, 194 [*HS1*, 139, 143, 145]): "Man, for millennia, remained what he was to Aristotle: a living animal, in addition capable of a political existence; modern man is an animal in whose politics his life as a living being is at stake." But life primarily means sex: "power talks *of* sexuality and *to* sexuality" (*HS1*, 147). Here, the gap between sexual democracy and biopower is minimal: in both cases, the point is not simply that politics is now also about sex; rather, sex has become the political issue *par excellence*. In the case of biopower, that is because sex is at "the junction between the two axes" of biopower, namely "the disciplines of the body" and "the regulation of populations" (*HS1*, 139). When it comes to sexual democracy, the reason is that sex is the frontier marking the extension of democracy.

At the same time, of course, sexual democracy diverges from biopower in a fundamental way: both talk "of" and "to" sexuality, but the former speaks of liberty and equality, while the latter uses a language of "regulation" and "discipline." This difference has to do, once more, with the public sphere: political deliberation introduces a distance, and therefore a critical dimension that is absent in Foucault's approach of norms. In the name of liberty and equality, the democratic logic thus transforms not only the contents of norms; at the same time, public discussions affect how we relate to norms. For example, being a man or a woman, incarnating a gender cannot mean the same thing once these formerly intangible identities are put into question. Instead of being transparent, norms have now become visible; they lose their obviousness and turn out to be problematic. As a consequence, we cannot identify with them as fully as in the past, when they were still perceived as our true selves: we only relate to them, as if from a remove. Put simply, once they become an object of public deliberation, norms do not seem so normal any longer.

The critical distance produced by public deliberation is absent in Foucault's approach of norms – just as it is in the habitus according to Pierre Bourdieu: social history is embodied, and this incorporation functions all the better for being involuntary and unconscious. *Masculine domination* illustrates this perspective: the French sociologist explains how "the schemes of perception, appreciation and action that are constitutive of habitus," which operate "below the level of the decisions of consciousness and the controls of the will, set up a cognitive relationship that is profoundly obscure to itself" (2001, 37). However, should we not question how this model devised in the context of rural Algeria in the late 1950s actually differs from the habitus in today's France? What the public sphere does to intimacy is dispel, at least in part, this obscurity:

the democratic habitus may escape our volition, but it does not
entirely elude our consciousness. Norms are never a pure creation
of the will; however, in democratic societies, we are not blind to
the normalization at work – whether we try to resist or comply,
bypass or even actively ignore it. The habitus is not simply acting
through us; we are also acting through the habitus, all the more so
since the public sphere opens a critical space.

Are we then to understand sexual democracy as a light, opti-
mistic counterpart to the dark pessimism of biopower? Should we
read the former as a liberal story of emancipation, and the latter
in radical terms of oppression? The question potentially leads in
two opposite, though complementary directions. The first has to
do with Foucault's reflections on power: he was soon to insist,
precisely in reaction against the prevailing interpretation of his
work in the wake of *DP* as a gloomy analysis of domination, on
the importance of resistance for its own sake, and not simply in
reaction against power: governmentality supposes real subjects,
not mere objects. If one defines, as Foucault does, power as a kind
of action on other actions, then, beyond the brutal imposition of
violence, the possibility arises of inventing new ways of life – not
against, nor outside, but from and within its very mechanisms.

The other direction opened by this question symmetrically
makes us reconsider sexual democracy in less sanguine terms.
The mediation of the public sphere cannot be reduced to its
critical dimension; it also feeds a normative understanding of
sexual democracy in racialized terms. This became clear in the
2000s, when Ronald Inglehart and Pippa Norris updated Samuel
Huntington's "clash of civilizations" to redefine it specifically as a
conflict between sexual cultures (Huntington 1993; Inglehart and
Norris 2003). This rhetoric has played internationally after 9/11, in
particular in Afghanistan, following a logic of expansionist imperialism; but it takes on a different meaning in "Fortress Europe,"
where it serves to justify the containment of immigration: "we"
need to protect our civilization from "them," presented as sexual
barbarians (through polemics on the Islamic veil, but also polyg-
amy and forced marriage, genital mutilations and more generally
violence against women).[4]

Hence tests imposed upon Third World migrants in the

Netherlands, in France, in Germany, and elsewhere: they are meant to exclude sexist (and even sometimes homophobic) "Others." Hence also all the attacks against Islam, throughout Europe: they circumvent accusations of racism in so far as they are framed in terms of gender and sexuality – of religious ideology rather than race. This is not entirely new, of course: the sexual dimension of civilization was already present at the time of colonization – which could be rationalized, in Gayatri Spivak's eloquent terms, as "white men saving brown women from brown men." However, this rhetoric is renewed as the conflation between "our" civilization and civilization itself now founded on the normative claims, not simply of culture, but more fundamentally of sexual democracy. Manifestly, just as biopower cannot be reduced to its somber version, sexual democracy should not be understood merely in sunny terms.

The Racialization of the Nation

Race may be the key term for this revision of both concepts. As we have just seen, the fact that sexual democracy is mediated by the public sphere also implies that it can also be appropriated (from a critical point of view, one would say instrumentalized) as a rhetoric serving xenophobic or racist ends. Not that sexual and racial democracy necessarily clash: there is nothing inevitable about this tension. Let us return to the example of *PaCS* and beyond, the French politics of marriage and reproductive rights for same-sex couples. How are we to understand what I have called (by contrast to the sacralization of marriage itself in the United States) the sacralization of filiation in today's France?[5] Instead of looking for culturalist answers that eventually boil down to the eternal Frenchness of France, I suggest paying attention instead to the recent politics of Frenchness in France: rather than explaining the nation by the nation, the idea is to focus on nationalism.

The naturalization of filiation is not inherent in French culture: far from belonging to immemorial France, its history is quite recent. After all, Napoleon's 1804 Civil Code established the social institution of matrimony as its foundation with the husband's presumption of paternity to a child born in wedlock. Only in 1972 did the strict separation between "legitimate" and "natural" children start fading from French law. But it was as late as the 1990s that French courts started deciding in favor of a biological definition of filiation (for example in paternity suits). Legal scholar Daniel Borrillo, a key promoter of gay and lesbian rights in France, has argued that the rise of this naturalist model, at the expense of the former civilist one, had to be understood as a reaction against the emergence of new claims for an inclusion of same-sex couples in the institutions of marriage and the family: the biologization of filiation would be the sign of a homophobic reaction – and indeed, many legal experts have voiced virulent homophobia in opposition to queer politics (Borrillo 2010).

I have offered a different (though not necessarily incompatible) interpretation, relying on the same chronology: the naturalization of filiation is not limited to family law, as filiation simultaneously defines nationality. Starting in the late 1980s, against the background of a rising extreme-right populism, with the National Front, French citizenship is redefined: *jus soli* recedes, thus increasing the importance of *jus sanguinis*. This is a way to resist the progress of family migration (namely, binational marriages and family reunification). In this context, the naturalization of filiation is opposed not only to gay rights, as Borrillo pointed out, but also to the naturalization (in a different sense, of course) of recent migrants, and more importantly their children: the racialization of the society makes it harder and harder, for those who were not born French, or even who are not of French "origin" (or indeed appearance) to become nationals.

This "biologization" of citizenship became most obvious through a polemical amendment to the 2007 immigration law that encouraged DNA tests for migrants trying to prove, in the face of bureaucratic skepticism when they request family reunification, that their children are actually theirs. It is also apparent in the tests (whether of bones or pubic hair) imposed upon young undocumented aliens who claim to be minors, in order to establish their true age (or so authorities claim, despite serious scientific doubt) (Cette France-là 2009a, 157–9, 2009b). In both cases, such biologization is reserved to foreigners; it can thus be understood not so much as a racial distinction from "us," but rather as a racialization of "them": only "others" are ostensibly defined in biological terms. Of course, this is an illusion: the racialization of the nation affects all – those who belong, and those who do not. Gays and lesbians know it all too well when they are denied access to filiation in the name of a naturalized filiation: some of "us" can end up on the other side, that of the "others." More broadly, the emergence of "whiteness" as an issue, also since the mid-2000s, only confirms that racialization is not solely for "them."

It is in the light of this biologized revision of the nation that we can go back to Paul Rabinow's ethnographic study of "French DNA" (Rabinow 1999). The American anthropologist recounts how an American biotech company named Millennium planned to collaborate with a French genetics laboratory, the Centre d'étude du polymorphisme humain [Center for the study of human polymorphism] (CEPH). Their alliance was stopped in 1994 by the French government lest this would imply forsaking to aliens (namely, Americans) "French DNA" – a remarkable phrase coined on this occasion. While irony is inscribed in the very title of the book, and even more explicitly in a blurb on the back-cover ("Who would have thought that there was such a thing as a genetic Napoleon Code?"), it is only in retrospect, after the infamous 2007 DNA Amendment, that the national issue can be fully perceived in its link with immigration. Indeed, 1994 is also the year when the first (so-called) "laws of bioethics" were adopted in Parliament, concerning (in particular) access to reproductive technologies (limited to different-sex couples, whether married or not, "of procreating age"): this was shortly after a 1993 law reforming citizenship to limit *jus soli* for the children of migrants. The laws of filiation, whether governing family or nationality, are in both cases defined (or redefined) in a (more) naturalistic framework.

Biopower, Race, and Sex

Sexual democracy and racial democracy do not necessarily stand in opposition: in France, as we just saw, the politics of the 1990s differ from those of the 2000s – and indeed, while marriage is now supposed to open up to same-sex couples under the presidency of the Socialist François Hollande, anti-immigrant policies are likely to remain unchanged. The point is not to presume the nature of the link between race and sex, but to assume its existence, whatever form it may take. Again, the example of (again, so-called) "bioethics" will prove useful, precisely because, in the French case at least, the term contributes to obfuscating the reality of biopolitics.[6]

Of course, one might think that bioethics has nothing to do with race. However, there are indications that the biologization of filiation contributes to a racialization of reproductive technologies. Think of surrogate motherhood: in the United States, in the second half of the 1980s, the Baby M case opposed the genetic surrogate mother, who refused to give up her parental rights to the couple who had hired her womb by contract. In response to the legal uncertainties concerning who the "true" parents are, many now choose to avoid any biological connection between the surrogate mother and the child – thanks to the development of gestational (as opposed to traditional) surrogacy. But it has also become common, remarkably, for white parents-to-be to hire non-white surrogate mothers, thus avoiding even the appearance of a biological link – thanks to race.

This racialized logic is not specific to the United States. Even (allegedly) color-blind France takes race into account when it comes to reproductive technologies. Access to gametes is conditioned upon biological resemblance – hair and eye, but also skin color. This, of course, may sound like common sense: why pair white children with black parents, or vice versa? However, it is worth noting that what seems absurd in the case of assisted reproduction is banal in the case of transnational adoption. Actually, in France, a white couple that would object to adopting a non-white child might be barred by social services. Why should filiation operate with different rules when we move from bioethics to the ethics of adoption? It seems clear that the biological dimension of reproductive technologies justifies, as if it were obvious, a biologization of filiation that opens the way for its racialization.

In order to explore further the relation between race and sex, it is time to go back to reading Foucault. To begin with, it is important to note how the philosopher offers, in *IFDS*, a slightly different version of biopower from what he presents that same year in *VS*: while he does distinguish "two absolutely heterogeneous types of discourses: on the one hand, the organization of law around sovereignty and on the other the mechanics of coercion exercised by disciplines" (*SMBD*, 38), Foucault does not so much oppose the two logics in diachronic terms as he analyzes their synchronic confrontation.

According to him, the tense coexistence of the two forms of power "makes more and more necessary a kind of arbitration discourse, a form of power and knowledge rendered neutral by its scientific sacralization" (*SMBD*, 39). This is exactly what happens in the case of French bioethics under the symbolic authority of wise men (and women), experts appointed to neutralize or depoliticize these issues. "It is on the side of the extension of medicine that you see how in a way the mechanics of discipline and the principle of law do, if not combine, perpetually exchange or struggle." Bioethics might thus be a good illustration of how, in today's governmentality, "the two heterogeneous strata of discipline and sovereignty meet" – or, to go back to an earlier point, how laws and norms interact (*IFDS*, 34–5 [*SMBD*, 39]).

We can now return to biopower according to Foucault. "Power talks *of* sexuality and *to* sexuality," as we have seen; but the famous phrase is preceded by an enumeration meant to illustrate his argument: "health, progeny, race, future of the species, vitality of the social body" (*VS*, 194 [*HS1*, 147]). When (bio)power speaks of sex, then it also speaks of race. Ann Stoler has powerfully emphasized the forgotten importance of race in the *VS*: her work illuminates how Foucault's "history of the West" overlooks its colonial Other, all the more paradoxically since it relies on an understanding of all kinds of Others – the mad, the perverts, etc. (Stoler 1995). However, as this historian and anthropologist of the (post)colonial world (Dutch and French, in particular) was the first to point out, remarkably, the lessons taught at the Collège de France at precisely the same time did focus on race – with a genealogy of racism through its mirror-image, the figure of the "war of the races."

Again, we can see how the philosopher himself immediately

puts into question chronological distinctions. It may appear that sex replaces blood, as seemingly we move from sovereignty to discipline; but in fact, just like for laws and norms, "the analytic of sexuality and the symbolic of blood, though they belong, in their very definition, to two very distinct regimes of power, have not happened in succession (no more than these powers) without overlapping, interacting, or echoing." Here comes the example of racism: "Nazism was probably the most naïve combination and at the same time the most cunning (the latter because of the former) of blood fantasies with the paroxysms of a disciplinary power" (*VS*, 196–7 [*HS1*, 149]).

Foucault developed his intuition in a later class that same year (*IFDS*, 226–8 [*SMBD*, 259–60]). Of course, the shift from sovereignty to discipline can be summarized as the passage from the old power to make die and let live to the new one of making live and letting die. That is the reason why suicide becomes a sociological issue, he argued in *VS* – or, one might add, why euthanasia is so problematic in our societies. But of course, as the example of capital punishment in the United States makes clear, the power to put to death does not belong to the past. Foucault raises the question himself: if biopower "has life as its object and objective," then "how is the right to kill going to be exercised?" Racism is a way "to establish a discontinuity of a biological kind," responds the philosopher, "within the biological continuum that is targeted by biopower." There is nothing new about the power to kill – except that it has to be made "compatible with the exercise of biopower." Such is the function of modern racism: race "is the condition that makes acceptable putting to death in a society of normalization."

Clearly, race is not a marginal element in the definition of biopower. It is inextricably linked to sex – just as it is in that of sexual democracy. The confrontation of the two concepts thus helps manifest this hidden dimension. *VS* is also a history of race. This is equally true of sexual democracy, which involves both the sexualization of race and the racialization of sex. The reason is simply that it defines "us" – in two distinct, though interrelated meanings: on the one hand, the public sphere permeates us, and thus contributes to our subjectivation; on the other hand, the rhetoric of sexual democracy serves to draw a line between "us" and "them."

There still remains a major difference between the two concepts. It is not, as we have seen, the opposition between the (liberal) politics of laws and the (radical) politics of norms. It has to do with the difference between discourse and rhetoric. Biopower is very much a matter of discourse; but this discursive practice is never simply a rhetoric: it is the very logic that structures norms. By contrast, the public sphere mediates the discourse of sexual democracy through a rhetoric, and thus introduces a distance within norms. In the end, the strategic choice to minimize or maximize the specificity of democratic societies is what justifies resorting to one concept or the other – biopower or sexual democracy. But their confrontation helps shed light on what they have in common – and, in particular, race.

Notes

1 On this, see my piece "Lieux d'invention. L'amitié, le mariage et la famille" [Friendship, marriage and the family] (Fassin 2004). The philosopher's lack of opposition to same-sex marriage finds confirmation in his personal life. On May 22, 2013, I interviewed his partner Daniel Defert (who founded the anti-AIDS association AIDES right after Foucault's death in 1984). As I was about to leave, he added these words (my translation): "Did you know that Foucault wanted us to get married? It was very funny. One day, he read in the gay press that some Presbyterian minister in Scotland celebrated same-sex weddings He says to me: 'Let's go!' So I tell him: 'Listen, it's absurd! We're not religious, and it will have no legal value. What are we going to look like?' I'm the one who didn't want to, but he did. I now regret it: it would have been symbolic. People put words in his mouth: 'No way Foucault would have supported gay marriage!'" As I echoed him with this quote – "Foucault would have had a good laugh" – Defert responded, "Well, no!" He then went on: "He actually wanted two things. He wanted us to get married, and he wanted us to adopt a child. We heard from a friend who had just adopted a Filipino child.

Foucault rose to his feet and grabbed his passport to travel to the
Philippines. I'm the one who said, 'Are you sure? Are we sure he'll
be happy?' We were afraid he would be harassed in school as a 'fag
baby.'"

This interview took place just a few days after the final approval
of the Taubira law opening marriage to same-sex couples in France
on May 17, 2013 – a context we had discussed earlier when I asked
Defert to join a manifesto published on December 12, 2012, calling
for a demonstration in support of the bill (http://www.liberation.
fr/societe/2012/12/12/mariage-pour-tous-le-16-decembre-manifes
tons-nous_867128, retrieved August 25, 2013). Conducted in the
apartment Defert had inherited from Foucault, it also reverberated
with another interview published a few months earlier by *Le Nouvel
Observateur* (November 6, 2013): as the political battle around the
bill was unfolding, his sale of Foucault's papers to the Bibliothèque
nationale de France revealed how (intellectual) legacy and (material)
inheritance are intertwined. Defert opens in these terms: "The history
of these archives would not have been the same had we been PACSed
[referring to the French *pacte civil de solidarité*] or married." As an avid
reader of Balzac, he understands how the Civil Code defines family
and property. While "Foucault left me his apartment with everything
in it," contrary to a surviving spouse, "I had to pay 65% taxes." As
the administration brutally ignored Defert's offer to donate Foucault's
archives to the State in exchange for a tax exemption, he had to sell his
own apartment in order to keep Foucault's. Defert clearly considers
today's sale for 3.8 million euros as payback. "For me, two things are
at stake: the indifference with which Foucault was treated in France
for a few years, and the difficulties of homosexual couples before
the PACS" (http://bibliobs.nouvelobs.com/essais/20121106.OBS
8175/daniel-defert-les-archives-de-foucault-ont-une-histoire-politi
que.html, retrieved August 25, 2013).

2 All of the following citations of Foucault in this section are excerpted
from "Le triomphe social du plaisir sexuel: une conversation avec
Michel Foucault" (*DE4*, 308–14 [*HS1*, 157–62]).

3 See my first conceptual definition in French in "Démocratie sexuelle"
[Sexual democracy] (Fassin 2005a).

4 I have tried to examine the tension between the critical and the
normative understandings of sexual democracy, and the political

contradictions that follow, in a variety of pieces that reflect on the
political urgency of this issue. See Fassin (2006, 2010a, 2010b, 2011a,
and 2011b).

5 The following argument is developed in my text "Entre famille et
nation: la filiation naturalisée" (Fassin 2009).

6 The following paragraphs borrow from my text "Sous la bioéthique,
la bio-politique" [Beneath bioethics, biopolitics] (Fassin 2012).

8

"A New Schema of Politicization":
Thinking Humans, Animals, and
Biopolitics with Foucault

Cary Wolfe

As is well known, Foucault argues in *HS1* that "for millennia, man remained what he was for Aristotle: a living animal with the additional capacity for a political existence; modern man is an animal whose politics places his existence as a living being in question" (134). Moreover, as Foucault famously defines biopolitics, it "is the power to make live. Sovereignty took life and let live. And now we have the emergence of a power that I would call the power of regularization, and it, in contrast, consists in making live and letting die" (*SMBD*, 247). Foucault develops this line of investigation later in his career. In *SMBD*, for example, he argues that a "new mechanism of power" arose in the seventeenth and eighteenth centuries, one that had "very specific procedures" and "new instruments." This new type of power, he argues, is "absolutely incompatible with relations of sovereignty," and it is based on "a closely meshed grid of material coercions rather than the physical existence of a sovereign" (35–6).

Foucault thus allows us to see, as Roberto Esposito points out, that for biopolitics the fundamental mechanism concerns not sovereignty and law but rather "something that precedes it because it pertains to its 'primary material'" (2008, 29). (As is well known, Foucault's main examples are medicine and the rise of the various "health" professions under the broader regime of "governmental-ity" and its specifically modern techniques of managing, directing, and enhancing the lives of populations via hygiene, population sciences, and so on, the better to extend and consolidate politi-cal power.) Even more importantly for our purposes, Foucault argues that this shift from sovereignty to biopower involves a new concept of the subject, one who is endowed with fundamental interests that cannot be limited to or contained by the simple *legal* category of the person.

In opposition to what Foucault calls *homo juridicus* (or *homo legalis*), we find in this new subject, *homo oeconomicus*, "an essen-tially and unconditionally irreducible element against any possible government," a "zone that is definitively inaccessible to any gov-ernment action," "an atom of freedom" (*BB*, 271). The subject of interest thus "overflows" the subject of right, "surrounds" him and, indeed, is the "permanent condition" of his possibility (274). *Homo oeconomicus* thus founds a new domain of "irrational rational-ity" that is of a fundamentally different order from sovereignty and the juridical subject. *Homo oeconomicus* thus says to the sovereign "you cannot because you do not know, and you do not know because you cannot know" (*BB*, 282, 283). But such a creature, of course – and for that very reason – poses a threat to power, one that will in time give rise to the regime of governmentality and its exercise of biopower (294–5), which will in turn involve new sciences and discourses: of ratios of birth and death, fertility and mortality rates, figures on longevity – in short, sciences of "popu-lations" whose task it is to manage this aleatory element by "a power that is not individualizing but, if you like, massifying, that is directed not at man-as-body but man-as-species" (*SMBD*, 243; see also 246, 249–50).

Foucault thus discloses a key element of the modern political landscape – the "radical transformation of the idea of *humanitas*," as Esposito puts it – that escapes the very political and legal con-cepts inherited from modernity. "*Humanitas* increasingly comes to adhere to its own biological material" (2008, 4), Esposito writes, and what is involved here is not so much the "animalization" of human populations but rather the exposure of how that designation simultaneously masks and makes possible the more fundamental operations of modern politics by means of what Giorgio Agamben calls "the anthropological machine, which each time decides upon and recomposes the conflict between man and animal" – a machine that depends upon (to use the terms that Agamben borrows from Aristotle) the distinction between *bios* (or political "form of life") and *zoë* (or "bare life") (2004, 75). To live under biopolitics, then, is to live in a situation in which we are all always already (potential) "animals" before the law – not just non-human animals according to zoological classification, but any group of living beings that is so framed. Here, the distinction "human/animal" – as the history of slavery, colonialism, and imperialism well shows – is a discursive *dispositif*, not a zoological designation. And it is all the more ironic, then, that the main line of biopolitical thought has had little or nothing to say about how this logic affects non-human beings – a cruel irony indeed, given how "animalization" has been one of its main resources.

   To begin to correct this problem, we need to insist on an important difference between Agamben and Foucault – or rather a set of differences whose consequences I want to unfold over the next few pages. While it is no doubt true – both in Foucault's own discourse and in point of fact – that sovereignty continues to be an important force in modern politics, Foucault's point is that it becomes recontextualized, and finally subordinated, to a fundamental political shift. Where Foucault allows us to disarticulate sovereignty and modern biopolitics, Agamben (as Jacques Rancière elegantly puts it) "matches them by equating Foucault's 'control over life' with Carl Schmitt's state of exception" (Rancière 2004, 300). And the result is an overly formalized symmetry between the figure of the sovereign and *homo sacer*, both of whom stand at the extreme opposite limits of a juridico-political order in which they are simultaneously included and excluded, inscribed in the law either by being abandoned by it (in the case of *homo sacer*) or establishing it by extra-legal means (in the case of the sovereign). As Agamben puts it, "the sovereign and *homo sacer* present symmetrical figures and have the same structure and are correlative: the sovereign is the one with respect to whom all men are potentially *homines sacri* and *homo sacer* is the one with respect to whom all men act as sovereigns" (1998, 84).

Now this exaggerated formal symmetry might seem of little moment – might seem merely academic, you might say – were it not for the fact that it leads Agamben to engage in a fundamental form of dismissal and disavowal of the embodied existence that we share with non-human animals (Elmer 2007, 20). "Agamben remains so fascinated by the hyperbolic opposition between meaningful life and mere animality," Jonathan Elmer argues, "between power and the absolute powerlessness of 'bare life,' that a trace of contempt edges into his description of those who have been reduced to the latter condition" – a fact which expresses itself in any number of odd ways in Agamben's work (2007, 30). For example, it leads him to condemn humanitarian aid groups by hewing to a logic that would allow the space between them and the Nazi death camps to become absolutely minimal. As Agamben puts it, humanitarian organizations "can only grasp human life in the figure of bare or sacred life, and therefore, despite themselves, maintain a secret solidarity with the very powers they ought to fight . . . The 'imploring eyes' of the Rwandan child . . . may well be the most telling contemporary cipher for the bare life that humanitarian organizations, in perfect symmetry with state power, need" (1998, 133–4). The problem here, as Rancière notes, is that Agamben subsumes under the same umbrella refugee camps, holding areas for illegal immigrants, the prison at Guantanamo, and much else besides – all of which are in turn assimilated to the fundamental paradigm of the Nazi camps as "the 'nomos' of modernity." And in this highly formalized space, "the executioner and victim . . . appear as two parts of the same 'biopolitical' body," and the polarity of state of exception and bare life "appears as a sort of ontological destiny" (2004, 301).

The only alternative to this logic in Agamben's work appears to be what in *The Open* he calls the "suspension of the suspension" of the anthropological machine that ceaselessly reconjugates the relation between the *bios* and *zoë*, human and animal, a radical *Gelassenheit* (or "letting be of Being," to use Heidegger's term) (2004, 91). As Agamben writes:

In our culture man has always been the result of a simultaneous division and articulation of the animal and the human, in which one of the two terms of the operation was also what was at stake in it. To render inoperative the machine that governs our conception of man will therefore mean no longer to seek new – more effective or more authentic – articulations, but rather to show the central emptiness, the hiatus that – within man – separates man and animal, and to risk ourselves in this emptiness: the suspension of the suspension. Shabbat of both animal and man. (2004, 92)

What Agamben offers us here, as Dominick LaCapra characterizes it, is a sort of "postsecular negative theology *in extremis*" that should give us pause because of "the linkage among an extremely negative if not nihilistic conception of existing social, political, and cultural reality" and a "desire for reenchantment of the world" (2009, 167).

Agamben's philologically driven formalism thus leads to a remarkable flattening of the differences between different political, ethical, and institutional conjunctures (this, essentially, is Rancière's complaint), a homogenization that is a direct consequence of the severe delimitation of the realm of the "genuinely" political. And as a result, as LaCapra notes, attempts to mitigate the legacy of slavery or apartheid, or protests against the genetic manipulation of life or the uneven effects of globalization, would not be recognizable as genuine historical or political undertakings (LaCapra 2009, 165).

Not surprisingly, such a view of what counts as "genuinely" political in Agamben's work leads to a similar flattening of the category of "the animal" itself, and this in two senses. First, as LaCapra notes, animals in all their diversity "are not figured as complex, differentiated living beings but instead function as an abstracted philosophical topos" (2009, 166) – what Jacques Derrida calls the "asininity" of the designation "*the* animal." And second – a consequence of the first – Agamben's position provides no means for a politically focused questioning of "the extent to which certain animals, employed in factory farming or experimentation, may be seen in terms of the concept of bare or naked, unprotected life" (LaCapra 2009, 172). What gets lost, in other words, is our ability to think a highly differentiated and nuanced biopolitical field, and to understand as well that the exercise of violence on the terrain of biopower is not always, or even often, one of highly symbolic and sacrificial ritual in some timeless political theater, but is often – indeed, maybe usually – an affair of power over and of life that is regularized, routinized, and banalized in the services of a strategic, not symbolic, project.

Having thus pried apart Agamben and Foucault, we are thus in a better position to emphasize two further dimensions of Foucault's thinking of the biopolitical: one positive or affirmative, and one negative or at least equivocal. The first derives from Foucault's rethinking of the political subject as one who is "before" the law, "underneath" and antecedent to the juridico-political order. What Maurizio Lazzarato calls Foucault's radical "displacement" of the problem of sovereignty doesn't neglect it but merely points out that "the grounding force will not be found on the side of power, since power is 'blind and weak'" (as Foucault puts it) – hence, its growing need, in an increasingly complex and differentiated field of operation, for the various techniques of management, surveillance, and so on that it deploys (Lazzarato 2002, 104). What we are dealing with here is not a withdrawal of sovereignty and the law, but rather, as Esposito puts it, how the pivot of real political power gradually shifts from the domain of legal codes and sanctions to "the immanent level of rules and norms that are addressed instead to bodies" (2008, 28). Politics, law, and economics now function primarily not in a "top-down" but in a "bottom-up" fashion, and become operators for the effective management of the health, well-being, and increase of the population, conceived now as an object of biological intervention. As Jeffrey Nealon characterizes it, "biopower forges an *enabling* link between the seemingly 'universal' categories of population or demography and the individual 'idiosyncrasies' of everyday life. And the proper name for that link is the 'norm'" (2007, 46). "Norms" are thus addressed neither to individual rights holders nor, in Esposito's words, to "their confluence in a people defined as the collective subject of a nation, but rather to the living being in the specificity of its constitution" (2011, 136).

But that very "specificity," precisely because of its own complexity and density, which increases all the more as new regimes of knowledge are brought to bear upon it, contains new challenges,

new "aleatory" elements that must be managed and directed. As
Lazzarato argues, three important points follow from this: first,
"biopolitics is the form of government taken by a *new dynamic of
forces* that, in conjunction, express power relations that the classical
world could not have known" (2002, 101); second, "the fundamental political problem of modernity is not that of a *single* source
of sovereign power, but that of a *multitude of forces* . . . If power, in
keeping with this description, is constituted from below, then we
need an ascending analysis of the constitution of power *dispositifs*";
and third, "biopower coordinates and targets a power that does
not properly belong to it, that comes from the 'outside.' *Biopower
is always born of something other than itself*" (103; all emphases in
original).

Here, then – with Foucault's emphasis on bodies "before" the
law – we find a potentially creative, "aleatory" element that inheres
in the very gambit of biopower, one not wholly subject to the
thanatological drift of a biopolitics subordinated to the paradigm of
sovereignty. Indeed, the political payoff of Foucault's analyses of
the mechanisms of governmentality resides in no small part in their
anatomy of how the machinery of power races to maintain control
over the forces it has brought into its orbit – forces that derive in
no small part from animal bodies (both human and non-human)
that are not always already abjected, as they are in Agamben.[1]
Quite the contrary, those bodies are enfolded via biopower in
struggle and resistance, and because those forces of resistance are
thereby produced in specifically articulated forms, through particular *dispositifs*, there is a chance – and this marks in no small
part Foucault's debt to Nietzsche (as both Esposito and Deleuze
have pointed out) – for life to burst through power's systematic
operation in ways that are more and more difficult to anticipate.[2]
Power/knowledge complexifies the political resource called the
"body," and complexity increases risk. Thus, as Lazzarato notes,
Foucault actually "interprets the introduction of 'life into history'
constructively because it presents the opportunity to propose a
new ontology, one that begins with the body and its potential,"
over and against the prevailing Western tradition of understanding the political subject as above all a subject of law" (2002, 100).
Indeed, Lazzarato argues, one of Foucault's key insights is that

without factoring "freedom" and the "resistance of forces" into the equation as constitutive, "the *dispositifs* of modern power remain incomprehensible" (2002, 104).

This compels us, then, to firmly distinguish between biopolitics in its declension toward sovereignty as constitutive, and biopolitics as a relation of bodies, forces, technologies, and *dispositifs* that, *by definition*, could entail no such formal symmetry between sovereignty and bare life of the sort we find in Agamben. Consequently, biopolitics is above all a "strategic" arrangement that coordinates power relations "in order to extract a surplus of power from living beings," rather than "the pure and simple capacity to legislate or legitimize sovereignty" (Lazzarato 2002, 103). Resistance and agency, then, though they may overlap at strategic points, are not by any means coterminous. Rather than remain within the subject/agency vs. object/abjection opposition, then, the power of Foucault's analysis is to demonstrate just how unstable and mobile the lines are between political subject and political object – indeed, to demonstrate how that entire vocabulary must give way to a new, more nuanced reconceptualizaton of political effectivity. And equally important is that Foucault's introduction of "life into history" – of the body in the broadest sense – into the political equation does not lead directly and always already to an abjection for which the most predictable tropes of animalization become the vehicle. For now, it becomes essential, as Lazzarato puts it, "to presuppose the virtual 'freedom' of the forces engaged to understand the exercise of power" (2002, 107). This reconceptualization of political subjectivity (if one wants to continue to put it that way) is in no small part what motivates a shift in Foucault's thinking in the 1970s, when he moves from theorizing power on the model of warfare to instead conceptualizing its multivalent and non-linear nature based upon "the potential, difference and autonomy of forces" (Lazzarato 2002, 105–6). Foucault's reorientation of the problem has the signal advantage of making the questions of freedom and power, questions of degrees and not of kind when it comes to the disposition of human and non-human bodies as those are networked with each other and with technologies, practices, and disciplines which may cluster and co-constitute them regardless of species designation.

Take, for example, the use of genetic markers and Estimated
Breeding Values (EBVs) in contemporary livestock breeding – a
practice which is of a piece with the increasingly pervasive use of
genetic knowledges in biosciences generally, as Donna Haraway
and Nikolas Rose (among others) have discussed in their very
different ways. EBVs constitute a statistical representation of an
animal's "genetic merit" based upon standardized measurements
(an animal's weight at X days old, or the depth or percentage of fat
in a particular part of the animal's body, and so on), whereas genetic
markers focus on actual genetic locations in the animal's genome
that are associated with various traits such as meat tenderness.
These are then indexed by private companies that conduct tests on
blood and hair samples to establish that a particular animal contains
a high level of valuable genetic material, in effect quantifying and
linking to genetic markers the value and future performance of the
animal and its offspring (Holloway and Morris 2012, 61). As one
study notes, such practices "are strongly promoted by state institutions and private companies in the UK which claim that they are
imperative to modernising and rationalising livestock breeding,"
in contrast to traditional breeding practices such as visual appraisal
(or breeding "by eye") and examination of records of breeding
ancestry (Holloway and Morris 2012, 62).

But such practices have also given rise to resistance in the
form of "biosocial collectivities," groups that form (as Rabinow,
Rose, and others have argued) in response to emerging scientific
discourses of power-knowledge, and often on the basis of shared
experience with the blindnesses and oversimplifications of these
new regimes (as in, for instance, collectivities formed by patients
who share medical experience with a particular condition and its
treatment) (Holloway and Morris 2012, 64). What is important
in the case of EBVs and genetic markers is that these collectivities include non-human animals as co-constitutive with human
beings in resisting the articulations of a biopolitical *dispositif* in
and through the body. Why specifically bio*political* and not just
bio*power*? Because such practices involve not just the insertion of
animal bodies into farming assemblages involving technologies,
human beings, land, statistical regimes, architectural spaces, and so
on, for the purposes of changing and "maximizing" those bodies,

but also the selection of individuals and populations as the bearers of particular traits to suit the particular ends of capitalist enterprise made possible, in turn, by a particular legal designation of the "person" from which animals are barred. What we have here, in other words, is not just the operation of a new "norm," but one whose benchmarks presuppose the production and sale of animal food products *as a commodity for profit* (Holloway and Morris 2012, 65–6).

In resistance to this new norm, these new biosocial collectivities assert the importance of care, an intimate understanding of the animal that one might even call "aesthetic," non-"expert" knowledges, and practices of husbandry that do not bear a direct linear relationship to efficiency and profit. For example, many breeders have pointed out that all sorts of factors – some under the control of the breeder, some not – have overriding influences on genetic composition, and those factors constitute a *complex* of human, animal, and inorganic relations that cannot be wholly anticipated, much less quantified. As one breeder puts it:

> I know damn well that there are an awful lot of influences that are involved in the way a lamb grows and it's not all down to genetics. There's a hell of a lot of external influences there . . . Because things like prolapses in sheep some of it is genetic, yes, but a lot of it is down to management. If you overfeed those ewes then they are more likely to prolapse . . . Same with mastitis and growth rates. I know they try to take account of different effects, such as climate and stuff, but even on my farm I've got different land types. I know that some fields are better than others, some might have a terrible time with worms or rain. Sheep do not do well when it's raining all summer, they hate it and don't grow. That is not a genetic effect. It is purely a climate effect and some sheep may fare better than others. (Holloway and Morris 2012, 69–70).

These complex interactions of qualitatively different factors are made manifest in the animal's body, and an experienced, successful breeder's constant adjustment to them is less like statistics and more like choreography, engaging all of the senses and involving both close visual assessment of the animal's comportment (what is often called "the stockman's eye") and deft bodily touch. In this light, if we take seriously everything that is meant in Foucault's lexicon of biopower by terms such as "bodies," "forces," "resistance" and their aleatory elements – and this is perhaps harder to see in the rhetorical glare of terms like "freedom" and "power" – then we are forced to understand power, freedom, and resistance as modalities of responding to an other who is also taken to be able to respond, but it is a responding that takes place on the basis of forces and capacities that are in no way transparent, or even necessarily accessible to, the subject who responds. In this sense, "resistance comes first" precisely because it resides not just at the level of the body, "before" the subject who takes thought, but also in the recursive relations of the body with its other – with all its others.

What all of this suggests is that the accent we find in Lazzarato's reading of Foucault makes sense – and with it, that we need to differentiate sharply between Foucault and Agamben, drawing out how a reading of biopolitics that focuses on *dispositifs* rather than sovereignty enables us to think a much more complex and highly differentiated biopolitical field. What is needed, then, is another *thought* of the biopolitical in which human and non-human lives are deeply woven together *de facto* even if, *de jure*, they "politically" have nothing to do with each other if we understand the political as constituted by sovereignty.

Of course, the dominant conjugation of the animal body (whether human or non-human) and the *dispositifs* of bipower in the biopolitical literature have been overwhelmingly thanatopolitical (thanks in no small part to Agamben's work). And it hardly needs pointing out that the practices of modern biopolitics have forged themselves in the common subjection and management of both human and animal bodies – a fact brought very sharply into focus in scholarship that examines the analogies between the technological manipulation of life in the factory farm and in the Nazi camps. As one writer notes, "the methods of the Holocaust exist today in the form of factory farming where billions of innocent, feeling beings are taken from their families, trucked hundreds of miles through all weather extremes, confined in cramped, filthy conditions and herded to their deaths" (Davis 2005, 9). In fact, the assembly line processes used to kill Jews in Nazi Germany derived from production models originally developed by Henry Ford (a notorious anti-Semite), who in turn reveals in his autobiography that the inspiration for his assembly-line method came from a visit to a Chicago slaughterhouse and witnessing its mechanized *disassembly* line for making meat out of animal carcasses (Patterson 2002, 72).

From the vantage of a Foucauldean biopolitics, with its emphasis on *dispositifs* rather than sovereignty, then, we are forced to conclude that current practices of factory farming and the like constitute not just some embarrassing sideline of modern life that has nothing to do with politics proper, and which can be well regulated by an adjacent set of anti-cruelty laws that do not intersect with politics as such in any fundamental way. Rather, such practices must be seen not just as political but as in fact *constitutively* political for biopolitics in its modern form. Indeed, the practices of maximizing control over life and death, of "making live," in Foucault's words, through eugenics, artificial insemination and selective breeding, pharmaceutical enhancement, inoculation, and the like are on display in the modern factory farm as perhaps nowhere else in biopolitical history. It can hardly be debated, I think, that "the animal" is, today – and on a scale unprecedented in human history – the site of the very ur-form of that *dispositif* and the face of its most unchecked, nightmarish effects. Such practices are part of a matrix that, under conditions of globalization, increasingly takes as its political object planetary life itself, at the level of "flesh," and they constitute a biopolitics that encompasses and conjoins the putatively opposed political regimes of liberal democracy, fascism, and communism. They involve the exponential expansion and routinization of mechanisms and logics that extend from the Chicago slaughterhouses of the turn of the twentieth century, through the assembly lines developed by Ford, to the Nazi death camps and back again, traversing what we are now forced to call a newly expanded community of the living.

Following Foucault's recasting of the problematic of biopolitics, we can thicken our sense of the fully political status of these developments even more. For example, a recent study by the Pew Commission on Industrial Farm Animal Production points out that factory farming may be good at producing edible animal

products at the lowest possible cost, but "there is evidence," as
The New York Times puts it, "that this model is economically
viable only because it passes on health costs to the public – in
the form of occasional salmonella, antibiotic-resistant diseases,
polluted waters, food poisoning and possibly certain cancers"
(Kristof 2010). A nearly 100-page report in 2008 by the Union
of Concerned Scientists lists in excruciating detail the costs – both
direct and indirect – borne by society for the mass-produced
and industrialized killing of animals for food. Between 1997 and
2005, US taxpayers handed over to concentrated animal feeding
operations (CAFOs) roughly $3.8 billion a year in the form of
"indirect" subsidies – chiefly in the form of government handouts
to growers of corn and soybeans, the majority of which is eaten by
livestock animals each year. Such subsidies artificially reduce the
price of meat, poultry, and pork, and other direct subsidies further
artificially reduce the costs of factory farming by shifting costs to
the taxpayer. Chief among these is the Environmental Quality
Incentives Program, which gives CAFOs about $100 million per
year, in effect forcing taxpayers to help pay the environmental
cleanup costs for factory farms. Added to these are the massive
but more difficult to quantify "external" costs of CAFOs, which
include environmental degradation and pollution of air and water
that results from the large amount of energy use and animal waste
generated by CAFOs, reduced quality of life for rural communities
(including lower property values), and so on. To even modestly
reduce the water and air pollution they create would cost CAFOs
more than $1 billion per year, and other external costs would likely
run into the billions (Gurian-Sherman 2008).

   One of these external costs – associated with the use of antibiotics in factory farms – is worth dwelling on for a moment. As a
recent *New York Times* article reports, 80 percent of the antibiotics
used in the United States go to livestock on factory farms – nearly
all of it administered in their food and water – and typically to
healthy animals to prevent them from becoming sick from the
cramped and squalid conditions they endure. In fact, the single
state of North Carolina uses more antibiotics for its livestock than
the entire country uses for its human population. Not surprisingly,
this has led to a startling increase in antibiotic-resistant pathogens –

chief among them, MRSA, an antibiotic-resistant Staphylococcus bacterium that annually kills more people than AIDS. It was recently found in 70 percent of hogs on one factory farm, and in 45 percent of employees at another (Kristof 2011, 10). When such pathogens, born of our own maltreatment of farm animals, pose a risk to national biosecurity, the results are depressingly familiar and send us back to our earlier discussion of "animal Holocaust": in England, millions of pigs, cows, and sheep shot and bulldozed into graves and burned during the foot-and-mouth disease epidemic of 2001; in California in the 1970s, the killing of nine million hens to thwart Newcastle Disease; in the spring of 2004, millions of chickens, turkeys, and ducks killed worldwide – 80 million alone in Southeast Asia, 19 million more in Canada – to combat H5N1 avian influenza (Davis 2005, 21–2).

The fundamental biopolitical logic identified by Foucault and developed later by Roberto Esposito is unmistakable here. As Foucault writes in his analysis of medicalization, the harmful effects of medication are "due not to errors of diagnosis or the accidental ingestion of those substances, but to the action of medical practice itself . . . precisely because of their efficacy," leading humankind "into a perilous area of history" (cited in Esposito 2011, 140–1). As Esposito notes, "as in all areas of contemporary social systems, neurotically haunted by a continuously growing need for security, this means that the risk from which the protection is meant to defend is actually created by the protection itself" – a logic that is, as we have seen, "inscribed at the heart of modern biopolitics" (2011, 141).

What we need to remember here is that biopolitics acts fundamentally not upon the "person" or the "individual," nor even, finally, on "the body," but rather at the even more elemental level of what Esposito calls "flesh," which is "nothing but the unitary weave of the difference between bodies. It is the non-belonging, or rather the intra-belonging," Esposito writes, "which allows what is different to not hermetically seal itself up within itself, but rather, to remain in contact with its outside" (2011, 121). To put it in systems theory terms, we might say that "the body" obtains at the level of autopoietic "organization" and its closure, while "the flesh" obtains at the level of "structure," opening the autopoietic unity to the flows of energy and organic material that both sustain it and potentially threaten it.[3] Flesh "is neither another body nor the body's other: it is simply the way of being in common of that which seeks to be immune," for which the distinction between "human" and "animal" is no longer an adequate lexicon, as even Nietzsche realized. "Flesh" thus becomes the communal substrate shared by humans with other forms of life in and through which "the body" is both sustained and threatened, and the more we attempt to maximize the former through the micrological manipulations of biopower, the more the threat increases. So when we consider the use of CAFOs to feed the majority of the population – its effects on public health (and therefore on public health policy and its escalating costs), the devastating, literally unsustainable effects on the environment, and the use of massive government subsidies to prop up the entire system – is it really possible to isolate all of these from the political "per se"? And if so, is it not a thin and impoverished understanding of the "political" that is the result?

As Foucault puts it in an interview from 1977:

> The political is not what ultimately determines (or overdetermines) elementary relations . . . All relations of force imply a power relation . . . and each power relation can be referred to the political sphere of which it is a part, both as its effect and as its condition of possibility . . . Political analysis and critique, for the most part, have to be invented – but so do strategies that will allow both modifying these relations of force and coordinating them in such a way that this modification will be possible and register in reality. That is to say that the problem is not really defining a political "position" (which brings us back to a choice on a chessboard that is already set up), but to imagine and to bring out new schemas of politicization. (*FL*, 211)

From this vantage, opposing factory farming would constitute a "new schema of politicization," not just in resisting the formative *dispositifs* of modern biopolitics in their most brazen form, but also in articulating with other dimensions of political resistance, such as opposition to the commodification and private ownership of life, and of other, non-human persons, in the services of late capitalism.

In this light, paying attention to the question of non-human animal life has the potential to actually *radicalize* biopolitical thought beyond its usual parameters.

Notes

1 See, for example, Esposito's discussion of Foucault's analysis of medicalization and urban space in Europe from around 1800 onward, in which the very processes that "make live" (to use Foucault's famous phrase) "contained something that internally contradicted it." As Esposito notes, "the first step is to isolate places where infectious germs may develop more easily due to the storage of bodies, whether dead or alive: ports, prisons, factories, hospitals, cemeteries." What is generated is a kind of "*quadrillage*, or pigeonholing, that placed individuals in an extensive system of institutional segments – family, school, army, factory, hospital – prohibiting, or at least controlling, circulation in the name of public safety. All the urbanization that developed in Europe starting in the middle of the eighteenth century took on the appearance of a dense network of fences between places, zones, and territories protected by boundaries established according to political and administrative rules that went well beyond sanitary needs" (2011, 139–40).

2 In Foucault's words, "where there is power, there is resistance, and yet, or rather consequently, this resistance is never in a position of exteriority in relation to power" (cited in Esposito 2008, 38; see also Deleuze 1988, 71).

3 On organization versus structure, see Maturana and Varela (1992, 46–7).

9

Parrhesia and Therapeusis: Foucault on and in the World of Contemporary Neoliberalism

Laurence McFalls and Mariella Pandolfi

In *NB*, Michel Foucault makes an incursion, rare in his scholarly work, into the political present. Leaping more than two centuries forward from the seventeenth- and eighteenth-century birth of classical liberalism and its critique of absolutist reason of state, Foucault devotes more than four weeks of lectures to postwar German political economy as an almost ideal-typical illustration of liberalism's fear of the state. Foucault's highly original interpretation of the *Wirtschaftswunder* of Germany's social market economy merits a brief recapitulation in light of the current crisis of the Euro-zone and European Union. In an undelivered section of his lecture notes, Foucault summarizes succinctly: "Germany's real miracle is to have made the jurisdiction of the state derive from the veridiction of the market" (*NB*, 96; [*BB*, 95] all translations from the French and Italian, here and throughout, are our own). That is, for Foucault, the historical effectiveness of German ordo-liberalism as translated into economic policy by Ludwig Erhard, the Federal Republic's first Finance Minister and second Chancellor, resided not in its technical validity but in its discursive ability to re-found the political legitimacy of the German state, absolutely discredited by the abominations and defeat of Nazism, on its subservience to the market price mechanism.

Typically misrepresented as a German variant of the social democratic "postwar consensus" on the need to balance state intervention and market mechanisms, Erhard's celebrated formula of *soziale Marktwirtschaft* (social market economy) was instead genuinely neoliberal in that, unlike classical liberalism's belief in the spontaneity of markets that could be unleashed by a limitation or withdrawal of the state, ordo-liberalism recognized the fragility of the market, whose inherent efficiencies depended on the state's expansion, preservation and restoration of social preconditions for the functioning of competitive free markets. Thus, the "social" element of the social market economy did not refer to a social democratic, political, or state-led decommodification of different life spheres such as family, education, or health but rather to their state-steered, usually indirect commodification as German social and economic policy from cartel legislation to apprenticeship programs aimed not to protect from the market but rather to perfect for the market. Although the practical effects of the *soziale Marktwirtschaft* may have resembled those of social democracy, its discursive logic was fully neoliberal. The political consequences of this logic, as we shall see, have become evident today as the European Union has become an instrument that amplifies Germany's neoliberal policy prescriptions.

Foucault's immediate interest in postwar German neoliberal political economy, as he explains in his lecture of March 7, 1979, arose from the French government's realignment, in the late 1970s, of its traditionally *dirigiste* [directive] economic policy with the German model (*NB*, 199–213 [*BB*, 192–207]), in a rapprochement that would ultimately lead to the deeper political integration of the European Union and to the creation of the single currency, the euro. Foucault could not, of course, predict either of these developments or the current European sovereign debt crisis. Nonetheless, we contend that Foucault in fact offers a key for understanding the current political and economic crisis of Europe and its brutal reinforcement of market reason. In this chapter, we shall show that Foucault's genealogy of liberal and neoliberal governmentality, presented in *NB*, anticipates the emergence, in the neoliberal era that followed Foucault's untimely death in 1984, of a novel, insidious mode of domination and subjectivation that we call "therapeutic." Benevolent and empowering in its discourse, the velvet cage of therapeusis rests on societal and individual-izing practices and techniques whose iron-fisted qualities have become particularly clear, as we shall expose, in the political and economic project of European integration, in the current crisis of that project, and in the post-liberal market order it portends. Foucault's presaging, in 1979, of the post-liberal present may well have encouraged his quest in the remaining years of his life for alternative forms of subjectivity. Indeed, we shall argue that his elaboration of the concept of parrhesia, in particular in *GSA2*, offers the only possible escape passage from the velvet-turned-iron cage of therapeusis. We shall sketch out this argument in two steps, namely through a brief exegesis of Foucault's lecture courses of 1979 and 1984, and through our own interpretation of contempo-rary European politics that builds on Foucault's prescient analytical and ethical insights.

From Market Truth to Subversion

Foucault's prescient critique of neoliberalism and its radicalization – or, as we would say, therapeutization – of biopolitics in *NB* follows (chrono)logically from his genealogy of the liberal state in its singularly Western European context of emergence as elabo-rated in *IFDS* and *STP*. Summarizing and developing ideas from these two previous lecture courses, Foucault recalls in the opening lectures of *NB* that liberalism arose from the internal and external dynamics of the European state system of the early modern period. In his genealogy of Europe's present, Foucault identifies two modes of political reason that emerged in Europe since the six-teenth century, one vertical in its logic, the other horizontal. The first, temporally, followed the vertical logic of the monopolization of legitimate violence. In the age of absolutism, nominal suzerains became effective sovereigns, acquiring the legal right "to make die and to let live" their subjects (*IFDS*, 214 [*SMBD*, 240]). Their logic of rule remained beholden to the imperial notion of the extensive growth of political and economic power according to the zero-sum games of conquest and mercantilism. The doctrinal innovations of sovereignty and reason of state, however, encouraged and reflected the development of intensive techniques for exploiting internal resources, though always under the guidance of the rational state. This logic of political development quickly reached its limits externally, notably in the Thirty Years' War, and internally, as the sovereign will to power met with resistance as well as its own incapacities.

The second, horizontal form of political reason arose in this context: the aristocratic, proto-liberal critique of the state sought, to be sure, to constrain sovereign authority but not to abandon social control, whose mechanisms became intensive rather than extensive. Succinctly, in Foucault's formulation, the liberal governmentality that arose from the critique of reason of state sought to govern more effectively by governing less (*NB*, 30 [*BB*, 28–9]). This new standard of efficiency was made possible by the invention (discovery) of the market as a (natural) regulatory mechanism whose empirical truth-value checked the sovereign's legislative ambition. The veridiction of empirical science thus replaced the jurisdiction of abstract reason. Finally, according to Foucault's (*NB*, 62 [*BB*, 61]) tripartite description of liberalism, the unbridled expansion of European political and economic power to the remainder of the planet compensated for the emergent nation-state's frustrated territorial expansion and freed the European economy from its internal limitations as well. Imperialism and colonialism were thus integral to the liberal project, as was racism, not only as a justification for Europe's domination of the outside world, but also as an efficient tool for normalizing and homogenizing the internal government of civil society within the boundaries of the nation-state (*IFDS*). Henceforth, the biopolitical, scientific management of the internal population under the "liberal state" (which would be an oxymoronic expression if the vertical and horizontal modes of authority were contradictory and not complementary) would, schematically, "make [its population] live and let [it] die."

After recalling this genealogy of biopolitics, of its birth in seventeenth- and eighteenth-century Western Europe, a context to which he returns in the final lectures of *NB*, Foucault makes his leap into the present. We have already seen that Foucault in four full lectures characterizes German ordo-liberalism as a discourse and set of policy technologies for the social engineering of an efficient market society. In four further lectures, he revisits American "anarcho-liberalism," inspired by Hayek, Mises, Friedman, and the Chicago School, as a discourse and set of policy prescriptions aimed at molding individuals into entrepreneurs capable of competing in a multiplicity of markets. Beyond the classic liberal American tradition of rugged individualism, i.e. the naturalistic theory of the spontaneously self-interested economic actor, anarcho-liberalism recognizes both that the governmental mechanism of self-interest can function outside the realm of material acquisition and that its functioning can require or benefit from the external manipulation of incentives. Foucault thus devotes more than two lectures to Gary Becker's theory of human capital as an illustration of American neoliberalism's generalization of the economic logic of market interests and incentives to the totality of human behavior, notably examining Becker's redefinition of the criminal from a moral agent or anthropological type to a rational actor indistinguishable in his cost, benefit, and risk analysis from any other *homo oeconomicus* (*NB*, 258–62 [*BB*, 248–53]). This rationally calculating subject of neoliberalism, however, differs from the classic liberal subject, according to Foucault, in that the neoliberal *homo oeconomicus* as a holder of human capital is no longer a "partner of exchange" engaged in social processes but "an entrepreneur of himself" (*NB*, 232 [*BB*, 226]), concerned only with maximizing himself, his human capital, as a source of revenue. As entrepreneur of the self, the human capitalist counts, calculates, and deploys his economic, cultural, technical, and physical resources including his body and genetic composition. The latter thus become not a fact or gift of nature but variables to be manipulated, and as a perturbed but prescient Foucault notes, such reconfigurations of the body and genes are not "science fiction" but "a currently ambient problematic" (*NB*, 233 [*BB*, 228]).

In short, whether in its German or American variant, neoliberalism, as Foucault elucidates it, distinguishes itself from classic liberalism in its denaturalization of the competitive free market as an autonomous, spontaneous, self-sustaining locus of veridiction that imposes itself negatively through the absence of intervention.

To the contrary, neoliberalism implies continuous corrective or ameliorative interventions upon societies and upon individuals to make them fit for competition as market societies and as entrepreneurs of the self. Like liberalism, neoliberalism denies reason of state's panoptic ambition rationally and legally to plan the totality of human interaction, leaving social coordination to the "invisible hand" of the market, but neoliberalism deploys a plethora of technologies for facilitating, encouraging, and enhancing market performance. The new and improved *homo oeconomicus* of neoliberalism is "eminently governable, [responding] systematically to systematic modifications introduced artificially into his environment" (*NB*, 274 [*BB*, 270]). As we shall elaborate in the second part of this chapter, we can thus extrapolate from Foucault and define neoliberalism as a therapeutic mode of government, one that legitimates its authority with claims of benevolence, of expertise, and even of empowerment of those whose conduct it guides.[1] Whether it be civil society or the entrepreneurial individual, the neoliberal subject ideally takes charge of its life through a panoply of practices of the self from self-help and self-reliance to self-marketing and self-governance. With the application of its therapeutic logic to virtually every life sphere, neoliberalism radically deepens the capillarization of biopower from the statistical aggregation of populations down to the genetic minutiae of sub-cellular life. To be sure, Foucault only implicitly anticipates such a radical biopolitics in his analysis of neoliberalism and its new subject, yet his subsequent turn towards the genealogy of ethical, ascetic, and "aesthetic"[2] constructions of the self strongly suggests that his glimpse of the emergent neoliberal subject sent him looking for a path of subversion if not salvation.

Thus, Foucault devotes the final five lecture courses of his life to the genealogical exploration of the relationship between subjectivity and truth in the Western tradition. The final two propose a genealogy of parrhesia, the courageous practice of speaking truth to power in an act of subjective affirmation and resistance. Of course, subjectivity, truth, and power constitute the three axes of Foucault's oeuvre, each element existing only in relation to the others and through social interactions. Because subjectivity emerges dialogically, it takes shape through different modes of speaking truth (veri–diction) in conjunction with different modes of power relations (governmentalities). At the beginning of *GSA2* (16–30; *CT*, 15–30]), Foucault distinguishes between four modes of veridiction, namely those of the prophet, who is the enigmatic mouthpiece of the future truth of destiny; of the sage, who unwillingly shares his understanding of the foundational, unifying truth of Being; of the teacher, who is obliged to perpetuate the truth of his technical knowledge; and of the parrhesiast, who dares to speak the truth about individuals and situations in their ethical singularity. Each mode of veridiction entails particular power relations between interlocutors, with that between the teacher and student, for example, being most complicit, symbiotic, and cowardly. Indeed, the lecturer Foucault, aspiring to parrhesia, mocks himself for his utter lack of courage (*GSA2*, 24 [*CT*, 24]).[3] Contrary to the teacher, who seeks only to reproduce his knowledge and ultimately himself in continuity with a tradition, the parrhesiast must be willing to risk losing his reputation, his friends and perhaps even his life when pronouncing his truth. He must ultimately lay his life entirely bare.

Through his genealogy of parrhesia in the ancient Greek, Hellenistic, Roman, and early Christian worlds, Foucault exposes the limits of political action and of philosophical critique as means for subverting the discourse, practices, and techniques of (bio) power in general and for escaping the veridictional cage of the market in particular. Only the ethical and "aesthetic" self-reappropriation of the body remains as a possible avenue for a different life. Originally a political concept from the Periclean golden age of Athenian democracy, namely the right and duty of the citizen to speak freely before the assembly, parrhesia became, with Socrates, an apolitical philosophical concern for the care of the self (*epimeleia heautou*) through the Socratic mission of overcoming the falsehood of opinion through remorseless frank questioning, even at the risk of violating the laws of the city and of condemnation to death. Whereas Socrates embodied philosophical reason and ethical life practice, after him it is possible to distinguish between philosophical and ethical parrhesia as represented respectively in the Platonic and Cynical traditions. Having devoted most of his 1983 lecture course to philosophical parrhesia, Foucault in 1984 analyzes ethical parrhesia, pursuing the distinction between the two forms through an exploration of the dialogues on the death of Socrates in the first half and then in the second developing the ascetic and ethical elements of parrhesia as pushed to their logical extreme in Cynicism. Literally dog-like in his *ēthos*, the Cynic, whom Diogenes best personifies, strips his life of all convention, from clothing and manners to knowledge superfluous to survival, in an exemplary performance of parrhesia. The pure Cynic represents radical alterity, a constant challenge to a life of conformity, but also a profoundly anti-political and potentially anti-philosophical or rather anti-metaphysical stance.

This sequence from political parrhesia to apolitical philosophical parrhesia to anti-political, anti-metaphysical ethical-Cynical parrhesia may coincidentally be chronological but it is, more importantly, logically inherent to the formal mode of action within the different types of parrhesiastic relationship. The political parrhesiast daringly speaks his truth to his interlocutor(s) in the name of their common good and in so doing succumbs to the rhetorical device of flattery, the appeal to passions and interests to arrive at the appearance of agreement.[4] The philosophical parrhesiast – as exemplified by Socrates' refusal, in the name of the well-being of the city, directly to participate in political life – thus adopts a critical, external stance towards politics and seeks a convergence of the *logos* of his and his interlocutors' souls, in what Foucault (*GSA1*, 344 [*GSO*, 374]) calls a move from the rhetorical to the erotic. By contrast, the Cynical parrhesiast does not seek to attain a reasoned, metaphysical convergence of souls, and much less to flatter, but rather performatively to provoke his interlocutors. His mode of interaction is neither rhetorical nor erotic but "aesthetic" in Foucault's sense of a perpetual subversive practice (cf. *GSA2*, 150–3 [*CT*, 162–5]).

Although Foucault devotes most of his final two lecture courses to philosophical parrhesia and to its champion Socrates, by the end of *GSA2* it is clear that only the radical, provocative alterity of the ethical and "aesthetic" parrhesia of the Cynical tradition responds to his personal aspiration for a different life, a life in truth, in a different world (311 [*CT*, 339]). We might speculate, on the basis of textual exegesis, why Foucault, after devoting the first half of his last lecture course to the Platonic dialogues on courage, the soul, and the death of Socrates, turns away from the metaphysical sentimentality of parrhesia in its erotic form in favor of an "aesthetic" of existence.[5] It is poignant, indeed, that Foucault (*GSA2*, 87–107 [*CT*, 141–55]), shortly before his own death, consecrates a lecture to Socrates' last words. Following Dumézil (1984), Foucault argues that Socrates' final request that a cock be sacrificed to Asclepius, the god of cure, signals his enduring commitment to his mission to cure himself and others of false opinions in keeping with philosophical parrhesia. Nonetheless, Socrates' philosophical parrhesia leads him to suicide in subordination to the laws of the city; the philosopher's life of truth has no effect on power relations or, worse still, reproduces their effects. Although Foucault (*GSA2*, 308 [*CT*, 338]) concludes the spoken portion of his final lecture course by affirming that the asceticism of Cynicism opened the possibility of a "true life of truth," neither there nor in his unspoken notes does he explain how the "aesthetic" truth of the Cynical ascetic can actually subvert the rhetorical "truth" of politics any more than philosophical truth can.

From Neoliberalism to Post-Liberalism: Foucault on the Contemporary Crisis of Europe

If the meaning of the last words of Foucault's final lecture course remains ambiguous, then we can only speculate as to what he might have thought or said about the expansion of neoliberal governmentality that followed his untimely death. Yet, as we propose to argue here, Foucault's analysis of liberal governmentality and his critique of neoliberalism in his lecture courses of the late 1970s carry the seeds of a powerful critique of our contemporary political economy, a critique that also holds the key to understanding the final Foucault's subversive project. For a conceptual overview of our argument, let us recall that Foucault turns to his critical analysis of neoliberalism in *NB* in order to elucidate liberal governmentality's phobia of the state. Despite its origins in a rational and empirical critique of reason of state, liberal governmentality did not supplant state authority but restrained it through the invention of universal individual rights and subordinated it to the interests of civil society through the gradual introduction of liberal democratic representative institutions. Neoliberalism, as we saw with Foucault, further subordinated the state to market veridiction by reducing its role to the encouragement of biopolitical techniques of individual and societal self-government in line with what we call (and elaborate further below) a therapeutic mode of domination. Reading between the lines, we can see that Foucault anticipates that this "therapeutic domination," present already within liberal biopolitics and expanded under neoliberalism, will become, as it is today, so pervasive that we can speak of post-liberalism, i.e. a mode of government that fully subordinates both life and what remains of the state to market veridiction and therapeutic techniques and that, in so doing, sweeps away the liberal subject of rights and the remnants of representative democratic authority. In light of this post-liberal, fully therapeutic present, Foucault's subversive project of parrhesia in the Cynical tradition, we shall contend, suddenly makes sense and offers slight hope.

As the explosion of Foucauldean political analysis since his death in 1984 suggests, we are not alone in believing that his work carries the seeds for a radical critique of the post-Cold War explosion of neoliberal governmentality and of its current paroxystic crisis. In our own work as a political scientist and an anthropologist, we have observed that Foucault's critique of neoliberal biopolitics has been essential to our own and to other scholars' understanding of the new forms of power, truth, and subjectivity that have proliferated in the post-Cold War neoliberal era, particularly in the rapidly expanding phenomenon of military-humanitarian intervention.[6] Usually on peripheral sites in the global South, these interventions have served as laboratories for new techniques of therapeutic government, of marketization, and of societal and individual self-organization and resilience in keeping with and perfecting neoliberal governmentality. Carried out with benevolence by an international, mobile corps of experts increasingly in collaboration with national military forces in a temporality of emergency and crisis management (Pandolfi 2003), this therapeutic mode of domination has shown the kinder, gentler face of neoliberalism, though the confusion of military and humanitarian genres has also pointed to the iron fist within the velvet glove (Pandolfi 2011). Since the beginning of the contemporary financial crisis in 2008, however, the laboratories of neoliberal intervention have moved from the periphery to the center, notably to Western Europe, where liberal biopolitics were born. Just as in the early modern period that Foucault analyzes in his lectures of 1976–9, the dynamics of the European state system in its global context have given a new impetus to biopolitical reason, showing the more brutal face of neoliberalism. Therefore, in order to argue that we are today witnessing the emergence of a new, post-liberal reason of government, from which the only escape lies in the parrhesia of the Cynical tradition, we shall sketch the genealogy of the current crisis of the euro and the European Union as harbingers of post-liberalism.

As Foucault summarizes (*NB*, 62 [*BB*, 61]), the advent of liberalism allowed European states to govern their populations efficiently and intensively in line with the empirical veridiction of the market and to convert their zero-sum mercantilist competition into global imperialist expansion. Pushing this history forward to the present, we can see that European liberalism, like the absolutist reason of state before it, had to confront its own limitations, most obviously in the cataclysmic wars of the first half of the twentieth century (cf. Polanyi 2010 [1944]). The exhaustion of European imperialist expansion and of the market as an efficient mechanism for regulating internal as well as external conflicts gave rise to totalitarian and other, less virulent state-led experiments, ending in the stalemate of the Cold War. (It is worth noting, however, that Foucault (*NB*, 93–4 [*BB*, 92–3]) implicitly foresees the end of this stalemate when he argues that socialism, whether in its social democratic or totalitarian form, unlike reason of state and liberalism, lacks its own governmental reason and will collapse under the veridictional weight of the market.) Decolonization within the bipolar postwar context consummated the idea of the sovereign territorial nation-state in liberal guise but also marked an end to European expansion, which had been vital to the liberal model.

With Europe divided and politically if not economically marginalized, postwar Western Europe reinvented itself in the project of European integration, though in its (con)federal self-imagination as a "Europe of fatherlands," it remained beholden to the logic of the liberal nation-state. Briefly hailed as "the end of history," the end of the Cold War indeed seemed to mark the final victory of liberalism, with the instauration or reinstauration of liberal democratic nation-states in eastern Central Europe and their relatively rapid integration into the European Union. The victory was short-lived, for the geopolitical and biopolitical conditions of liberalism no longer obtained. The world was no longer a stage onto which Europe could literally and figuratively project its internal contradictions and conflicts, and Europe's populations were no longer the relatively homogeneous and stable entities subject to the rational government of the still fundamentally liberal welfare state. Instead, migration, global financial and trade flows, transnational networks (of culture, communication, terror) and the like made Europe the scene of world tensions. At the same time, new (neoliberal) technologies for individualizing social risk disaggregated nation-state populations as a unit of government.

Within this general post-Cold War context (which Foucault foretells), it is possible to interpret the European Union's strategy of eliminating boundaries and promoting common citizenship and new "governance" mechanisms as an attempt to construct a super-state to compete with the other emergent global super-powers, be it under the logic of an evanescent globalized liberalism or of imperial neo-mercantilism. Or it is possible to see this Europe as the laboratory of a new, post-liberal form of political reason, namely one that fragments social relations not into neo-medieval territorial units ("the Europe of regions") but into countless, deterritorialized transversal categories of individuals. While Europe's discourse of citizenship may be couched in classic liberal language, its invariable coupling with the discourse of "governance," i.e. individuals' and groups' participation in mechanisms of their expert government outside the traditional representative mechanisms of territorially based liberal democracy, points to its subscription to a post-liberal political reason. European "citizenship" suggests neither a European super-state nor a European patchwork of fluidly shifting sub-state units, but a Europe of individuals and populations engaged in a constant, multifaceted entrepreneurship of themselves and perhaps even in a redefinition of human experience.

Still only in emergence, post-liberalism, as we use the term, refers not to a surpassing of liberalism's veridiction through the market but to an enhancement of it that strips the liberal and neoliberal subject of any autonomy. Well beyond neoliberalism's familiar reinforcement and redeployment of market mechanisms and privatization of social services, post-liberalism more fundamentally, even ontologically, redefines the human experience, replacing the liberal subject with what Dillon and Reid (2009) call the "biohuman." From liberal governmentality post-liberalism retains the "conduct of conduct" through the manipulation of interests, and from neoliberal economic theory it adopts the idea that the market as a locus of veridiction is not natural but rather a fragile social construct. Unlike both classic liberalism and neoliberalism, however, post-liberalism collapses the distinction between the individual, subjected to anatomo-political discipline, and the collectivity, subjected to biopolitical government. The post-liberal subject is not the fragmented subject of post-modernity but rather a composite subject, contingently pieced together genetically and socially. Humans, of course, have always been such constructs, but today they are subjected to social scientific discourses and biomedical technologies (ranging from "intersectionality" to genetic engineering) that allow the radical biopolitical self-government of individual bodies to be understood and understandable as particularly configured and manipulable exemplars of the human species in its diversity, with each susceptible to its particular vulnerabilities.

The discursive coupling of diversity and vulnerability is central to contemporary post-liberal governmentality. A host of new social technologies for preventing or alleviating potential or actual vulnerabilities and for encouraging resilience and adaptation have proliferated, with eligibility for programs depending on the (self-) labeling of particular individuals as vulnerable by virtue of their identification with any number of the countless socially, demographically, or biologically constructed and targeted categories of vulnerability (migrants, the elderly, pregnant women, etc.). At the same time, diversity has become a "human resource" to be managed, cultivated, and turned into a source of resilience, creativity, initiative, and employee loyalty. As the positive and negative sides of the same coin, diversity and vulnerability are to post-liberalism what liberty and security were to classic liberalism (*NB*, 66–8 [*BB*, 65–6]). Liberal governmentality harnessed the mechanism of interest by producing and consuming individual freedoms, but it also promoted public and private social insurance schemes for mutualizing the risks of individual liberty. Post-liberal governmentality also harnesses the mechanism of interest, but it does so by a proliferation of forms of diversity and vulnerability that leaves the two terms as well as individuals and populations indistinguishable.

Post-liberalism's simultaneous government of individuals and populations can most easily be understood through one of the biomedical practices that inspire it, namely "personalized medicine," or the use of genetic, molecular, and environmental profiling for the optimization of individual patients' preventive or therapeutic care in realization of what Foucault already in 1979 saw as an emergent "ambient problematic." Similarly, social profiling (also called "post-demographics"), even if it is denounced as racist or discriminatory, has become a powerful tool not only of law enforcement but also of marketing (thanks notably to internet data manipulation) and post-welfarist social policy in general. Our presentation here of post-liberalism's political logic has necessarily been schematic. Our point, however, is to underscore that the mushrooming and naturalization of concepts of diversity, vulnerability, and resilience and especially of social technologies for designating and governing them have become omnipresent, effecting an epistemic rupture redefining the human experience. Whereas the tension between the transcendent and immanent qualities of the liberal subject as a holder simultaneously of universal abstract reason and of particular concrete interests defined the relatively coherent subjective experience of liberal governmentality (see Dillon and Reid 2009), the post-liberal subject leads a life of constant, incoherent, and fragmentary reconfiguration in line with ever-new technologies and practices of the self.

The political reason and subjectivity of post-liberalism are not emerging in contemporary Europe alone, but, as the sovereign debt crises and the potential implosion of the common-currency euro-zone call into question the fiscal, financial, economic, and political viability of a growing number of member states and of the European Union as a whole, Europe faces its moment of truth, in the strong epistemic sense of the word. On the one hand, the systematic dismantling of state capacities and public services removes the final vestiges of liberal representative democratic accountability in favor of markets; on the other, the discursive confusion surrounding this process forecloses effective political understanding and action. In the public debates surrounding the economic and therefore political crisis of Europe, several superposed layers of governmental discourse erupt to the surface, revealing the competing but at times complementary logics of reason of state and of classic, neo-, and post-liberal governmentalities at work in political thought, practices, and technologies. In the states most targeted by the financial markets and in turn by disciplining measures on the part of the EU Commission, metaphors of, and direct references to, war and territorial conquest (notably by Nazi Germany) evoke the geopolitical reason of state and feed into right-wing populist fantasies of restoring the glory of the nation-state. At the same time, the liberal truth criterion of the market remains unassailable as the final arbiter in political debates. Market verdicts leave no option but austerity and retrenchment, and protest movements such as Occupy, Attac, or Common Good have articulated no alternative truth regime, except perhaps a return to the abstract universalism of the rational jurisdiction of reason of state as opposed to the empirical veridiction of the market. Finally, the neoliberal logic of expert technical intervention to correct or prevent market imperfection and failures has become evident in the leading role played in the current European crisis by the nebulous aggregate of international experts organized around institutions such as the International Monetary Fund, the World Bank, the European Central Bank, the European Commission, and the World Trade Organization. Formally intergovernmental, these agencies, through which an enlightened cosmopolitan elite circulates, have become an autonomous source of authority, formulating if not dictating national government policies on the basis of their alleged technical competency.[7]

Regardless of the substantive contents and validity of experts' claims to legitimate authority in the current crisis, these claims clearly, and in an exacerbated manner, take the form of therapeutic domination (McFalls 2010). Defined succinctly as an impersonal and exceptional mode of command, therapeutic domination entails the expert application of an instrumentally rational technical procedure, typically a treatment protocol, to a subordinated individual or population in a situation of emergency, crisis, or disease, always to the supposed benefit of the treated. Implicit in this mode of domination is a historical and cultural decontextualization of technical action in a temporality of urgency. Therapeutic domination thus forecloses political debate, suspends democratic procedures, and foregoes consequentialist questions of responsibility in the name of immediate efficiency. In the case of contemporary Europe, the sovereign debt crisis, arising from the banking crisis of 2008, morphed over the course of 2011, for whatever reason, justified or not, into a permanent emergency with an endless cycle of summits, ultimatums, and last-chance appeals, each of which progressively strips away states' possibilities politically to counter market truths. Whatever its outcome, the European crisis augurs a post-liberal world of fully therapeutic government, where there is no future, there are no politics, only an eternal present in which the veridiction of the market, finally freed from the jurisdiction of the state, leaves the post-liberal biohuman at the mercy of all market-tried-and-true technologies of the self.

Such a world of total therapeusis raises the question of whether and how resistance, and hence the possibility of change, might occur. Implicit, as we have seen, in Foucault's critique of (neo-) liberal biopolitics, the therapeutic mode of domination is particularly impervious to resistance (McFalls 2010; Pandolfi & McFalls 2009). Like any mode of authority, therapeutic domination legitimates itself rhetorically with normative appeals of beneficence. The particular rhetorical genius of the therapeutic discourse, however, resides not only in its substantive claim to care – indeed, it is suspiciously close to philosophical parrhesia's *epimeleia heautou* – but also in its exceptional and impersonal form. Put most simply, it can short-circuit any criticism with the questions: who could be against saving a life (and especially, as the advertising rhetoric of humanitarian oranizations' self-marketing so effectively shows, the life of an anonymous child)? And who could oppose applying the technically most efficient procedure in an emergency? To do so would be pathological and justify further therapeutic intervention. By reducing the stakes of politics to the survival and autonomous resilience of the diversely vulnerable, post-liberal therapeutic domination effectively reduces politics to the technical management of an endless series of catastrophes, real, impending, or imagined, without any concern for coordination or overarching order, that being left to the impersonal immediacy of the market.

In light of the emergence of this post-liberal dystopia that Foucault's critique of neoliberalism anticipates, we can understand why Foucault, near the end of his life, pleads in favor of parrhesia in the ethical and "aesthetic" form of the Cynical tradition. While Foucault remains elusive about what a reactivation of the cynical *ēthos* and "aesthetic" would entail today, he does – again with prescience – suggest some possibilities and limits for a subversive parrhesia in the face of the iron cage of post-liberal therapeusis. In the second hour of his lecture of February 29, 1984, Foucault (*GSA2*, 163–76) identifies three posterities of ancient Cynicism in Western culture: religious, political, and aesthetic. First, he considers the debt to Cynicism of Christian asceticism, particularly in its monastic and heretical doctrinal as well as spontaneously anti-ecclesiastic forms.[8] Second, Foucault points to revolutionary, activist, and leftist life-styles as modern – primarily nineteenth-century – attempts to scandalize and provoke with an exemplary life of truth, evoking the today paradigmatic figure of the suicide bomber, "as practice of a life for truth right up to and including death (the bomb that kills even the one who places it)" (*GSA2*, 170 [*CT*, 185]). Foucault casts doubt on the subversive potential of a parrhesia that ultimately reverts to the emotive rhetoric and self-defeating conformity of political action. Finally, he holds up the figure of the artist, who in the modern age becomes not just an exceptional person, but especially a violent expositor of the cultural possibilities of life. Although Foucault (*GSA2*, 174 [*CT*, 189]) celebrates the permanent violence of modern art as a "wild eruption of the true," he also recognizes its marginality to the massively effective political technologies of the present.

Where, finally, does Foucault leave us then? Inasmuch as *GSA2* proposes a solution to the problem of contemporary post-liberal governmentality foreseen implicitly in *NC*, the "late" Foucault offers us only the narrowest of escape routes from therapeutic dystopia. It is an escape route that Giorgio Agamben has been trying to open up politically, philosophically, and ethically through his analyses of the foundational violence of the law, of alternative forms of life, and of the art of existence. In his recent examination of Christian monasticism as an alternative form of life as "art," Agamben (2011, 47) suggests where Foucault was heading: "[T]his analogy [of monastic life as a form of art] must not be understood in the sense of an aestheticization of existence, but rather in the sense, which Michel Foucault seemed to have in mind in his final writings, of a definition of personal life in relation to an uninterrupted practice." The art of such a life does not consist in its pursuit of exceptional beauty but rather in the continuous mastery of an entirely personal practice of the self. Personal, singular, contextualized, and quotidian: these traits are, of course, antithetical to the impersonal, extraordinary form of therapeutic domination; they also correspond to the courage of the parrhesiast, who abandons prophetic, philosophic, and scientific truth in favor of the singular ethical truth of a life in context. Only the extreme courage to pursue our own ethos, continually and not exceptionally, to give content to an alternative form of life, outside the laws of scientific, philosophical, and prophetic truths can – perhaps – burst the cage of the post-liberal present.

Notes

1 We have developed the concept of therapeutic domination within the framework of our work in the anthropology of humanitarian intervention (Pandolfi and McFalls 2009). In a cross-reading of Foucault and Max Weber, we understand the peculiar mode of authority exercised by the international aid community over local beneficiaries on contemporary sites of intervention as an original form of legitimate domination implicit in Weber's sociology of domination (McFalls 2008; 2010).

2 We place the concept "aesthetics" in inverted commas in order to

avoid appearing to partake in the reading/critique of Foucault as an aestheticist. Foucault's use of the term, as we shall argue, refers to an ethical practice of life that can be an "art" in the broad sense of the term.

3   "*Tout le monde sait, et moi le premier, que nul n'a besoin d'être courageux pour enseigner*" [Everyone knows, and me first of all, that no one needs to be courageous to teach]. At the beginning of this lecture, Foucault complains about the unilateral format of a lecture course and expresses his preference for the interactive intimacy of a seminar.

4   The relationship between parrhesia and rhetoric is complex, raising "*tout un foyer de questions, tout un réseau d'interférences, proximités, intrications, etc., qu'il faudra essayer de débrouiller*" [a whole hotbed of questions, a whole network of interferences, proximities, intrications, etc., that it will be necessary to try to clear up] (*GSA1*, 53 [*GSO*, 53]). Although the two forms of speech are evidently not the same, Foucault concludes (*GSA1*, 344 [*GSO*, 374]): "You understand why Periclean parrhesia necessarily had to lead to something like rhetoric, that is, that use of language that allows one to win out over others and to unite them, by persuasion, under this command, within the form of this asserted superiority."

5   Indeed, Foucault (*GSA2*, 143 [153]) concludes his courses on the death of Socrates self-derisively: "*Alors cette fois promis, j'ai terminé avec Socrate. Il faut bien, comme professeur de philosophie, avoir fait au moins une fois dans sa vie un cours sur Socrate et la mort de Socrate. C'est fait. Salvate animam meam*" [So, as promised, I concluded with Socrates. It's quite necessary, as a professor of philosophy, to have given at least one course on Socrates and the death of Socrates. It's done. Save my soul].

6   For a sample of this scholarship of Foucauldean inspiration and a selected bibliography, see the essays collected in Fassin and Pandolfi (2010).

7   The imposition of expert authority at the expense of democratically elected governments has been most evident in Greece and Italy so far, but even in hegemonic Germany, the nominal center-right governing coalition has been replaced on the now high political issues of the economy and European policy by a *de facto* grand coalition of the Christian Democrats and the opposition Social Democrats.

8   Giorgio Agamben (2011, 177–8) follows this avenue, exploring notably the subversive potential – albeit unrealized – of the Franciscan

property-less form of life outside the violence of the law and the Western "paradigm of operativity" that confounds ethics and the law: "*Ma è certo che solo a partire dalla ripresa del confronto in una nuova prospettiva potrà eventualmente decidersi se e in che misura ha ancora un senso o se, invece, il dominio planetario del paradigma dell'operatività esige di spostare il confronto decisivo su un altro terreno*" [But it is certain that only from the resumption of the comparison in a new perspective will it eventually be determined whether and to what extent . . . it still has a sense or if, instead, the planetary dominance of the paradigm shift of operativity requires the decisive shift to another terrain] (Agamben 2011, 178).

10

Foucault, Marx, Neoliberalism: Unveiling Undercover Boss

Toby Miller

This chapter seeks to do two things. First, at a theoretical/ exegetical level, it demonstrates important affinities between Foucault and Marx(ism): I contend that an opposition between them is misplaced, and their work can be fruitfully combined. Second, at an applied level, I draw on biopower and governmentality to understand the creation and popularity of neoliberalism through brief studies of two major institutions: the US news media and university administration. I hope to show that these quite distinct sites can explicate the oft-ignored Marxist connection to biopolitics. And in keeping with my title, fans of *Undercover Boss* will not be disappointed. Unless they are.

Foucault and Marxism

At a theoretical level, Foucault was forever critically engaging the humanistic Marxism of Jean-Paul Sartre and the structuralist Marxism of Louis Althusser (who taught him). It is worth recalling Foucault's recommendation to "open Althusser's books," and the latter's contention that "something from my writings has passed into his" (*FL*, 14 and Althusser 1969, 256). As Foucault said of their relationship, "I followed" (*RM*, 55).

There is a significant link between Althusser and Foucault in their theorization of subjects, objects, representation, and inter-pretation. The accusation of functionalist Marxism sometimes leveled at Althusser, because of his totalizing view of ideological apparatuses, is similar to certain critics' lament for the absence of an outside to power in Foucault. Of course, there are major meth-odological differences as well as similarities. Althusser investigated problematics and their underpinning ideology in the context of the real. Conversely, Foucault looked at statements, their precondi-tions, and their settings in discursive formations, then moved on to research-related archives. Only Althusser privileged science (Miller 1994).

Foucault's principal quibble with Marxism lay in its focus on class, to the comparative exclusion of struggle, and the totalizing certitudes of ideology critique. He complained that the latter half of the grand dialectical couplet received less than equal treatment. In particular, he sought to understand material manifestations of power that were not simply used to accrete *bourgeois* dominance or state authority – hence his archival readings of prisons, hospitals, and asyla. These commitments revealed that the micropolitics of forming and controlling subjects could not be read off from macro-economic blocs, and were as much to do with dispensing power as accumulating or exercising it (*PK*, 58 and Foucault 1982, 782).

Foucault's concept of biopower drew extensively on Marx to construct homologies between civil and military training via "docile bodies." Comparing the division of labor to the organiza-tion of infantry, *DP* has many Marxist features in its account of how disciplinary power developed alongside capitalism as elites addressed the interrelated tasks of developing and maintaining a productive and compliant labor force and social order. One can pick up on these insights to consider post-industrial forms of soci-ality (Sibilia 2009).

Perhaps the most subtle and complex engagement between Foucault and Marxism emerged over the state and the way he expanded Roland Barthes' term "governmentality," which Barthes coined during the high point of his own Marxism to describe market variations and the state's attempt to claim responsibility for them (when the outcome was positive) (1973, 130).

Foucault developed this ironic, ugly neologism to account for "the way in which the modern state began to worry about individuals" (*RM*, 4) by asking: "How to govern oneself, how to be governed, how to govern others, by whom the people will accept being governed, how to become the best possible governor." These issues arose as twin processes: the displacement of feudalism by the sovereign state, and the similarly conflictual Reformation and its counters. Daily economic and spiritual government came up for redefinition. While the state emerged as a centralizing tendency that sought to normalize itself and others, a devolved religious authority produced a void, via ecclesiastical conflicts and debates about divine right. The doctrine of transcendence fell into crisis, and royalty came to represent managerial rather than immanent rule (*FE*, 87–90). Despite the concept's origins and, I think, utility, there has been an enthusiastic uptake of this account of governmentality by *converso* anti-Marxist leftists drawn to the *bourgeois* promises of neoliberalism in response to their own disappointments with ideology critique. This move mistakes description for prescription (Rose 1999 is one of dozens renowned for such maneuvers).

And in terms of progressive social movements, Foucault's participation and inspiration cannot be doubted. Foucault's political actions were often shared with Sartre or inspired by his example, for all that the *a priori* reasoning subject at the heart of existentialism was foreign to Foucault's projects, like its equivalent in *bourgeois* Anglo-Yanqui liberalism. Foucault joined the Maoist Gauche Proletarienne, helped develop *Gai Pied*, and was a founder of the Groupe d'Information sur les Prisons. It is also worth noting that his research and public intellectualism inspire leftists living under authoritarian regimes such as the Argentine *junta* (Friera 2004).

Biopower

The presumed opposition between Foucault and Marxism also forgets the fundamental anti-imperialism that underpinned much of his work. His 1970s lectures on biopolitics were close partners when he investigated how colonialism gave Europe new life by pauperizing the rest of the world (*SMBD* and *STP*). During the emergence of capitalism and imperialism, "biopower" subjected bodies to regulation, self-surveillance, and self-discipline. This complex governmentalization was initiated in asyla, hospitals, prisons, schools, and plantations. Biopower made the relationship of populations to their environments a central strut of governance in eighteenth- and nineteenth-century Europe, as productivity and health were linked to climatic and geographic surroundings. Each part was subject to human intervention and hence governmental interest, via forecasting, measuring, and estimating (*STP*, 245).

With the upheavals of the seventeenth century, such as the Thirty Years' War and rural and urban revolt, the conditions for implementing new modes of social organization arose. In eighteenth-century Europe, the government of territory became secondary to the government of things and social relations. Biopower freed the arts of government from the pre-modern motifs and *idées fixes* of the sovereign and the household. The population displaced the prince as a site for accumulating power, and the home was displaced by the economy as a newly anthropomorphized and international dynamic of social intervention and achievement. The populace became the province of statistics, and the nation was bounded not by the direct exertion of juridical influence or domestic authority, but by forms of knowledge that granted "the people" life. City, country, and empire substituted for household, with all the hierarchical dislocation that implies, as the epidemic and the map displaced the kitchen and the church (*FE*, 98–9).

Government was conceived and actualized in terms of climate, disease, industry, finance, custom, and disaster – literally, a concern with life and death, and what could be calculated and managed between them. Wealth and health became goals to be attained through the disposition of capacities across the population once "biological existence was reflected in political existence." Biopower brought "life and its mechanisms into the realm of explicit calculations" and made "knowledge-power an agent of transformation of human life." Bodies were identified with

politics, because managing them was part of running countries
and empires, with "the life of the species . . . wagered on its own
political strategies" (*FE*, 92–5, 97; *HS1*, 143).

Governing people came to mean, most centrally and critically, obeying the "imperative of health: at once the duty of each
and the objective of all." So even as Revolutionary France was
embarking on a regime of slaughter, public-health campaigns were
underway, as the state constructed a Janus-faced "game between
death and life" (*RM*, 4, 277). Modern capitalism was articulated
to the modern state's desire to deliver a docile and healthy labor
force to business; but not only to business, and not merely in a
way that showed the lineage of that desire. Cholera, sanitation,
and prostitution were figured as problems for governments to
address in the modern era, through "the emergence of the health
and physical well-being of the population in general as one of the
essential objectives of political power." The entire "social body"
was assayed and treated for its insufficiencies. In shifting its tasks
from naked, controlling power to generative, productive power,
government in general increasingly aimed to "'make' live and 'let'
die," as well as "take life or let live" (*SMBD*, 241).

The critical shift here was away from an accumulation of power
by the sovereign, and towards the dispersal of power into the population. The center invested people with the capacity to produce
and consume things, insisting on freedom in some compartments
of life, and obedience in others (Foucault 1994c, 125). Out of that
came the following prospect: "Maybe what is really important
for our modernity – that is, for our present – is not so much the
étatisation of society, as the governmentalization of the state" (*FE*,
103). The "problem of the central soul" of the state was immanent
in "multiple peripheral bodies" and the messy labor of controlling
them. Such a move allowed for "transformation not at the level of
political theory, but rather at the level of the mechanisms, techniques, and technologies of power" (*SMBD*, 29, 37, 241).

Drawing on Barthes, Foucault proposed a threefold concept of
governmentality to explain life today. The first element utilizes
economics to mold the population into efficient and effective
producers. The second is an array of apparatuses designed to create
conditions for this productivity, via bodily interventions and the

promotion of fealty and individuality. The third translates methods between education and penology, transforming justice into human "improvement." Put another way, we might understand this as the indoctrination of the state by the social and the infestation of sovereignty with demography (*FE*, 102–3).

Governmentality centers the population as desiring, producing, and committed subjects who stand ready both to fight for the state and to question its actions. In Foucault's words, the market has latterly become "a 'test,' a locus of privileged experience where one . . . [can] identify the effects of excessive governmentality" (*EW1*, 76). This is a way of resituating management of the social squarely within civil society – a further transformation in governmentality. As he argued, "civil society is the concrete ensemble within which these ideal points, economic men, must be placed so that they can be appropriately managed" (*BB*, 296).

For Foucault, governance organizes the public by having it organize itself, through the material inscription of discourse into policies and programs of the state and capital via technology. He defines a technology as "a matrix of popular reason." It has four categories: "technologies of production" make for the physical transformation of material objects; "technologies of sign systems" are semiotic; "technologies of power" form subjects as a means of dominating individuals and encouraging them to define themselves in particular ways; and "technologies of the self" are applied by individuals to make themselves autotelically happy (*TS*, 18). This analysis is not distant from Marxism, and it opens up neoliberalism to inspection.

Neoliberalism

Neoliberalism was one of the most successful attempts to reshape individuals in human history. Its achievements rank alongside such productive and destructive sectarian practices as state socialism, colonialism, nationalism, and religion. Neoliberalism's lust for market regulation was so powerful that its prelates opined on every biopolitical topic imaginable, from birth rates to divorce, from suicide to abortion, from performance-enhancing drugs to altruism.

Neoliberalism provided more than "a political alternative" to mixed-market social welfare. Its singular triumph over thirty years was to sustain a "many-sided, ambiguous, global claim with a foothold in both the right and the left" (*BB*, 218) through a seeming rejection of tyranny and promotion of transparency. The neoliberal clerisy enlisted philosophical liberals and conservatives alike by opposing labor and welfare, remaining agnostic about elections (other than when governmental outlays were at stake), and maintaining that individuals could govern themselves. Neoliberalism stood rhetorically against elitism (for populism); against subvention (for markets); and against public service (for philanthropy).

I use the past tense to describe neoliberalism because of the Global North's descent into an economic *oubliette* since 2008, via the delayed disasters of derivatives deregulation and the New International Division of Labor. The ensuing crisis has forced the clerisy, from Beijing to the Bourse, to pick over the social ruins they oversaw. Ultimately, neoliberalism sank under the weight of contradiction, buried beneath its own blend of individuation and authoritarianism. But even as its wreckage is everywhere to be seen, neoliberal ideology continues to bob about and hinder reform. Its hold over the world via the "Washington Consensus" may be over, but its tentacles still control much of ordinary life and policy-making. The vibrant debates on blogs between world-renowned economists since 2008 are dramatic death-throes, as grownups throw stones at one another over deficits and spread sheets in the hope of an enduring hegemony that seems hopelessly compromised (Quiggin 2010).

Foucault's biopolitical insights into neoliberalism's birth in the 1970s provide "a way of thinking about this problem before it became actual," before it "ruined people's lives and wrecked social, political and economic institutions" (Tribe 2009, 694). He did not simply equate the concept with a stage of economic development; nor did he fall for the *canard* that it sought to withdraw the state from economic activity. Rather, Foucault explained that neoliberalism governed populations through market imperatives, invoking and training them as ratiocinative liberal actors *per medio* biopower.

Neoliberalism's "whole way of being and thinking" (*BB*, 218) was spread by neoclassical economists who knew everything and spared no one their analyses and prescriptions. Many of us looked on, bemused, as these demagogic true believers denounced or ignored work done by sociologists, anthropologists, artists, historians, linguists, and social movements, while promoting their own capacity to comprehend the totality of human life without reference to class, gender, race, culture, ideology, or collective identity, other than as acts of individual rationality. In certain ways, their lives backed up their scholarship, of course.

Charles Ferguson's documentary *Inside Job* (2010) and associated research exposed the fact that leading economists opined on the public interest before, during, and after pocketing hefty sitting and speaking fees as corporate consultants and conference lounge lizards (also see Folbre 2010). These revelations have prodded the sacerdotal *elite* to consider adopting a code of ethics to govern their cartoonish conduct and abandon the charade of double-blind manuscript reviewing in their journals because so many evaluators had financial investments in perspectives they were supporting "intellectually" (Berrett 2011; Jaschik 2011). Meanwhile, the average Gringo economist was charging a hundred dollars per paper review, in keeping with the profession's rent-seeking *Weltanschauung*, which sees salaries rise by 3.8 percent with each article penned in a house journal (*The Economist* 2011).

Given the fervor accompanying this extraordinary, self-appointed claim to omniscience and omnipotence, it comes as no surprise that economics has a religious origin. When the Trinity was being ideologized within Christianity, something had to be done to legitimize the concept at the same time as dismissing and decrying polytheistic and pagan rivals to the new religion's moralistic monotheism. Hence *oikonomia*, a sphere of worldly arrangements that was to be directed by a physical presence on Earth that could represent the will of the deity. God gave Christ "the economy" to manage, so "the economy" indexically manifested Christianity (Agamben 2009, 9–10).

Neoliberalism sought to create "an enterprise society" (*BB*,

147, 218) through the pretense that the latter was a natural (albeit never-achieved) state of affairs and people were intelligible through the precepts of selfishness, with the market privileged as "the interface of government and the individual" (*BB*, 253). At the same time, consumption was turned on its head. Internally divided – but happily so – each person was "a consumer on the one hand, but . . . also a producer" (*BB*, 226).

This trend reached its rhetorical apogee when Mexican President Vicente Fox (2000–6) asked reporters: "*¿Yo por qué?   ¿Qué no somos 100 millones de mexicanos?*" [Why me? . . . Aren't there a hundred million Mexicans?] (quoted in Venegas 2003). In other words, each person must assume responsibility for his or her material fortunes. The fact that not every one of the other hundred million Mexicans exercised control over the country's money supply, tariff policy, trade, labor law, and exchange rate might have given him pause. Similarly, George Bush Minor's Presidential *mantra* was "making every citizen an agent of his or her own destiny" (quoted in Miller 2007). Paradoxically, this discourse flourished by imposing competition as a framework to regulate everyday life through the most comprehensive statism imaginable (*BB*, 145). It did so through a mediatized anthropomorphism that drew on biopower.

Communicating Biopolitically

The backdrop to neoliberalism was the anthropomorphization of the economy and the intensification of globalization via an international division of labor, regional trading blocs, globally oriented cities, and an anti-labor ethos of deregulation.

How was this hegemony achieved? The media and education were central to that remarkable achievement, because a popular unity was established between the assayed social body of biopower and the anthropomorphic figure of the economy. The neoliberal right won many struggles enacted over culture, sometimes in concert with the new right of cultural studies – the prelates of creative industries, and their doctrine of "prosumption" – and sometimes in concert with conservatives, when making nationalism into a cultural and commercial norm. New media technologies deepened the biopolitical impact of neoliberalism by seeming to oppose the state and speak to the multifaceted ability of people to make their own media – and destinies (Ritzer and Jurgenson 2010). But this achievement drew on an earlier shift in media coverage of economics plus its suzerainty over educational administration.

English-language media references to "the economy" as a living subject, with needs and desires, derive from coverage of the Depression. At that time, press attention shifted from relations between producers and consumers of goods (a labor-process discourse of the popular newspapers) and onto relations between different material products *of* labor. There was a similar change in emphasis from use-value to exchange-value. The discursive commodities "the economy" and "the market" were given life and value through being textualized, then fetishized as empirical truths in the newspapers of the day (Emmison 1983; Emmison and McHoul 1987).

In other words, the crisis of the 1930s and the diffusion of Keynesianism ushered "the economy" into popular knowledge. This process bore some relationship to material reality, but like all statistical forms, it textualized biopolitical interests and conflicts. The discursive framework "the economy" came to be theorized as an entity with needs and emotions. This invention was *constructed* rather than merely *described* by economics (Arminen 2010). From that time, "the economy" began to thrive and suffer in bodily and emotional ways, just like a person, and become subject to biopolitical promotion and security.

While the press helped to anthropomorphize the economy, the neoliberal drive to economize all forms of life had a reciprocal effect. Perhaps neoliberalism's most powerful impact on the media was the financialization of news and current affairs. Foucault identified cash-operated US think tanks like the American Enterprise Institute as the intellectual hand-servants of this practice, vocalists of a "permanent criticism of government policy" (*BB*, 247). Today they do "research" in order to pen op-eds in newspapers and provide talking-points on cable news.

Neoclassical economic theory is deemed palatable on US

television in a way that other theoretical vocabularies are not. In addition, stories are presented in terms of their monetary significance to investors. TV parrots the market's specialized vocabulary, assumes a community of interest and commitment to fictive capital, and takes the deep affiliation and regular participation of viewers in stock prices as watchwords. The heroization of business executives by fawning journalists became part of a doubling of time dedicated by television news to the market across the 1990s. In 2000, finance was the principal topic on ABC, NBC, and CBS nightly news, and second only to terrorism in 2002. Promoting stocks where one had a personal financial interest became *de rigueur* for anchors and pundits. By 2002, even the New York Stock Exchange was worried by this tendency, and called for regulation requiring reporters to disclose their investments, so egregious had been their complicity with the dotcom overinvestment of the 1990s (Miller 2007).

Business advisors dominate discussion on dedicated finance stations like CNBC and Bloomberg, and are granted the status of seers when they appear on MSNBC, CNN, or the broadcast networks. The focus of much "news" has become stock markets, earnings, profits, and portfolio management. Journalists stalk politics in order to discredit democratic activities that might restrain capital. Labor news has been transmogrified into corporate news, and politics is measured in terms of its reception by business.

For example, during his time as Chair of the Federal Reserve, Alan Greenspan was filmed getting in and out of cars each day as if he were *en route* to a meeting to decide the fate of nations, each upturned eyebrow or wrinkled frown subject to hyper-interpretation by a bevy of needy followers. This obsessive pattern repeated as a farce in the latter part of the decade, when financial markets crumbled into self-indulgent, infantile fury and tears.

The trend is international: leading sources of wholesale video news, such as Reuters, make most of their money from finance reporting, which infuses their overall delivery of news. Primarily political journalists at Reuters refer to themselves as "cavaliers" and their primarily financial counterparts as "roundheads" – severe metaphors from the English Civil War (Palmer et al. 1998). The focus falls on stock markets in Asia, Europe, and New York, reports on company earnings, profits, and stocks, and portfolio management (Martin 2002; 2004).

Journalistic veneration of the market is ever ready to point to infractions of this anthropomorphized, yet oddly subject-free sphere, as a means of constructing moral panics around the conduct of whoever raises its ire. Even the global financial crisis hasn't eroded faith in reactionary solutions to a radical problem, as the bizarre press coverage of the Gringo financial meltdown indicates (Pew Research Center 2009; Thompson 2009). Meanwhile, the leftist media, which had investigated Enron and other sites of malfeasance for years, remained ridiculed or ignored.

Another telling instance of neoliberal biopolitics can be discerned in US universities' mimetic managerial fallacy, a process whereby administrators construct corporate life as their desired other and "codes of business judgment have presented themselves as universal knowledge" (Bruno and Newfield 2010). Universities are increasingly prone to puerile managerial warlockcraft superstitions about "excellence," "quality control," and "flatter structures." In addition, academic institutions have come to resemble the entities they now serve, as colleges are transformed into big businesses/government secretariats. Major research schools, particularly private ones, are also landlords, tax havens, and research-and-development surrogates, whose trustees look for returns on collective and individual investments (Giroux and Myrsiades 2001; Giroux 2007).

One can find instances of the mimetic managerial fallacy in any university administration, but it's hard to go past one collegecrat informing the *New York Times Magazine* that "being president of the University of California is like being manager of a cemetery: there are many people under you, but no one is listening. I listen to them" (Solomon 2009).

But he is not really alone, this poor pseudo-isolate: the seemingly solitary life at the top is actually quite sociable, because the mimetic fallacy has seen non-teaching managers increase their proportion from a tenth to a fifth of employees across US schools in the last three decades. The upshot of such ecstatically parthenogenetic managerialism is that more and more senior and junior administrative positions are created. Universities have added so many managers (a 240% increase from 1976 to 2001) that faculty

amount to just a third of campus workers. And whereas senior
faculty members are frequently replaced by assistant professors or
adjuncts, senior managers tend to be replaced by those of equivalent rank (Deresiewicz 2011; Martin 2011). Reach out and feel the
love. *Apparatchiks* are just a coquettish glance away.

Consider the Chancellor Who Came in from the Cold thanks
to the reality television show *Undercover Boss* (2010) on CBS,
which was nominated for an Emmy as "Outstanding Reality
Program" in 2010 and 2011 and won the next year (Emmys
2012). It follows corporate executives as they venture *incognito* into
factories to experience grassroots life in their companies. To me,
this smacks of unreconstructed Maoism. It's all rather reminiscent
of Deng Xiaoping being sent off to the Xinjian County Tractor
Factory during the Cultural Revolution for some political re-
education courtesy of participant observation of the working class
(Wang 2003).

But no. Part of the wider reality-television phenomenon,
Undercover Boss is a banal example of game shows taken into the
community, *cinéma-vérité* conceits, scripts written in post-produc-
tion, and *ethē* of Social Darwinism, surveillance, neoliberalism,
and gossip. Makeover shows like this one target economically
underprivileged viewers, offering them a lifestyle they cannot
afford to sustain. The genre emphasizes the responsibility of each
person to master their drives and harness their energies in order
to secure better jobs, homes, looks, and lovers. It is suffused with
deregulatory nostra of individual responsibility, avarice, possessive
individualism, hyper-competitiveness, and commodification.

Timothy White, the then Chancellor of the University of
California Riverside (UCR) who went on to run the California
State University system, appeared on *Undercover Boss* in 2011 (CBS
2011). It began and ended in tears. He cried about personal loss.
He cried about student debt. He almost cried about putting in
false teeth and wearing a Groucho mustache as part of his thrilling
disguise. He looked very miserable as he tried to function as an
athletic coach, a library assistant, a science adjunct – you name it.

But then he removed the disguise. He came out, out of the
closet of the *faux* proletariat. And his young mentors in these
various failed real jobs were rewarded. Student loans? Forgiven.

Poor athletic facilities? Sorted (a promise of US$2 million for capital improvements). Untenured junior faculty? Supported. It was magic, provided by unnamed benefactors.

What an absurd moment – but a teachable one, as we Socratic folks like to say. It cloaked the horrors of a system that puts children of the working class into generational debt and wastes millions of dollars on anti-educational sports programs. The cloak was one-off charity, made available to those lucky enough to be subject to childish deceit by a media corporation and a public servant.

The mimetic managerial fallacy also stimulates surveillance. Regional accrediting institutions that vouch for the quality of US degrees have been in place for well over a century. But since the 1970s, there have been vast increases in auditing work: from outside the university, on the campus itself, within departments, and in how faculty members see themselves. For example, we have seen ever-increasing performance-based evaluations of teaching at departmental and decanal levels, rather than in terms of the stand-ard of an overall school. Such methods are used by 95 percent of departments (for the impact on feminist professors and faculty of color, see Valdivia 2001).

Grants and commodification are valorized over publication, and administrators refer to "change" as an unproblematic good that they adore and admire. This means more obedience, more external review, more metrification of tasks, more forms, less autonomy, and less time to research. "Change" refers, really, to managerial mistrust of academics. It is a new kind of conformity, to national and international governmentalization and commodification. The picture is starkly sketched in Gaye Tuchman's telling ethnography *Wannabe U* (2009).

Administrators frequently link budgets to outcomes, in keeping with the prevailing beliefs of public-policy mandarins – their restless quest to conduct themselves like corporate captains. As successive superstitions come along – the 1990s variety was Total Quality Management – administrators fall in line with beguiling *doxa*. Along the way, faculty–student ratios worsen, and report-ing, surveillance, and administration grow in size and power. Many of us who have actually worked for business, the military, or government know what laughably inefficient institutions they can be – but folks who watch academics research and teach from the perch of administration frequently have *ressentiment* in their eyes and underachievement on their *résumés*, kicking down even as they kiss up.

Conclusion

Foucault's work has under-appreciated ties to Marxism. These are evident in his biopolitical activism and research. They provide a way for us to comprehend neoliberalism, and how the latter has been formed by, and in turn has helped to revise, crucial cultural nodes such as the news media and university administration.

The next challenge is to develop two tendencies. The first should be a program of research into the ongoing biopoliticization of everyday life via an anthropomorphizing economism. The second tendency must engage in activism, working with social movements that oppose neoliberalism to help them construct a counter-discourse to the ratiocinative, calculating fraud at the heart of the *bourgeois* media and higher education.

11
Assembling Untimeliness: Permanently and Restively
Paul Rabinow

Knowing how to end: Masters of the first rank are recognized by the fact that in matters great and small they know how to find an end perfectly, be it the end of a melody or a thought . . . The better of the second rank always get restless toward the end.

> – Friedrich Nietzsche (1974, 160)

La philosophie a à être dans un extériorité permanente et rétive par rapport à la politique, et c'est en cela qu'elle est réelle [Philosophy has to stand in a permanent and restive relation to politics, and it's in this that it is real. (editor's translation)]

> – Michel Foucault (*GSA1*, 326 [*GSO*, 354])

Nietzsche's assertion is heartening as it provides a trope with which one can comfort oneself. It is a relief during periods of wandering and *stultia* [troubled irresolution] to know that one might in due course arrive at the heights of the second rank. The fiction of such an imagined and imaginary station is reassuring for a number of reasons. For one, I (along with my co-workers) have certainly been restless in finding a more or less honorable ending and exit from our recent work as embedded practitioners in a center of synthetic biology (Rabinow and Bennett 2012; Rabinow and

Stavrianakis 2013). For another, the quotation that serves as my epigraph, paragraph 281, is followed shortly by paragraph 283, "Preparatory Human Beings," in which he eagerly anticipates a more virile age in which heroism will be carried into "the search for knowledge" and men will "wage wars for the sake of thoughts and their consequences" (Nietzsche 1974, 160). That challenge has been taken up throughout the twentieth century and the first decade of the twenty-first with committed ardor by an assortment of intellectual masters as well as hordes of lower rank prophets, sages, and technicians, both in the academy and in corporate, governmental, and other institutional walls. Nietzsche's hope is tragic; seen with hindsight, it is at most a form of black comedy. In sum, it is hard to imagine the eternal return of such a virile gay science as something even the strongest could endure or that contemporary artists and thinkers of whatever rank should seriously consider finding a form to accommodate perfectly or otherwise.

Foucault's emphatic and empathic assertion is encouraging, if ambiguous and exigent. It provides an orientation to the bedeviled question of how those committed to thinking might best be situated in relation to those waging power struggles, especially those claiming to do so (even in part or in passing) for the sake of thoughts and its consequences. Foucault's litotes (remarkably close to those of Max Weber) is neither a call for contemplation per se nor an advocacy of scientific or unruffled Stoic *ataraxia* [composure]. Rather, it proceeds from an acknowledgment that power relations permeate human actions and passions and that therefore there is always a problem in establishing a relationship to them if one is to think with and through actual situations as one's object and proving ground.

John Dewey argued for a comparable but not identical approach (albeit in a different vocabulary). Thinking, Dewey held, arises from troubles in pragmatic situations. What attitude should a thinker adopt to troubled practices and situations? Dewey's answer: a pragmatic and reconstructive one. "Pragmatic" means engaged directly in the troubled situation and "reconstructive" means intervening with the goal of inflecting the situation so as to make it a milieu in which humans are more likely to flourish.

Foucault proposes a permanent and restive relation to politics (as well as science and subjectivity) as a key anchor point in a mode of thinking he calls philosophical. Although the adjective "permanent" might seem innocuous, actually it is not. Working at establishing a permanent philosophical and anthropological relationship to politics, science and the self is a life-long work requiring incessant attention and rectification. Such work requires the elaboration and practice of an array of the elements of a *bios tekhnikos* [skillful life] in the service of what Foucault called a *bios filosofikos* [philosophical life]. Such a form of life, a mediated and monitored form of work on the self and others, the acceptance of a kind of perpetual discomfort with the situations one observes in close proximity – a permanent adjacency – but has the capacity to intervene only in a restrictive and singular manner.

If the call for a permanent relationship might seem innocuous, the term "restive" cannot be elided with any ease. It is hard not to wonder what is at stake for Foucault in the use of this term. "Restive" has a similar semiotic range in both English and French: one core meaning is "recalcitrant." "Recalcitrant," it seems to me, however, conveys something that is too fixed and static. The German *widerspenstig* – "unruly, against one's will" – picks out a slightly different dimension of experience that unsettles what might otherwise be a general adolescent sulky or defiant stubbornness. However, even that stance still sounds too reactive and defensive to make "restive" such a valorized term. Yet another connotation in English – "uneasy and on the verge of resisting control" – is more enlightening. It indicates a mode of vigilance, an alert wariness.[1] Such vigilance should include caution about preemptory negativity. Vigilance requires attention to specifics and a suspension of unwarranted judgment. Judgment without inquiry renders one vulnerable to aligning with those who claim to know the significance of things, events and situations in advance of their unfolding or assembling.

Finally, a "verge" is a border, potentially available as a zone of adjacency. Thus, to say that "restive" means in part "on the verge of resisting control" evokes both an actively maintained observational position – an element of the repertoire of *bios tekhnikos* – and an *ēthos* – a dimension of a *bios filosofikos*. It should include finding or making a prime location to observe those resisting control or those seeking to exercise control. The dynamics and rationality of control, however, while demanding attention, is not necessarily the unique or even the most salient aspect of politics, science, or subjectivity. Power, after all, is productive.

Assemblages

One of the things that entails a distinctive form of production is the assemblage. Although the term "assemblage" is widely used, only a few critics have taken it seriously as either an object of knowledge or an objective of design. In order to provide the elements for this double target, a few elements need to be specified. An assemblage is not a totality, a seamless whole; it is not a pre-existing thing of the world with pre-given properties.[2] Assemblages, however, once they are made or happen, do become things in the world, things characterized by a specific form of functional coherence and efficacy. Assemblages have an ontological status – a variant of what Ian Hacking has called historical ontology (Hacking 2004). Assemblages are real; they have existence, forms, effects; certain assemblages include affects as elements. Assemblages make some things and events possible and others improbable.

They differ, however, from what has traditionally been understood as "a thing" or "an object" in being composed of heterogeneous parts that retain – to a degree, as they are combined and recombined into new interrelations – their original properties. They retain these qualities because they enter into an assemblage through establishing relations of exteriority – not interiority – with the other entities with which they have been brought into proximity and with which they interact.[3] The fact that an assemblage brings together entities in the world into a proximity in which they establish relations between and among themselves while remaining external to each other and thereby retaining their original properties has a number of ramifications.

The first is that the order of an assemblage is, as Manuel DeLanda puts it, "contingently obligatory instead of logically necessary" (DeLanda 2006, 11). It follows that "while logically necessary relations may be investigated by thought alone, contingently obligatory ones involve a consideration of empirical questions" (11). Given that conclusion, it follows that the practice of thinking about and with assemblages would itself have to be more than discursive or theoretical. One form of creative work consists in an act of creation; one, however, that contributes to bringing together diverse elements into a form – an assemblage – that preserves their diversity while opening up hitherto unknown or unavailable capacities.

Praemeditatio malorum: A Presumption of Evil

In his 1981–2 lectures at the Collège de France, peculiarly entitled "The Hermeneutics of the Subject" (*HS*), Foucault introduced an extended set of archaeological investigations into the techniques of the care of the self in the ancient world. Of direct interest here is his exploration of the linking of memory as a preeminent site of the integration of life and thought with a set of techniques that were grouped under *meletē*, the term translated as "meditation." The goal of this generalized apparatus connecting the present and memory through reasoned examination of one's actions was taken to be the medium through which an ethical life could be capacitated. An essential dimension, taken for granted and assumed, was that the future was unknowable, uncontrollable, and certain to bring with it dangers and evils. Regardless, nothing new and significant for the manner in which one led one's life was looming in the future, only more of the same. Stoic and other philosophers developed techniques, exercises, and practices for facing such a future, and consequently the past and the present.

The older significance of the term *meletē* has been covered over both by subsequent Christian, Enlightenment, and modern uses, which differ in essential ways from the objects and objectives Roman philosophers such as Seneca addressed. The Stoic scope of the term *meletē* is resolutely mundane in Max Weber's sense of "this-worldly." It refers to a set of practices formed to engage the everyday world and its perpetual, if sporadic, dangers, evils, and turbulence. These practices and their associated techniques were not designed to transcend this quotidian world for another beatific one, but rather as a means of preparing oneself to face actual dangers so as to be able to lead, as best one could, a reasonable and composed life despite them. Given this perspective, meditation and its practices contributed as an essential component of a form of life – a *bios* – understood as a permanent preparation for a life-long test of the self. This life-long preparatory work afforded one the capacities for a testing of oneself and of what one thinks and how one practices what one thinks.

In the ancient world, both Greek and Roman, albeit in diverse manners, meditation was habitually linked to memory: truth in the form of recognition, the rent subject brought back to a repaired state of wholeness (*HS*, 460). The function of the practices and exercises that Foucault groups under the term *askēsis* were designed to provide the equipment of true discourse on which one would be able to call for aid, for assistance, when the need arose. Foucault provides a crisp definition of *meletē*, the collection of practices, maxims, and exercises, as "the exercise of thought on thought" (*HS*, 455). The constant goal of these practices was not epistemological, however, but rather the self-transformation into an ethical subject, the test of oneself as the subject of truth. The challenge was to constitute the subject (oneself and others) as the subject of true knowledge and as a subject of right action. This permanent task was understood as being undertaken against and within the world that is perceived, recognized, and practiced as a test – the site of experience and an exercise in ethical being (*HS*, 484–7).

For those undertaking the practices of *meletē* – and of course most would not follow this rigorous path – the self-surveillance passed through an act of reason. But how was reason to be practiced as an element of *meletē*? "Reason is a gaze looking down, as it were, and a gaze that enables reason in its free employment to observe, check, judge, and evaluate what is taking place in the flow of representations and the flow of passions" (*HS*, 457) – the flow of representations and the flow of passions as the object of reason and the objective for reason to surveil, modulate, mediate, and meditate on.

A privileged domain of these exercises (and the manner in

which memory was activated within them) was called the work of *praemeditatio malorum*, the premeditation or presumption of evils. Throughout ancient times there was a constant and pervasive mistrust of the future. The future preoccupied; it preoccupied the mind, led away from memory, from recognition and identity. Training to prepare for nefarious events was required so as not to be taken off guard when they arrived. One of the ways one achieved this preparation was through an exhaustive review of evils. This preparatory work did not constitute a remedy, it would not prevent evils and demanding trials from taking place; rather, it was a means of preparing oneself to face them in a reasonable, that is to say, composed manner. For example, Seneca wrote to a young friend: "to exhort you for the future, to lift your soul aloft against misfortune, to foresee her offensives not as possible events, but as bound to occur" (*HS*, 470). Fundamentally, all of this work was a way of sealing off the future as best one could.

The future was troubling. Thus, Plutarch argues that those who turn toward the future were *stulti*, and hence have forgotten or neglected to take care of the self. Those afflicted with *stultitia* have not taken care of themselves. They are prey to the flow and overflow of representations of the external world and cannot discriminate among them. Those afflicted with *stultitia*, almost all of us, are afflicted by irresolution and restlessness. The *stulti* need help (*HS*, 131).

The ultimate problem, as these Stoic philosophers understood it, was that turning toward the future negated attention to the present (*HS*, 465). It followed that in order to ward off at least the part of troubles magnified by representations and passions of specific dimensions of the future as it appeared in the present, the future needed to be systematically nullified. Achieving such containment required a type of disciplined practice. The *praemeditatio malorum* was designed to achieve this nullification of the future through a reduction of the imagination, a restriction of its scope to the simple and stripped-down reality of the present. Practical exercises were designed to achieve this defensive disposition: since one could not know or work directly on the future, one had to work on what was available in the present, and what was available was imagination. If the site of *praemeditatio malorum* was the imagination, the site of the soul's trouble and agitation as concerns the future, one needed equipment to prepare oneself to diminish, ward off, or at least identify the source of these troubles. The *praemeditatio malorum* was a form of preparation "realized through the test of the non-reality of what we actualize in this exercise of thought" (*HS*, 473). Preparedness was the exercise of thought upon thought, in this case focalized in and on the imagination and the flow of representations and associated passions. It was a test of reality and of one's relationship to that reality.

★

In my view, Foucault and Gerhard Richter, an unlikely couple, provide different but serendipitously synergistic attempts in philosophy and art (as well as criticism and ethics more broadly) worthy not so much of direct emulation as of possible aid for the *stulti*, those restless and troubled seekers filling Nietzsche's imaginary second ranks. Foucault and Richter can be seen to converge on a common problematization. Both move toward a reversal of recent and distant relations of the past and future – and their relationships with the present – as sites of *meletē*. Both seem to indicate in their work the worth of adopting this topos as one characteristic of how things might be better assembled today. Contrary to the ancients, today, for these inquirers, the past is not the site of self-recognition, at least in a redemptive form. The problem of leaving the past behind in the proper manner requires work and discrimination, not simply negation; preparing for the future requires a tempered imagination and at least some glimmer of hope. How to achieve that tempering, preparation and obdurate faith in work requires (among other things) a new form of *meletē*.

Richter or Foucault's goal is certainly not to simply erase or obliterate the past any more than to seal off the future – quite the contrary. In both cases, however, there is a distinctive kind of reduction of the present and the future involved in their work. There is an acute attention to the present. Sharpening and orienting that attention draws on extensive and intensive experience as well as a rich acquaintance with tradition understood archaeologically (and at times genealogically, perhaps more so in Richter's case). Further, for both of these artists of contemporary life, the reduction performed both in and on imagination is certainly equally a matter of taming the drive to a free flow of representations and its associated theorizing, which knows in advance what is good or bad, right or wrong, in motion or stasis.

Both Foucault and Richter have equipped themselves so as to work in the actuality of the present. They have both, in very different ways, equipped themselves to work toward a near future that might be remediative of the present. They both seek to make today introduce a difference in relation both to the past and to the future. Their prodigious and varied outputs, permanent and restive, demonstrate a tempered form of the *stulti* that Plutarch sought to avoid.

Foucault and Richter had work to do – their own work. But what is work?

> *Travail: ce qui est susceptible d'introduire une différence significative dans le champ du savoir, au prix d'une certaine peine pour l'auteur et le lecteur, et avec l'éventuelle récompense d'un certain plaisir, c'est-à-dire d'un accès à une autre figure de la vérité* [Work: that which is susceptible to introducing a significant difference into the field of knowledge, at the price of a certain pain for the author and the reader, and with the eventual recompense of a certain pleasure, which is to say of an access to a different figure of the truth]. (*DE4*, 367 [n.a.])

This quote beautifully describes the work of philosophy or science taken most broadly. The question remains open, however, how it would need to be transformed or modified if it were to frame the work of an artist.

Gerhard Richter's October 18, 1977 Paintings: Assemble and Accompany

Examining Gerhard Richter's attempt to render something visible – the suicide/murders of members of the Baader-Meinhof gang – provides us with an object and perhaps a lesson in how a permanent and restive *ēthos* can be put to work to bring new capacities in the world. It is instructive. A case study of how one can work with and about that productivity in relation to politics, science, and subjectivity is the theme under consideration in what follows.

Richter has produced an immense corpus of artistic work as well as actively contributing to generating a weighty body of conflicting critical response. Both the art works and the criticism are diverse. It is striking that perhaps his two most influential critical commentators, Benjamin H.H. Buchloh and Robert Storr, have accompanied Richter for decades now with their commentary and their company. This accompaniment is willed and mutually valued. Richter has provided these critics liberal access to repeated interviews and exchanges; they have produced copious and sincere reflections on his work. These reflections and Richter's responses to them do not converge on a stable or consensual interpretation or even communication points.

Robert Storr, for a time a curator at the Museum of Modern Art (MOMA) in New York (during which he organized a major Richter exhibition around the controversial October 1977 paintings), and subsequently Dean of the School of Art at Yale, has written several monographs on Richter's work. Storr's prose is jargon free (by art world standards) and his interpretations are not contested directly by Richter, thereby providing at least the appearance of his endorsement of Storr's interpretations.

It would not be mistaken to read instrumental motives into this state of affairs given Storr's previous position as a curator at MOMA and given Richter's sought-after and carefully orchestrated success in the marketplace. That self-promotion, while part of the story and consistently effective, is nonetheless neither unique to Richter nor does it constitute the whole story. Part of Richter's strategy, intentionally designed or not, has been to transform the role of the avant-garde artist rebelling against the reigning regime (in this case avant-gardist) by drawing attention to his lifestyle or the content or form of his work. Richter looks conventional; he makes money; he lives a comfortable life; he paints pictures of his children; he works tirelessly.

A refugee from the former East Germany, Richter insistently presents himself as permanently non-ideological and anti-theoretical. Storr willingly takes him at his word and provides a lucid and reliable presentation of Richter's work. That American clarity, of course, guarantees neither the interpretation's veridical claims nor its comprehensiveness. It does, however, I argue, constitute a part of the dynamics of assemblage that Richter is restively designing, that is to say, shaping and inflecting.

Richter appears to be a long-time friend of Buchloh and has even produced a painting (blurred of course) of the two of them in discussion. Yet, Richter rarely agrees with the aesthetic, veridictional, or ethical claims of Buchloh's jargonized, Adorno-like, high discourse. With a persistent regularity, in response to a theoretical assertion, Richter simply claims not to understand what Buchloh is talking about; at other times he directly disagrees. In these exchanges, Buchloh appears textually like a character out of Thomas Mann (more *The Magic Mountain* than *Doctor Faustus*, more Settembrini than Zeitblom) in his insistence on theorizing everything; he barely seems to notice, or in any case does not remark on, the fact that year after year, Richter refuses to acknowledge the core of his claims. This fact, of course, does not mean that Buchloh's interventions are erroneous.

It is admirable, if highly unusual, that this interpretive dissonance does not seem to stand in the way of their discussions, repartee or friendship. Here is one example.

BB: It seems to me that you introduce process-related painting as just one of painting's many possibilities, while not insisting, as Ryman did, that it is its only aspect.

GR: Then why should I go to such lengths to make it so varied?

BB: Because you are setting out to call off all the aspects there are, like a catalogue; because you're really trying to pursue both a rhetoric of painting and the simultaneous analysis of that rhetoric.

GR: If all this were just a matter of display – the way the yellow, tatter-edged area rises up against the blue green background – how could it tell a story or set up moods?

BB: A mood? You mean it really sets up an emotional experience?

GR: Yes, and aesthetic pleasure, too.

BB: That's something different. Aesthetic pleasure I can see, but absolutely not a mood.

GR: So what is a mood?

BB: A mood has an explicitly emotional, spiritual, psychological quality.

GR: That's exactly what is there.

BB: Fortunately only in the weakest parts.

GR: Surely you don't think that a stupid demonstration of brushwork, or of the rhetoric of painting and its elements, could ever achieve anything, say anything, express any longing.

BB: Longing for what?

GR: For lost qualities, for a better world – for the opposite of misery and hopelessness.

BB: The longing to be able to present culture as a contemplative spectacle without losing credibility?

GR: I might also call it redemption. Or hope – the hope that I can after all effect something through painting.

BB: Again, this is all so generalized; effect in what sense? Epistemological, emotional, psychological, political?

GR: All at once, I don't know . . .

BB: It's the contradiction of knowing full well that the means you are using won't achieve what you aim for, and at the same time not being prepared to change those means.

GR: That's not a contradiction, it's a perfectly normal state of affairs. The normal mess, if you like. And that couldn't be changed by choosing a different means and methods.

BB: Do your paintings invite acts of faith, or analyses? What matters more to you?

GR: Either would be fine with me. In your case they invite you to analyze; others find them an invitation to perform acts of faith. (Richter 1986, 180–2)

★

The question arises as to why Richter authorizes (in the double sense) these interviews. Perhaps there is a simple act of friendship involved. But the consistent over-the-years pattern of theoretical elaboration and demurral or refusal would seem to indicate that something more is at stake. Something else, additionally, it would seem, is being set in motion. The question that interests me is less whether there is an art market and how Richter is playing the game (as he surely is), but how critical discourse and Richter's painting are being made to function in this heterogeneous and dynamic milieu.

A main argument of this chapter is that this enduring critical dissonance between and among the critics and the artist is part of an assemblage that Richter is permanently and restively building and rectifying. It is as if Richter is acknowledging and affirming the unsurpassable existence of a critical discourse, whether or not he agrees, concurs, or is bypassed by it intellectually or otherwise. Richter, after all, is not operating primarily in the veridical field of true and false: he is a painter. As with his abstract paintings – *abstrackte Bild* – he is making a space for, making visible, rendering framed, a thing of the world: color and line and volume in one medium and theorizing, concepts, casuistry and sophism, in the other. Both domains exist: they are things of the world, the modern world as well as some contemporary scenes. Richter is assembling some of the discursive vectors that surround his work; whatever his motives (friendship, patronage, market-oriented, curiosity, etc.), he is assembling diverse and heterogeneous elements. Through form-giving he is creating something. That, after all, is what he does.

One response to this interpretive discord would be to attempt to mediate it. For example, one might try to bring the critics together at a symposium, let them speak and then have a modera-tor propose some form of arbitration. Such hermeneutically guided discussion and triage would lead in this case to a thin soup. In any case, neither required American-style politesse, nor persevering German clarification, nor arch French stylization would further, in my opinion, what Richter is abetting and facilitating.

Storr provides one powerful alternative interpretation when he analogizes Richter's approach to that of Brecht. Storr writes:

> Rather than identification with the characters, Brechtian drama creates distance between them and the audience; rather than involving the public with the action, as was true in classical dramaturgy, it confronts the public with difficult choices; rather than smooth transitions from scene to scene it presents discontinuous self-contained episodes; rather than emotional release, it leaves the viewer with unsolved problems and persistent intellectual and spiritual discomfort. Richter's paintings do much the same. (2000, 137)

Whether Storr realizes it or not, Richter's interviews and publications do much the same with his own critical work. Richter assembles and accompanies both Storr and Buchloh. Richter keeps these critical discourses in close proximity to his paintings, but he does so in such a way that the heterogeneity among the interpretations as well as between the discourses and the paintings is given a form.

Within the assemblage, consequently, Richter assembles elements that act so as to cause one to question things ("Who is more convincing?"; "Why is he talking to these critics?"; "Is any of this talk significant?"; "How does that swatch of green paint relate to this discourse?"). Although assembling problems is already a feat, perhaps a mark of something more is that at times we get a strong sense that the stakes are more than this problem of interpretation or that dispute over quality, but rather a problematization. Again:

> GR: Surely you don't think that a stupid demonstration of brushwork, or of the rhetoric of painting and its elements, could ever achieve anything, say anything, express any longing?

Moody, isn't he!

Assembling October 18, 1977

> Ezra Pound's Modernist call to arms was "make it new." For Richter, a product of Utopia's ruin, it would seem that the precondition for making anything new – at least any abstract picture – is to make something old or evocative of things already known, so that the known style and the old ideal can be annulled, undone, unmade.
> – Robert Storr (2009, 68)

In mid-winter 1989, fifteen paintings were exhibited at a small museum in Krefeld (outside Cologne). The museum was the former house of Mies van der Rohe, hence a tribute of sorts to high modernism. Buchloh observes:

That this group of paintings was first exhibited in a building by Mies van der Rohe seems an appropriate historical accident, for Mies is the architect who constructed the only German contribution to public monumental sculpture in the twentieth century, devoting it to the memory of the philosopher Rosa Luxemburg and the revolutionary Karl Liebknecht, both of whom had been murdered by the Berlin police. The coincidence establishes continuity between a bourgeois architect in the Weimar state of the 1920s and a bourgeois painter in West Germany of the 1980s. And indeed both artists differ from most of their contemporaries in their ability to tolerate, in public view, the challenges to the very political and economic system with which they identify as artists. (Quoted in Storr 2000, 31)

Yet one must wonder, as Buchloh does not, what it means to be a bourgeois in the twenty-first century. Mies had a clearer vision of how modernist architecture would accommodate capitalism and the persona of the architect than does Richter, even though Richter lives in comfort and his paintings sell readily at high prices. Furthermore, Mies's problems (political, aesthetic, and ethical) are not the same as Richter's. In fact, it is the whole world of political ideology including modernism that Richter is attempting to leave behind without forgetting it. Hence Buchloh's comparison is seductive but ultimately misleading.

The overt subject matter of the series of black-white-grey canvasses would be known to all Germans of a certain age and education: the officially proclaimed suicide or suspected murder in prison of two of Germany's most illustrious political terrorists. Richter's grey, black, and white paintings include portraits, scenes of the confrontation and arrest, the physical setting of the prison cells, the hanged body of Gudrun Ensslin, eerie almost tender portraits of the leading woman, and a funeral procession. Storr's claim that "studied separately, but even more so together, the fifteen paintings are among the most somber and perplexing works of art in modern times" is an uncontroversial one (Storr 2000, 28).

Venue

The series was acquired in June 1995 by the Museum of Modern Art in New York. Exactly how this happened is a subject of debate as there was a sense that a promise of sorts had been made to the museum in Frankfurt. There is the countervailing story, however, that the Museum's trustees, one of whose members had been killed by the Red Army Faction, refused to pay for the paintings. Regardless, by shifting the context, the paintings were placed within an art historical series rather than as illustrations of a political interpretation; by shifting the venue of their presentation, the form of their presentation was altered (Storr 2000, 34). It is in this light that Richter's claim that neither political intent nor historical truth were at issue makes some sense. The paintings both evoke and annul the historical and political elements that would almost inevitably be evoked by viewers who were aware of these elements and had been moved by them in one fashion or another. As an act of memory they would be caught in a small set of possible associations.

We can agree with Storr that here Richter was, as always, trying to make something new. Part of the artist's capacity was to see that their actuality would change if they were located elsewhere as well as that he had the standing, power, and resources in the art world to make this transfer happen and seem worthy of debate.

By including a change in venue in his assemblage, and knowing that Storr would provide a certain reading while allowing Buchloh and others to provide quite different readings, Richter knew that the paintings stood a chance of retaining a lasting actuality. As he wrote:

> This means that they are documents and they are not illustrative materials . . . The reviews [in the United States] were inspiringly different from the German ones. Here one was so affected by the subject matter that the paintings were almost exclusively viewed in political terms – or even as a kind of family affair . . . People abroad did not let their expectations and bias obscure their view of the paintings. (Storr 2009, 36)

Although it is clear what Richter means, it is more accurate to say that "people abroad" had a different and probably more diverse set of expectations that would obscure their view of the paintings in different and diverse ways. And they have.

Mode

We should take seriously Richter's disclaimer: "These pictures possibly give rise to questions of political content or historical truth. Neither interests me in this instance" (Storr 2009, 130).

He knows perfectly well that the pictures would give rise to questions, debates, accusations and defenses of what they presumably represented in terms of political content and/or historical truth. Among the many things Richter was attempting to achieve was to move the debate away from remaining in a deadening perpetual oscillation between the polarities of politics and theory. Richter was neither aligning himself with the existing sides of the debate and the politics (he recognizes some validity or coherence for each), nor was he dismissing the whole affair. Rather, he was attempting to set something else in motion: make something taken to be past visual in the present.

Richter refers to the paintings as a "leave-taking" (from violent struggle and ideology). Storr adds that the same is true of epochal and revolutionary criticism. Storr observes that the previous forms and norms of revolutionary criticism today function so as to conserve the past, not to challenge the recent past or near future. "As historical paintings they remain eloquently unresolved; as a contemporary requiem they stop short of transfiguration." They heighten and/or reawaken tensions, but do not resolve them. Those portrayed are neither heroes nor anti-heroes as they would have been in the modernist tradition. Rather, there is an activation of memory, not its erasure – but such activation is not designed to achieve either a stable integration of positions in the present or a clear identification with past figures. If anything, these "somber and perplexing" paintings yield a range of troubled reactions.

The past, however, does not disappear – quite the contrary.

The leave-taking is not from painting, either – quite the contrary – but how is it done? And here, I believe, a contemporary form of *meletē* enters in. Crucial to this leave-taking is a mood shift.

Mood and Trope: Metalepsis

Let us remember that the practices of *meletē* were a form of preparation and preparedness, with a subset of these practices directed at composing a relationship to the future. The *praemeditatio malorum* was a specific form of preparation "realized through the test of the non-reality of what we actualize in this exercise of thought" (*HS*, 473). Preparedness was the exercise of thought upon thought, in this case focalized in and on the imagination and the flow of representations and associated passions. It was a test of reality and of one's relationship to that reality. In this instance, that reality was death, evil, and incapacity to act directly on events and situations.

Let us also remember that Richter was adamant, even indignant, when his friend Buchloh sneered at the possibility that he was attempting to create a mood in the October 18, 1977 paintings as well as equally, albeit in multiply different ways, in all of his work. Predictably, Buchloh was following the line of criticism of mood (*Stimmung*) as essentially anti-rational and politically nefarious, which Adorno (and Pierre Bourdieu) had articulated as an attack on Heidegger (Adorno 1973; Bourdieu 1991).

So what is mood? The French scholar Gérard Genette, in a long chapter on "mood" in *Narrative Discourse: An Essay in Method*, quotes the definition of "mood" from the authoritative French dictionary *Littré*. "Mood" (*mood* in French as well): "Name given to different forms of the verb that are used to affirm more or less the same thing in question and to express . . . the different points of view from which the life or the action is looked at" (Genette 1980, 182). This capacity to vary points of view is what narrative mood aims at achieving. To achieve this goal, it specifically concentrates on designing and structuring the place and function of distance and perspective. The successful use of mood as a means favors modal variations as its primary means for the regulation of narrative stylization.

But how specifically is mood put to work in narrative? The answer is that it can be deployed in many different ways. Of those diverse ways, the pertinent trope for the problems we have been considering is metalepsis. Metalepsis (*transumptio* in Latin) is an old trope that appeared in the ancient handbooks but has come to occupy a much broader and more inventive place in modern literature, albeit one that has received less attention from many critics, including those who practice it. Technically, metalepsis is achieved, Genette tells us, through "the act that consists precisely of introducing into one situation, by means of a discourse, the knowledge of another situation" (1980, 234). Its strength and its unsettling dynamics arise from its deployment of "a boundary that is precisely the narrating (or the performance) itself: a shifting but sacred frontier between two worlds, the world in which one tells, the world of which one tells" (234). Staying on the verge in a metaleptic narrative is extremely difficult. Whence the uneasiness that Borges so well puts his finger on: "Such inversions suggest that if the characters in a story can be readers or spectators, then we, their readers or spectators, can be fictitious" (234).

Metalepsis is troubling, Genette argues, because of its simultaneously unacceptable and persistent insistence that the extra-textual is always textual. What is bothersome here is the challenge that "the narrator and his narratees – you and I – perhaps belong to the same narrative" (1980, 236). Achieving an effective metaleptic narrative requires more than technical skill. It requires the ability to effectively produce a mood: one in which distance and perspective are troubled, uncertain, and significant; one in which the spectator feels herself observed and involved.[1]

A metaleptic trope has an additional and significant characteristic. Metalepsis is the only one of the canonical tropes that operates in an explicitly historical register. Metalepsis takes up the past, or an aspect of the past, or rather the enduring presence of something past, and makes it function within a different narratological milieu – above all an assemblage for Richter – thereby subordinating it to a different function and thus transforming it and making it present.

One germane aspect of this historical and transformative mode of dealing with unresolved tensions has been explored by the American literary and cultural critic Harold Bloom, especially in his well-known *The Anxiety of Influence* (1973). Metalepsis, he writes, is a return of the dead, but very much in the poet's own dress, his own colors (1973, 141). This sentence sounds like it was written about Richter, not only his October 17, 1977 paintings but also others, such as his infamous painting of his "Uncle Rudi" in his Nazi uniform.

Such making present can be done in any number of ways. Its general form, however, is beautifully captured by James D. Faubion when he says metalepsis is "a calling up of the past precisely in order to acknowledge at once its weight and its failure, its incapacity to determine the present and the future, which is what allows it to establish a mood of hope, of positive possibility" (Faubion, personal communication).

Finally, this mode of this re-presenting is not ironic – the modernist mode *par excellence*. It seeks to do more than negate or displace or trouble the apparently real. The challenge of the metaleptic in literature and, it seems, in some painting and philosophy, is not to freeze distance and perspective. Rather, it is to provide the elements through which a form of possibility is made actual through the bringing into the present of something (sign, event, mood, etc.) that has passed but remains pertinent and salient. The skill is making this feat happen without precisely fixing exactly how it remains pertinent and salient. Unless there is a metaleptic implication of the viewer into the presentation, it will remain either nostalgic or ironic.

Of course, Walter Benjamin's famous interpretation of Paul Klee's Angelus Novus looking back at the ruins of history while being blown into the future by its raging flames and wind comes obligatorily to mind. And a number of critics including Storr have made the connection of Klee's angel to the painting Richter made of his daughter facing backward peering into the void. It is obvious, however, that neither Richter nor Foucault still held to a belief in history as the site of progress.

Foucault in his last works looked back to the Greek and Hellenistic philosophers. He drew much from them but whatever else he was doing in these explorations it was not affirming the possibility of mimesis or advocating Seneca or Epictetus as an exemplum to guide us in the present. Although this chapter is not the place to explore this claim, having spent the last three of his lecture series at the Collège de France (and of his life) exploring Greek and Hellenistic philosophy, in an interview of the period Foucault could not have been more emphatic: "*Toute l'Antiquité me paraît avoir été une profonde erreur*" [All antiquity seems to me to have been a profound error] (*FL*, 319). It was a profound error because it was committed to mastery of the self either as a means of the preparation to rule or to endure fate's slings and arrows. In either case there was an explicit unitary model of how to be. Foucault rejected both the goal and the venue, but not the practices – or the significance of mood as a vital accompaniment of *ēthos*. Of course, naturally, it goes without saying that accepting the problem and refusing older solutions was something Foucault's later lectures struggled with when defining the parameters of design.

Rather, Foucault was indicating both the impossibility of a direct return as well as a possible problematization, building on the awareness of the historical distance and altered perspective of these philosophers so as to make possible (but not certain) the assemblage of new lines of flight or at least the plausibility and worth of attempting to do so.

★

Thus, in contradistinction to Buchloh's claim that history painting as a genre is no longer possible for a true artist, one can see Richter's series as an attempt – metaleptically – to paint historically without the comfort of a philosophy of history or an understanding of representation in art either as giving direct access to the world or to being thoroughly incapable of doing so. Storr underscores this point when he says, "The problems it poses are out of a tradition, and they manifest the tradition's struggle to adapt to new circumstances" (Storr 2000, 131). The challenge is how to make history painting contemporary or more accurately how to present historical elements in a contemporary assemblage such that new visibilities and sayable things become actual, inducing motion and affect.

Notes

1 For a phenomenology of vigilance, see Duval (1990).
2 For a full systematic formal theory of these elements, see DeLanda (2002).
3 "While [an entity's] properties are given and may be denumerable as a closed list, its capacities are not given – they may go unexercised if no entity suitable for interaction is around – and for a potentially open list, since there is no way to tell in advance in what way a given entity may affect or be affected by innumerable other entities. In this view, being part of a whole involves the exercise of a part's capacities but it is not a constituent property of it. And given that an unexercised capacity does not affect what a component is, a part may be detached from the whole while preserving its identity" (DeLanda 2006, 10).
4 "*La pédagogie de Klee; Apprendre à déduire mais aussi à réduire les phé-nomènes. Tout le génie de Klee est là: à partir d'une problématique très simple et parvenir à une poétique d'une force remarquable où la problématique est totalement absorbée. Autrement dit, son principale de base est primordial, mais son imagination poétique, loin d'être appauvrie par la réflexion sur un problème technique, ne cesse au contraire de s'enrichir. L'imagination, cette faculté merveilleuse, ne fait rien d'autre, si on la laisse sans contrôle, que de prendre appui sur la mémoire. La mémoire fait ressort au jour des choses res-senties, entendues ou vues*" [Klee's pedagogy: to learn to deduce but also to reduce phenomena. That's the whole genius of Klee: from a very simple problematic to attain a poetics of remarkable force where the problematic is totally absorbed. In other words, his founding principle is primordial, but his poetic imagination, far from being impoverished by reflection on a technical problem, on the contrary never stops being enriched. The imagination, this marvelous faculty, does nothing else, if one leaves it unfettered, than to take support from memory. Memory acts as a springboard to the day of things deeply felt, heard or seen] (Boulez 1989, 146–7).

12

Constantine Cavafy: A Parrhesiast for the Cynic of the Future

James D. Faubion

In the final two years of his lectures at the Collège de France, Foucault's prevailing preoccupation is parrhesia. The term is Greek, and from the Greek – ancient and modern – it might most readily be translated as candor, freedom and frankness of speech, speaking fully what is on one's mind. From Euripides through Aristotle, parrhesia is the privilege of the Athenian citizen, the citizen of the assembly. Its logic ties speech to opinion, to the sincere expression of belief and commitment. Its scene is the scene of political oratory. Within it, the parrhesiast does not cater to what the people want to hear. He does not pander. Whether he speaks the truth as such is another matter. In the Aristotelian theorization of oratory, what truth he speaks is indeterminate at best. Foucault's preoccupation with parrhesia is not, however, limited to its ancient semantics, and if he attends to the relationship of the parrhesiast to the democratic assembly, he does so in order to inscribe in a more precise geometry the architectural foundations of the lectures as a whole. As I have suggested elsewhere (2011), those foundations might be seen to constitute a triangle, whose points come together at the intersections of three vectors. One of these is the vector of parrhesia conceived not merely as frank speaking, but the frank speaking of the truth, and in particular the truth of and about *ēthos* (*GSA2*, 25 [*CT*, 25]). Another is the vector of the ethics of the care of the self. The third is that of the governance of others. In its interior, the triangle thus formed encloses the philosopher, the philosophical life as a distinctive ethics, a distinctive mode of being and working in the world. Somewhat surprisingly, Plato – no democrat – comes to occupy its center stage (*GSA1*, 171–225 [*GSO*, 187–243]).

The triangle is tidy enough in the first installments of the lectures. As the lectures proceed, however, it opens and, in opening, becomes less a schema of elucidation than of problematization, a schema of queries to which Foucault turns and queries whose resolution he does not reach. In opening the triangle, Foucault begins to register his often oblique but nevertheless increasingly palpable skepticism both of the continuity of philosophy as an ethically integrated way of life and of its relevance to the governance of others. He also opens and explicitly raises the question of whether the triangle linking parrhesia, the care of the self, and the governance of others survives in any other way or ways of life. What seems in his judgment to preserve the way of the philosophical parrhesiast beyond antiquity is in fact not the Socratic or Platonic or Aristotelian but "the more typical form of ancient philosophy" (*GSA1*, 318 [*GSO*, 346]; here and throughout, translations from French are my own), Cynicism, whose inaugural figure is Diogenes, younger contemporary of Plato. The Cynic has three cardinal features. First, he sides with nature against conventional ornaments and propriety; he is a "free man" and is "in his life, the truth in its manifest state" (*GSA1*, 319 [*GSO*, 347]). Second, he speaks, and speaks with candor, not merely to his common fellows but above all to those in command, those who rule; he is the original speaker of the truth to power (*GSA1*, 319–20 [*GSO*, 347–8]). Third, he is utterly without fear, and in announcing the truth courageously and regardless of the risks he might thus run, he redeems himself, but also renders a service to "humanity as a whole" (*GSA1*, 319 [*GSO*, 348]).

The portrait is compelling, but it is also puzzling. We might suppose that what is natural is simply the case – "the truth" in this particular sense. The grounds of the Cynic's confidence that nature as he purports to know it is nature in its truth are, however, unclear. The anthropologist has to point out that every conception of the divide between human nature and mere artifice – Diogenes' conception included – remains under the typically subliminal influence of conventional presumptions, of *doxa*, of the taken for granted. The puzzle deepens, moreover, as Foucault begins to look beyond antiquity for the descendants of Diogenes – of Cynicism as the thematics of "life as the scandal of the truth," of a style or form of life as the "place of the emergence of the truth" (*GSA2*, 166 [*CT*, 180]). Philosophers have no prominent place within his horizons – though as latter-day parrhesiasts, receive an early nod (*GSA1*, 322 [*GSO*, 349–50]). More exemplary Cynics, however, emerge in three other domains – and they hold their surprises. As McFalls and Pandolfi have also pointed out in their contribution to this volume, one is the domain of the early Christian ascetic, of that ascetic who "lived out and made a work" of life as a "witnessing of the truth itself" (*GSA2*, 167 [*CT*, 181]). Nearer to us is the domain of the militant, of that militant who has rendered militancy itself "a witnessing" (*GSA2*, 170 [*CT*, 184]). The third domain is that of the artist, that distinctly "modern" artist who has "established a relationship with the real that is no longer of the order of ornamentation, of the order of imitation, but instead of the order of rendering naked, of unmasking, of scouring, of excavation, of violent reduction to the elementals of existence" (*GSA2*, 173 [*CT*, 188]). The ascetic, the militant, the modern artist: sometimes their truths converge, but the contrary is more often the case.

All the same, Foucault's intuitions merit developing – and they point not to any simple epistemological relativism but instead to the pluralization of ethics and so of *ēthos*, whose truths are not given but instead are made. They are thus "poetic" truths, not in the strictly aesthetic sense but – as McFalls and Pandolfi have also underscored – instead in the broader ancient sense of the term. In what follows, I turn to a modern artist whose Cynicism I find more instructive than the French cases in point – Charles Baudelaire, Edouard Manet, Gustave Flaubert – that Foucault himself offers. I turn to Constantine Cavafy, whose case may shed particular light on the puzzle of Cynical parrhesia precisely because it is incomplete. It illustrates a long struggle to give form to an ethics grounded in an *ēthos* of the realization – the recognition and the manifest exercise – of feeling, of passion-in-action. By his own reckoning, however, Cavafy can do no more than give that *ēthos* a discursive form (and even then not altogether frankly). He is incapable of translating it into the substantive character to whose truth he would himself be at once creator, witness and testament. He remains only a theorist – the theorist of a Cynicism whose fulfillment must await a future in which it could see and live in the light of the full day.

A Note on Method

My approach to Cavafy is bioethnographic – treating the man, but the man above all as a creature of his sociocultural and historical environment. Fortunately, Cavafy's home, the Alexandria of the late nineteenth and early twentieth centuries, is enough of an open social and cultural book to allow for detailed sociocultural cartographies (Haag 2004; Keeley 1996). Cavafy himself has been the subject of extensive biographical attention since shortly after his death from esophageal cancer in 1933. Alexandrian Timos Malanos is the first to publish his conversations with and recollections of the poet and his world (Malanos 1935, 1957, 1981). Many others – biographers and editors – ensue (Gialourakēs 1959, 1975; Daskalopoulos 1988; Papoutsakis 1963; Peridēs 1948; Pieridēs 1943; Saregiannēs 1964; Savidis 1983, 1985, 1987; Tsirkas 1958, 1971). Peter Bien's overview of Cavafy's life and work is the first in English to benefit from the opening of the poet's archive (Bien 1964). The best biography of Cavafy in English remains Robert Liddell's (Liddell 1976). Aesthetico-biographical engagements with Cavafy extend from E.M. Forster's introduction of the poet to Anglophone audiences, to Marguerite Yourcenar's introduction to and – with Konstandinos Dēmaras – translation of his poems into French (Cavafy 1978), to George Seferis' juxtaposing him with T.S. Eliot, to Gregory Jusdanis' analysis of the context and form of his poetics, to the editorial manifesto of a 1983 issue of *The Journal of the Hellenic Diaspora* that might serve to mark the advent of an ever growing number of treatments of him as breaking ground for a gay literature (Editors 1983; Forster 1923; Jusdanis 1987; Seferis 1966). Panagiotis Roilos' *C.P. Cavafy: The Economics of Metonymy* is a major recent contribution (Roilos 2009).

The prevailing thesis that much of Cavafy's oeuvre is autobiographical rests with many others on the presumption that, between the lyrical author and his oeuvre, a unilinear relation of cause and effect must hold, and a relation that in its "optimal" – or least hermeneutically vexing and most sincere – modality is equivalent to that between a particular sensibility or point of view and its written avenue of representation. Though worthy in general of some skepticism, the presumption is warranted enough in the case at hand; Cafavy seems himself to have understood the relation between author and oeuvre just so. One of the notes recovered from his archive reveals him worrying over truth, falsehood, and sincerity (or honesty: *eilikrineia* [Cavafy 1983, 21]). Another of them has him bemoaning his own lack of courage for hesitating to write more candidly about his erotic passion:

> It passed through my mind tonight to write about my love. And yet I will not do it. What power prejudice has. I have freed myself from it; but I think of those who are enslaved, under whose eyes this paper might fall. And I stop. What pusillanimity. But let me inscribe a letter – T – as a symbol . . . of this moment. (Cavafy 1983, 27; here and throughout, translations from Greek are my own)

Hence, the Cavafy of the capital "T" (Gialourakēs 1959), whose symbol Malanos thought to stand for the oppressive *teikhē* or "fortress walls" of the poem of the same name, published just a few months before the poet wrote the note in question (Gialourakēs 1959, 63). It is now widely thought to be the first initial of an unidentified man's name, but could just as readily (also) stand for the Orthodox cross in any of its darker connotations. Both notes were written in 1902 (see also Faubion 2004, 45–6). The poet was already 39 years old – and evidently not very happy with himself.

Becoming Poet

In fact, Cavafy had ample cause for unhappiness much earlier in his life. He was born into great luxury, the youngest child of a family ensconced in a mansion on Alexandria's opulent rue Cherif and among the crème de la crème of a cosmopolitan Greek diaspora. His father, however, died in 1860, when he was only seven, and had not bothered to accumulate an estate that would sustain his family in the style to which it had become accustomed. Even so, Cavafy's mother Kharikleia had funds enough to settle with Constantine and his elder brothers in Liverpool in 1872. Two years later, the four would move to London, where they would enjoy the company of their magnificently wealthy kindred during another year abroad (Liddell 1976, 26). They returned to Alexandria in 1877, but to an Alexandria in which Egyptian nationalist sentiments were brewing and the European diaspora the object of their increasing animus. The situation came to a head in 1882. The French and British installed a fleet off Alexandria's shore. On June 11, 1882, a riot erupted in the city. Its outcomes are uncertain; that it constituted "the massacre of the Christians" is almost certainly hyperbole. The British fleet did not act immediately (it would bombard and destroy much of the city and much of the Cavafy home precisely a month later), but the British state did order its citizens to evacuate. The Cavafy family, naturalized British citizens one and all, did so (Liddell 1976, 30–1), setting forth for Constantinople, where Kharikleia had been born and raised as the daughter of a gem merchant. Constantine's brothers would all return to their jobs in Alexandria by the end of October 1882. Kharikleia remained in greater Constantinople with her three younger children. Her father seems himself to have fallen significantly in his fortunes. He could not – or did not – provide for his daughter and grandsons beyond accommodation at his villa in the Bosphorus village known in Greek (and in one of the poet's works) as Neokhori. Nor were the poet's paternal Constantinopolitan relatives forthcoming. The brothers in Alexandria sent support, but (if their epistolary apologies are to be taken seriously) it was nothing more than a pittance. In the nocturnal backstreets of Constantinople, Cavafy had his first homosexual junkets – and would determine to become a poet at the same time.

Kharikleia brought her sons back to Alexandria in 1885. The elder Cavafys were gainfully employed, though only gainfully. It is unclear whether the latter supported their younger brother in order to allow him the leisure to further what the whole of his devoted and doting family already expected to be a literary career. In any event, one can find no parallels with Sartre's Flaubert here: nothing to inspire the myth of a family idiot (quite the contrary); nothing to encourage a disdain for the writerly life (quite the contrary); nothing to invite the son to legitimate himself only in following dutifully in the footsteps of his father (quite the contrary) (Sartre 1981). Constantine had occasional remuneration as a journalistic essayist from the outset. Later he worked for his brother Aristidēs at the Cotton Exchange. Liddell notes that as early as 1889 he had begun to work in the British Irrigation Office "in the hope of getting a salaried post" (Liddell 1976, 53). He adds that "such an arrangement was by no means uncommon in Egypt at that date" – but the young man's hope was somewhat misplaced even so, since Liddell further adds that such an appointment was "against regulations" (54). In fact, Cavafy never received such an appointment. Instead, he stepped as a temporary replacement into a position that the departure of a regular employee had left vacant. He took up residence in a second-story flat above the demimonde of Alexandria's rue Lepsius. He remained an irrigation clerk from 1892 until December of 1921, when he informed his superiors at the Office that he would not renew his contract.

Jeffreys' research establishes that Cavafy was deeply affected by his sojourn in London. His London cousins were the immediate descendants of an alliance both matrimonial and entrepreneurial that commenced with his uncle George Cavafy's marriage to Maria Thomas, the daughter of one of the partners in a firm that would be known by 1829 as Ionnides and Company, after the father of another partner, Constantine Ionnides. It was a big success. By the 1870s, the poet's collateral relatives and their business colleagues had made both entrepreneurial and matrimonial alliances with such other notable London families as the Cassavettis. Most of them rivaled the aristocracy in their resources. In what Jeffreys asserts to have been the interest of "flaunting their status," they made substantial aesthetic investments (Jeffreys 2006, 59). They had evidently also internalized a sufficient sense of distinction to make wise investments. "Remarkably," in Jeffreys' judgment, "the business savvy of these aesthetic patrons was matched by a discerning eye and an almost bohemian relish for high aestheticism" (2006, 59).

What Cavafy learns from his likely wide-eyed exposure to the aesthetes (and perhaps also to some of the social scandals they fostered) and to their aestheticist works is arguably twofold. The first is the principle that art is a value in itself: "art for art's sake." Read at the first order, the principle amounts to aesthetic absolutism, the rejection of the notion that art should in any circumstance be the instrument of any non-aesthetic end. Read at the second order, it identifies an objective structural possibility (whose objectivity nevertheless belies its very shallow socio-historical depth). A good Calvinist could have found his calling in clerking at the Irrigation Office. Cavafy could regard it only as what we would now call his day job. Though he carried out his duties with responsibility and diligence, he plainly regarded doing so as merely instrumental, the means of the support of the subject – the person and the poet – he essentially was. As a person, he remained throughout what Liddell terms a *mondain*, a "man of the world," fond of exclusive invitations, fond of mingling with high Alexandrian society, fond of the attention it gave him, attention (if positive) won as much because of the social capital he had inherited as because of the literary stature he acquired. He was a dandy, with a taste for well-cut suits. Roilos appropriately looks to aestheticist precedent in accounting for the penchant, noting further Cavafy's approval of the luxurious dandies that recur in his poetic corpus (Roilos 2009, 62–4). Clerking did not make for a luxurious dandyism, but it did allow the dandy his indulgences. It also compromised his more essential task. Recalling in his notebook the visit of an aspiring poet who complained of having to peddle his labor and struggle to find publishers:

> I didn't want to leave him in his error and I said a few words to him, something like the following. Unhappy and burdensome, his position – but how dearly my little luxuries cost me myself. In order to obtain

them I went off my natural course [*grammē*] and became a government
clerk – how laughable – and I waste and I lose so many precious hours
of the day (to which must be added as well the hours of fatigue and
torpor to which they give way). What damage, what damage, what
betrayal. While that impoverished [young man] doesn't lose any time
whatever; he is always there, a faithful and dutiful child of Art. (1983,
32)

Betrayal perhaps – but little self-deceit at this juncture.

Second, Cavafy learns and absorbs all the trademarks of
decadence – Greek revivalism, the favoring of the painterly and the
sculptural, the embrace of fantasy, sensualism and (homo)eroticism,
the preoccupation with desire and the melancholy of its remaining
unrequited, the disdain of bourgeois respectability, the cultivation
in the aesthetic garden of the Flowers of Evil, and again the dandyism that Roilos has underscored. Jeffreys can point to Cavafy's
earliest poems as his most solid and incontestable support, though
Cavafy ultimately rejected almost all of those poems as "wretched
trash" (1983, 64). Cavafy's official corpus is thus constituted of a
"rejected" as well as a "canonical," an "unfinished" and a "hidden"
or "unpublished" component. Jeffreys is, however, further correct
in identifying traces – sometimes glaring traces – of aestheticist
principles and preferences in many of Cavafy's later poems. Roilos
amply confirms the glare in his careful readings of both the early
and the later poems (Roilos 2009). Traces of aestheticism do not
an aestheticist make, to be sure. Nor does Jeffreys assert that they
do. This said, the conclusion is inescapable that such principles
and preferences exercise on Cavafy an enduring influence. Roilos
reads the aestheticist decadence of an "antieconomy of jouissance"
from the beginning to the end of Cavafy's oeuvre (Roilos 2009,
167–72).

The Poet (Im)proper

Between 1911 and 1924 unfolds the decade and a half of what
virtually all of Cavafy's readers regard as his maturation as a poet

(cf. Jusdanis 1987, xvi–xvii; see also Roilos 2009). If Cavafy remains a master of irony and something – more than something – of an aesthete throughout, he leaves behind the poetical principles of the Romanticism and the Symbolism that mark his first poetic efforts in favor of the increasingly inimitable "visionary" or "dramatic" realism appropriate to an investigation of the scope of human feeling always "in progress." If with less consensus, a majority of his readers note a parallel maturation of the thematic of homosexuality or the homosexual voice. Masked, occluded, imprisoned in the early poetry, homosexuality and the formulae of homoerotic desire begin to emerge in Cavafy's works as early as 1904, though as Edmund Keeley notes, in none of his published works until a decade thence (1996, 45; see also Alexiou 1983). Rendered in the passive or middle voice at first, more often than not as autoerotic fantasy, homosexuality becomes, as Alexander Nehamas has shown, an increasingly "active" motivation in the later poetry, the motivation of an active subject, and its scenes less nocturnal, less ephemeral and anonymous, more greatly enriched with a complexity of sentiment (Nehamas 1983). For many readers (Anton 1995; Malanos 1957; Tsirkas 1958, 1971), the homoerotic poetry is further testament to the poet's coming to terms, literally and figuratively, with his own sexual "instinct" or "proclivities," even if its testament is "implicit" (Malanos 1957, 60). Cavafy does not indeed write anything that could be construed as overtly confessional poetry. As Keeley further notes, the poet stops short of making public "poems in which a first-person speaker [is] an active participant in a context that establishe[s] the sex of the loved one unambiguously" (1996, 45 – a considerably easier feat in Greek than in English, though not easy even so). But then, the majority reader might add, as goes the man so go his poems. Biographers agree that in multiple arenas of his life, Cavafy was a virtuoso of both impression management and the fine arts of discretion.

Parrhesiast manqué. Decadent aestheticist in the closet. Of more immediate pertinence here, however, is the aestheticism that he develops while dwelling in his closet, which is an aestheticism of his own colors and an aestheticism that stands at neither an aestheticist nor a decadent extreme. Cavafy's aestheticist elders made his aesthetico-ethics an objective but still merely potential structural possibility. His family had cast him early on as an artist in the making. One would only be coy in refusing to entertain whether the neo-classicism, the sensualism and the homoeroticism that were the hallmarks of aestheticist style and aestheticist daring further impelled, even seduced him toward making himself into one. They could have done nothing else – however conscious of their allure he might or might not have been. Yet, he develops an aestheticist subject position whose devotion is not merely to art and to art alone. Its extra-aesthetic dimension is not merely instrumentalistic. Instead, of decadent hedonism and of art for the adult Cavafy, so of virtue for Aristotle: it is a means to a good of which it is only one constituent but it is also good in itself. Just here the poet reaches beyond the aesthetic in the strict sense of the term toward a broader ethical poiesis.

If Cavafy's readers have been tempted to read him as an ethicist at all, they have been tempted to read him as a hedonist (Jusdanis 1987, 24; Keeley 1996, 80). In yet another contemplative notation written in 1902, the Cavafy who is still seeking his pleasures in the dark backstreets of Constantinople invites a diagnosis of hedonistic arrogance: "I don't know if perversion brings power. Sometimes I think so. But it's certain that it is the wellspring of greatness" (1983, 29). At least it invites such a diagnosis if every perversion is presumptively pleasurable. Even with the presumption granted, however, hedonism functions here as a means to greatness, not as an end in itself. Several other poems, moreover, connect the same principle with degeneracy and dissolution. "He Vows" of 1915, written (until the final line) with the caesurae that are one of Cavafy's most idiosyncratic formalistic lineaments, does so with great economy:

> Every so often he vows   to lead a better life.
> But when night comes again   bearing its own counsel,
> and its own allowances,   and its assurances,
> when night comes again   with its own energies
> he falls back, beaten down, back to the deadly joys. (2007, 139)

To be sure, Cavafy shows persistent sympathy in his poems early and late for the dissolute – but those who are redeemed serve not

Hēdonē but instead another god. The youth of "Days of 1896," published (daringly) in 1927, is one of several cases in point:

> On occasion, as necessary,
> he covered his expenses   acting as an intermediary,
> engaging in transactions   that others regarded as shameful.
> He developed into such a character   that to be seen
> in his company   was to risk one's reputation.
>
> But that's not the whole of it;   that's really not very fair.
> The memory of his beauty   deserves much better.
> There is another quality   by which he may be
> seen to be far more sympathetic,   a modest
> and sincere child of Eros,   who without
> a second thought   placed, even above
> his notions of honor   and his own reputation,
> the pure sensual delight   of his pure flesh.
>
> Above his own reputation?   But society,
> exceedingly prudish,   always got it wrong. (2007, 343)

The corpus includes other encomia, to yet other gods, and in a more direct voice: to the soldiers of the Akhaian League who fought to the death against the Spartans; to Queen Kratesikleia, who willingly embraced bondage in Egypt in order to protect her Sparta from siege; to the Byzantine queen Anna Dalassēnē, who "never spoke those cold words 'mine' and 'yours'" (2007, 344); the loyal Else of the unpublished "Lohengrin"; and Simeon Stylites, of whom a Cavafian visitor to Beirut writes a friend, "Before we were born – I am twenty-nine years old,/ you I think are younger than I – / before we were born, imagine it/ [he] climbed up a pillar and ever since remains there before God" (1989, 278). All these figurae manifest Cavafy's cardinal virtue: courage. They act in the face of conventional disapprobation; they march fearless and without self-pity into futility. They display precisely the virtue that Cavafy declares himself to lack. Another notation from his journal of 1902: "I recognize that I am a coward and that I cannot act."

The notation nevertheless continues, and what it affirms is the poet's priority over the man (the Greek *andreia*, "courage," also glossed as "manliness," is usually if not exclusively ascribed to men alone) he could not be: "I only speak. I don't think my words are superfluous. Someone else will act them out. But my many words – of me the coward – will facilitate activity. They will clear the ground" (1983, 26). Not the coward but the poet; not the laughable Irrigation Office clerk but the poet – but here the ethical call takes what, after Forster, one can identify as a characteristically Cavafean "slant," a characteristically Cavafean turn toward the ironic, the seriously if not terribly ironic (Forster 1923). In 1902, Cavafy is still writing the sort of affected, derivative aestheticist poetry that he will later condemn. The condemnation is, however, already implicit in this self-assessment. His youthful "perversions," of far fewer strictures to his mind than those in which he deemed Baudelaire to have been enclosed (Cavafy 1983, 42), would be the experiential catalysts of his poetic imagination. They would not, however, be in and of themselves its telos. Unlike his aestheticist predecessors, Cavafy will not rest with the valorization of the beauty of perversion any more than he will rest peacefully solely with the valorization of art for art's sake. In 1902 precisely, he comes to understand his poetry as an ethical instrument, a means of breaking a lance, of preparing the way for practices, for commitments that convention, in its inadequacy, in its unreflective straightforwardness, does not countenance, does not yet permit to exist. He will always be concerned with poetic form. If not yet in his poetry then at least as the subject-as-subject that he would become, he nevertheless turns away in 1902 from the pure aesthetic (see Bourdieu 1984, 1993) to a poetry of purpose. He renders programmatic – and even more programmatic in the *Ars Poetica* shortly to follow – a functional poetry, a poetry of reference, even if its reference is proleptic, to lives yet to come. In its exemplifications, which will proliferate as the corpus unfolds, it remains referentially proleptic even when its settings are of the Hellenistic past. Thus precisely Cavafy's corpus cannot be placed at the formalist and most purely aesthetic extremes of modern cultural production. It carries too much functional import to warrant doing so (Faubion 2010).

All he can offer are words – but they will open the way, provide the templates and the guidelines for the transformation of motive into act, the subjective swirl of feeling and experience into a coded, organized, hence communicable and communicative mode of being in the world, a way of life, "a form of life" in very much the sense that Wittgenstein would distill into its logically and linguistically simplest tokens in the *Philosophical Investigations* (Wittgenstein 1958). Cavafy indeed characterizes one of the procedures he follows in revising his own work as "philosophical" (1995, 341). All the same, he is not a philosopher of language. Words are the medium of his form-giving enterprise, but it is an enterprise that might thus be pursued in many other media besides the linguistic. Cavafy had read his Keats and remains loyal enough throughout his poetic career to the Romantic testament of the "Ode on a Grecian Urn," which later aestheticism only made more emphatic. Not merely is life short and *tekhnē* enduring – a phrase, it is worth noting, that comes down to us from the Hippocratic aphorisms, not from any aesthetician. It is also that, for the Keats of the "Ode," for the aesthetes and for the Cavafy of such poems as "Before Time Changes Them" and many others besides, human life is animation in all its brevity and art and art alone its only eternal preservative. The more that Cavafy turns away from the letter of established aestheticism, however, his aesthetic preservationalism functions in two distinct temporal registers: one "out of time," (as in his "On the Ship"); the other, which is also spatial, a projective chronotopy, the landscape of a more liberal future. This is the futurist Cavafy that Roilos has found Filippo Tommaso Marinetti to have admired (2009, 10).

Philosophical Cavafy: in the *Ars Poetica*, written some time in 1903 (and written in English), he contrasts the writing of poetry to the paralyzed inaction that might follow from the "seemingly highest . . . philosophy of the absolute worthlessness of effort and of the inherent contradictions in every human utterance" (1995, 340). Even so, the poet, who produces not works of "immediate utility" but instead of "beauty" (341), belongs ultimately with the philosopher. The two stand together on the same side of the divide between the theoretical and the practical life. They think; they rely on "guesswork" (340); they put their thoughts into words. In the

Ars Poetica as elsewhere, Cafavy underscores that others are or will be left to translate his words into concrete actions. Yet the poet, on the side of the philosopher, is not in the end a philosopher, and for two reasons. First, the poet always remains an artist. He is thus not obligated to give all sides of an issue, to proffer only unqualified, eternal truths. In his treatment of feeling especially, he can offer only "one side," which "does not mean that he denies the obverse" (340). The truths of the poet in his articulation of the feelings are transient truths, "sometimes very transient, sometimes of some duration" (340). Their validity rests entirely in their applicability, their possible reference. Pointing to three of his earliest published (though later rejected) poems, Cavafy asserts:

> If even for one day, or one hour I felt like the man within "Walls," or like the man of "Windows" the poem is based on a truth, a short-lived truth, but which, for the very reason of its having once existed, may repeat itself in another life, perhaps with as short duration, perhaps with longer. If "Thermopylae" fits but one life, it is true; and it may, indeed the probabilities are that it must. (343)

History repeats itself. History is in any event most likely to repeat itself – if only in bits and pieces. The poem – if a good one – is the effective sign of its iterability and reiteration.

The poem might also be the sign of a feeling or an action yet to come, a potential but – if good – an effective sign of the iterability of an iteration. Take the example of the titular player in the early but unpublished "Pawn":

> . . . he is saved from all perils
> and he manages to reach the last line in time.
>
> How triumphantly he gets there in time
> to the formidable last line;
> how readily he approaches his own death!
>
> For here the Pawn will perish
> and all his pains were only for this.
> He came to fall in the Hades of chess

>   to resurrect from the grave
>   the queen who will save us. (1989, 237)

Commenting in the *Ars Poetica* on some version of the poem, Cavafy observes that "it deals mainly with the domain of *theory translated into action*" (1995, 343). The Pawn is a "pioneer," a "hero," but no poet, no philosopher. "A great artist or a great philosopher is not brought to quite the same sacrifice." "Great" here can only mean "ground-breaking," for Cavafy continues:

> it may be said, however, that he also undergoes sacrifice in another way by his never being appreciated as is his need during his lifetime, by even after his death a great part of his struggles and his toil being underrated or ignored, and by his making discoveries and laying foundations which, necessarily imperfect in his case, do not and cannot bring him honour or profit, but being perfected and brought to fruition by others bring those others – whose *prospatheia* [effort] has been but small – honour and profit. (1995, 343–4)

It's a tough job, but the great artist or philosopher is nevertheless called to do it. It is also a job of the grandest proportions. The pawn is "fit" for his task. "The theorist is fit for other work" (344–5) and his work in the end is of superior honor:

> The millions that will be saved by the retreat of the "queen" owe their happiness to [him]. To the hero thanks are due too; he by his sacrifice realizes or rather hastens the good planned. But even without him the good planned would have been realised. (345)

Visionary of the good of millions, the poet-schematist will have his day and his glory and in that day be the chief "benefactor" of his own visions (345). The parrhesiast in principle, even if sotte voce, lays the groundwork for the Cynic in fact. Cavafy the man was modest – sometimes. Cavafy the poet-theorist, even if a parrhesiast manqué, is not. But then, as George Steiner wrote somewhere of Alexander Solzhenitsyn, "the great know no modesty."

Envoi

In "On the genealogy of ethics: overview of a work in progress," Foucault famously (for some, infamously) asks why everyone's life might not become a work of art (*EW1*, 261). The echoes (surely misleading) are high aestheticist – Baudelairean and Wildean. In any event, late in his final lectures, the rhetorician gives way to the historical observer. In his review of Plato's Socratic dialogues, he says, he sought to recover "the moment of the establishment of a certain rapport between the care of a beautiful, a striking, a memorable existence – undoubtedly archaic, ancient, traditional within Greek culture – and the preoccupation with truth-speaking" (*GSA2*, 150). He continues:

> What I wanted to recover is how truth-speaking, in the ethical modality that appears with Socrates . . . has interfered with the principle of existence as something to be fashioned in all its possible perfection . . . how this principle has not only been replaced, but taken up again, inflected, modified and reelaborated by that of truth-speaking as something that one must confront courageously, how the objective of the beauty of existence and the task of taking account of oneself within the play of truth have been combined. (*GSA2*, 150 [*CT*, 162])

He thus invites us to place Cavafy's corpus in a long stream of the resolution of the dynamics of aesthetic and ethical autopoiesis, from the Homeric corpus, through Plutarch's *Lives* and the Benedictine and Franciscan creeds, to the Nietzschean, the Emersonian and indeed the aestheticist as such. Cavafy's corpus belongs to the Cynical current of that stream, but its turn is novel. Even if its resolution was never achieved and remained instead always "in progress," it pointed and still points toward the truth of a self made frank in being manifest – and in being manifest made frankly the truth, and a truth at least in part of the subject's own making – in its synthesis of the given and the fashioned, of nature and culture, however the divide between the two might be conceived. Cavafy's is a Cynicism that neither disowns nature nor takes it for granted. It is neither aestheticist, nor Diogenean, nor any repetition of the high Romantic synthesis of the two. Here's one use of Foucault, then: he invites us to render Cavafy a Cynical modern, a modern Cynic. It has mileage.

References

Adorno, T. (1973) *The Jargon of Authenticity*. K. Tarnowski and F. Will (trans.). Northwestern University Press, Evanston.

Agamben, G. (1998) *Homo Sacer: Sovereign Power and Bare Life*. D. Heller-Roazen (trans.). Stanford University Press, Stanford.

Agamben, G. (2004) *The Open: Man and Animal*. K. Attell (trans.). Stanford University Press, Stanford.

Agamben, G. (2009) *What Is an Apparatus? and Other Essays*. D. Kishik and S. Pedatella (trans.). Stanford University Press, Stanford.

Agamben, G. (2011) *Altissima povertà. Regole monastiche e forme di vita*. Neri Pozza, Vicenza.

Ajavon, F-X. et al. (2004) *Abécédaire de Michel Foucault*. Vrin, Paris.

Alexiou, M. (1983) Eroticism and poetry. *Journal of the Hellenic Diaspora* **10**, 45–65.

Althusser, L. (1969) *For Marx*. B. Brewster (trans.). Penguin, Harmondsworth.

Althusser, L. (1971) *Lenin and Philosophy and Other Essays*. B. Brewster (trans.). Monthly Review Press, New York.

Andrews, D. (2008) Kinesiology's inconvenient truth and the physical cultural studies imperative. *Quest* **60**, 46–63.

Anton, J. (1995) *The Poetry and Poetics of Constantine P. Cavafy*. Harwood, Chur, Switzerland.

Arminen, I. (2010) Who's afraid of financial markets? *International Sociology* **25**(2), 170–83.

Badiou, A. (2005) *Metapolitics*. J. Barker (trans.). Verso, London.

Barker, J. (ed.) (2007) *The Anthropology of Morality in Melanesia and Beyond*. Ashgate, Aldershot.

Barthes, R. (1973) *Mythologies*. A. Laver (trans.). Paladin, London.

Barthes, R. (1977) *Roland Barthes by Roland Barthes*. R. Howard (trans.). Macmillan, New York.

Barthes, R. (1978) *A Lover's Discourse: Fragments*. R. Howard (trans.). Hill and Wang, New York.

Barthes, R. (2002a) *Le Neutre*. Seuil, Paris.

Barthes, R. (2002b) *Oeuvres complètes*. Seuil, Paris.

Bauman, Z. (1988) *Freedom*. Open University Press, Milton Keynes.

Bauman, Z. (1993) *Postmodern Ethics*. Blackwell, Oxford.

Bellon, G. (2007) "Je crois au temps": entretien avec Daniel Defert. Revue *Recto/Verso* **1** (http://www.revuerectoverso.com/spip.php?article29) (last accessed March 26, 2012).

Bellori, G.P. (1672) *Le vite de' pittori, scultori e architetti moderni*, Rome, N. P.

Berrett, D. (2011) The "inside job" effect. *Inside Higher Ed* (http://www.insidehighered.com/news/2011/04/19/economists_start_probing_their_own_ethics) (last accessed December 15, 2012).

Bersani, L. (1995) *Homos*. Harvard University Press, Cambridge, MA.

Bersani, L. (2000) Sociality and sexuality. *Critical Inquiry* **26**(4), 641–56.

Bersani, L. (2004) Fr-oucault and the end of sex. Lecture delivered at a conference entitled "Foucault in Berkeley: Twenty Years Later," University of California, October 16.

Bersani, L. and Dutoit, U. (1998) *Caravaggio's Secrets*. MIT Press, Cambridge, MA.

Berthold-Bond, D. (1995) *Hegel's Theory of Madness*. SUNY Press, Albany.

Bien, P. (1964) *Constantine Cavafy*. Columbia, New York.

Binkley, S. and Capetillo, J. (2011) *A Foucault for the 21st Century: Governmentality, Biopolitics and Discipline in the New Millennium*. Cambridge Scholars, Newcastle upon Tyne.

Blencowe, C. (2012) *Biopolitical Experience: Foucault, Power and Positive Critique*. Palgrave Macmillan, New York.

Bloom, H. (1973) *The Anxiety of Influence: A Theory of Poetry.* Oxford University Press, New York.

Borges, J.L. (1962) *Ficciones.* Grove Press, New York.

Borrillo, D. (2010) La parenté et la parentalité dans le droit: conflits entre le modèle civiliste et l'idéologie naturaliste de la filiation. In: Dorlin, E. and Fassin, E. (eds.) *Reproduire le genre.* BPI/Beaubourg Publishers, Paris, 127–36.

Boulez, P. (1989) *Le pays fertile: Paul Klee.* P. Thévenin (ed.). Gallimard, Paris.

Bourdieu, P. (1977). *Outline of a Theory of Practice.* R. Nice (trans.). Cambridge University Press, Cambridge.

Bourdieu, P. (1984) *Distinction: A Social Critique of the Judgement of Taste.* R. Nice (trans.). Harvard, Cambridge, MA.

Bourdieu, P. (1991) *The Political Ontology of Martin Heidegger.* P. Collier (trans.). Stanford University Press, Stanford.

Bourdieu, P. (1993) *The Field of Cultural Production.* R. Johnson (ed. and trans.). Columbia University Press, New York.

Bourdieu, P. (2001) *Masculine Domination.* R. Nice (trans.). Stanford University Press, Stanford.

Bourdin, J.-C. (2008) *Michel Foucault: savoirs, domination et sujet.* Presses Universitaires de Rennes, Rennes.

Bourg, J. (2007) *From Revolution to Ethics: May 1968 and Contemporary French Thought.* McGill-Queen's University Press, Montreal.

Bröckling, U., Krassmann, S., and Lemke, T. (eds.) (2011) *Governmentality: Current Issues and Future Challenges.* Routledge, New York.

Bruno, I. and Newfield, C. (2010) Can the cognitariat speak? *e-flux journal* **14**(3) (http://www.e-flux.com/journal/view/118) (last accessed December 15, 2012).

Brunon-Ernst, A. (2012) *Beyond Foucault: New Perspectives on Bentham's Panopticon.* Ashgate, London.

Bührmann, A.D. and Ernst, S. (eds.) (2010) *Care or Control of the Self? Norbert Elias, Michel Foucault, and The Subject in the 21st Century.* Cambridge Scholars, Newcastle upon Tyne.

Burchell, G., Gordon, C. and Miller, P. (eds.) (1991) *The Foucault Effect: Studies in Governmentality.* University of Chicago Press, Chicago.

Butler, J. (1993) *Bodies that Matter: On the Discursive Limits of "Sex."* Routledge, New York.

Butler, J. (1997) *The Psychic Life of Power: Theories in Subjection.* Stanford University Press, Stanford.

Butler, J. (2000) *Antigone's Claim: Kinship Between Life and Death.* Columbia University Press, New York.

Butler, J. (2004) *Undoing Gender.* Routledge, New York.

Campbell, T.C. (2011) *Improper Life: Technology and Biopolitics from Heidegger to Agamben.* University of Minnesota, Minneapolis.

Canguilhem, G. (1994) The death of man, or exhaustion of the cogito? In: Gutting, G. (ed.) *The Cambridge Companion to Foucault.* Cambridge University Press, Cambridge, 71–91.

Carter, K. (2008) *Race: A Theological Account.* Oxford University Press, Oxford.

Cavafy, C.P. (1978) *Présentation critique de Constantin Cavafy, 1863–1933, suivi d'une traduction des poèmes par Marguerite Yourcenar et Constantin Dimaras.* Gallimard, Paris.

Cavafy, C.P. (1983) *Unpublished Poetic and Ethical Notes (1902–1911).* G.P. Savidēs (ed.). Ermēs, Athens (in Greek).

Cavafy, C.P. (1989) *The Greek Poems of C.P. Cavafy.* M. Koliatis (trans.). Aristide Caratzas, New Rochelle, NY.

Cavafy, C.P. (1995) *Ars Poetica.* In: Anton, J., *The Poetry and Poetics of Constantine P. Cavafy.* Harwood, Chur, Switzerland, 339–45.

Cavafy, C.P. (2007) *C.P. Cavafy: The Canon.* S. Haviaras (trans.). Harvard University Press, Cambridge, MA.

CBS (2011) *Undercover Boss.* http://www.cbs.com/primetime/undercover_boss/video (last accessed December 17, 2012).

Cette France-là (2009a) La technologie du soupçon: tests osseux, tests de pilosité, tests ADN. *Cette France-là*, 06.05.2007 | 30.06.2008, vol. 1, 157–9.

Cette France-là (2009b) Le sexe de l'immigration. *Cette France-là*, 06.05.2007 | 30.06.2008, vol. 1, 108–11.

Chauncey, G. (1995) *Gay New York: Gender, Urban Culture, and the Making of the Gay Male World, 1890–1940.* Basic Books, New York.

Chun, W. (2006) *Control and Freedom: Power and Paranoia in the Age of Fiber Optics.* MIT Press, Cambridge, MA.

Chun, W. (2011) *Programmed Visions: Software and Memory.* MIT Press, Cambridge, MA.

Cicchini, M. and Porret, M. (eds.) (2007) *Les sphères du pénal avec Michel Foucault: histoires et sociologie du droit de punir.* Antipodes, Lausanne.

Connolly, W. (2005) *Pluralism*. Duke University Press, Durham.

Cooper, D. (1967) Introduction. In: Foucault, M., *Madness and Civilization: A .History of Madness in the Age of Reason*. Tavistock, London, vii–ix.

Courtine, J.-J. (2012) *Déchiffrer le corps: penser avec Michel Foucault*. Editions Jérôme Millon, Grenoble.

Daskalopoulos, D. (1988) *Cavafy: Notes in the Margin*. Diatōn, Athens (in Greek).

Davidson, A. (2001) *The Emergence of Sexuality: Historical Epistemology and the Formation of Concepts*. Harvard University Press, Cambridge, MA.

Davis, K. (2005) *The Holocaust and the Henmaid's Tale*. Lantern Books, New York.

Dean, M. (2010) *Governmentality: Power and Rule in Modern Society*. Sage, London.

Defert, D. (2001) Chronologie. In: Foucault, M., *Dits et Écrits*, Gallimard, Paris, 13–90.

DeLanda, M. (2002) *Intensive Science and Virtual Philosophy*. Continuum Books, London.

DeLanda, M. (2006) *A New Philosophy of Society: Assemblage Theory and Social Complexity*. Continuum Books, New York.

Deleuze, G. (1988) *Foucault*. S. Hand (trans.). University of Minnesota Press, Minneapolis.

Deleuze, G. and Guattari, F. (1983) *Anti-Oedipus: Capitalism and Schizophrenia*. B. Massumi (trans.). University of Minnesota Press, Minneapolis.

Deresiewicz, W. (2011) Faulty towers: the crisis in higher education. *The Nation* (http://www.thenation.com/article/160410/faulty-towers-crisis-higher-education) (last accessed December 15, 2012).

Derrida, J. (1978) Cogito and the history of madness. In: *Writing and Difference*, A. Bass (trans.). University of Chicago Press, Chicago, 36–76.

Derrida, J. (1994) "To do justice to Freud": the history of madness in the age of psychoanalysis. *Critical Inquiry* **20**, 227–66.

Descartes, R. (1985) *The Philosophical Writings of Descartes*, vol. 1. J. Cottingham, R. Stoothoff, and D. Murdoch (trans.). Cambridge University Press, Cambridge.

Descartes, R. (1998) *Meditations and Other Metaphysical Writings*. D.M. Clarke (ed.). Palgrave Macmillan, New York.

Dillon, G. and Reid, J. (2009) *The Liberal Way of War: Killing to Make Life Live*. Routledge, Oxford.

Dreyfus, H.L. and Rabinow, P. (1982) *Beyond Structuralism and Hermeneutics: Michel Foucault*. University of Chicago Press, Chicago.

Dreyfus, H.L. and Rabinow, P. (1986) What is maturity? Habermas and Foucault. In: Hoy, D. (ed.) *Foucault. A Critical Reader*. Blackwell, Oxford, 109–22.

Dumézil, G. (1984) *Le moyne noir en gris dedans Varennes*. Gallimard, Paris.

Dupont, N.A. (2010) *L'impatience de la liberté: éthique et politique chez Michel Foucault*. Editions Kimé, Paris.

Duval, R. (1990) *Temps et vigilance*. Vrin, Paris.

Dworkin, R. (2000) *Sovereign Virtue: The Theory and Practice of Equality*. Harvard University Press, Cambridge, MA.

The Economist (2011) What good are economics journals? (http://www.economist.com/blogs/freeexchange/2011/03/economics_3)(last accessed December 15, 2012).

Editors (1983) Statement. *Journal of the Hellenic Diaspora* **10**, 5–6.

Elmer, J. (2007) Torture and hyperbole. *Law, Culture, and the Humanities* **3**(1), 18–34.

Emmison, M. (1983) "The economy": its emergence in media discourse. In: Davis, H. and Walton, P. (eds.) *Language, Image, Media*. Basil Blackwell, Oxford, 139–55.

Emmison, M. and McHoul, A. (1987) Drawing on the economy: cartoon discourse and the production of a category. *Cultural Studies* **1**(1), 93–111.

Emmys (2012) *Undercover Boss* (http://www.emmys.com/shows/undercover-boss) (last accessed December 17, 2012).

Eribon, D. (1992) *Michel Foucault*. B. Wing (trans.). Harvard University Press, Cambridge, MA.

Eribon, D. (2001) *Une morale du minoritaire*. Seuil, Paris.

Eribon, D. (2004) *Insult and the Making of the Gay Self*. M. Lucey (trans.). Duke University Press, Durham.

Esposito, R. (2008) *Bios: Biopolitics and Philosophy*. T. Campbell (trans.). University of Minnesota Press, Minneapolis.

Esposito, R. (2011) *Immunitas: The Protection and Negation of Life*. Z. Hanafi (trans.). Polity, Cambridge.

Evens, T.M.S. (2008) *Anthropology as Ethics: Nondualism and the Conduct of Sacrifice*. Berghahn, Oxford.

Farquhar, J. (2002) *Appetites: Food and Sex in Post-Socialist China*. Duke University Press, Durham.

Fassin, D. and Pandolfi, M. (eds.) (2010) *Contemporary States of Emergency: The Politics of Military and Humanitarian Interventions*. Zone Books, New York.

Fassin, E. (2001) Same sex, different politics. "Gay marriage" debates in France and the United States. *Public Culture* **13**(2), 215–32.

Fassin, E. (2004) Lieux d'invention. L'amitié, le mariage et la famille. *Vacarme* **29**, 120–3.

Fassin, E. (2005a) Démocratie sexuelle. *Comprendre, revue de philosophie et de sciences sociales* **6**, 263–76.

Fassin, E. (2005b) *Genre et sexualité: politique de la critique historique*. In: Granjon, C. (ed.) *Penser avec Michel Foucault: Théorie pratique et critique politique*. Karthala, Paris, 225–50.

Fassin, E. (2006) La démocratie sexuelle et le conflit des civilisations. *Multitudes* **26**, 123–31.

Fassin, E. (2009) Entre famille et nation: la filiation naturalisée. *Droit & société* **72**, 373–82.

Fassin, E. (2010a) Homosexuels des villes, homophobes des banlieues? *Métropolitiques* December 1 (http://www.metropolitiques.eu/ Homosexuels-des-villes-homophobes.html) (last accessed August 6, 2013).

Fassin, E. (2010b) National identities and transnational intimacies. Sexual democracy and the politics of immigration in Europe. *Public Culture* **22**(3), 507–29.

Fassin, E. (2011a) A double-edged sword: sexual democracy, gender norms, and racialized rhetoric. In: Butler, J. and Weed, E. (eds.) *The Question of Gender: Joan W. Scott's Critical Feminism*. Indiana University Press, Bloomington, 143–58.

Fassin, E. (2011b) From criticism to critique. *History of the Present. A Journal of Critical History* **1**(2), 265–74.

Fassin, E. (2012) Sous la bioéthique, la bio-politique In: Borillo, D., Fassin, E., and Hennette-Vauchez, S. (eds.), *Raison publique*, May 15 (http://www.raison-publique.fr/article523.html) (last accessed August 4, 2012).

Faubion, J.D. (2004) Cavafy: Toward the principles of a transcultural sociology of minor literature. *Modern Greek Studies: Australia and New Zealand* **11–12**, 40–65.

Faubion, J.D. (2010) In passing: Cavafy and the theoretico-poetics of liminality. In: Roilos, P. (ed.) *Imagination and Logos: Essays on C.P. Cavafy*, Harvard University Press, Cambridge, MA, 1–29.

Faubion, J.D. (2011) *An Anthropology of Ethics*. Cambridge University Press, Cambridge.

Faubion, J.D. (2012) Foucault and the genealogy of ethics. In: Fassin, D. (ed.) *A Companion to Moral Anthropology*. John Wiley & Sons, London, 67–84.

Faye, E. (2009) *Heidegger: The Introduction of Nazism into Philosophy in Light of the Unpublished Seminars of 1933–1935*. K. Harries (trans.). Yale University Press, New Haven.

Ferguson, J. (1994) *The Anti-Politics Machine: Development, Depoliticization and Bureaucratic Power in Lesotho*. University of Minnesota, Minneapolis.

Folbre, N. (2010) Ethics for economists. *New York Times* (http://economix.blogs.nytimes.com/2010/11/08/ethics-for-economists) (last accessed December 15, 2012).

Forster, E.M. (1923) The poet Constantine Cavafy. In: *Pharos and Pharillon*. Alfred Knopf, New York, 110–17.

Foucault, M. (1961) *Folie et déraison. Histoire de la folie á l'âge classique*. Plon, Paris.

Foucault, M. (1963) *Naissance de la clinique: Une archéologie du regard médical*. Presses Universitaires de France, Paris.

Foucault, M. (1964) *Folie et déraison. Histoire de la folie á l'âge classique*. Plon, Paris.

Foucault, M. (1965) *Madness and Civilization: A History of Insanity in the Age of Reason*. R. Howard (trans.). Pantheon, New York. British edition published by Tavistock in 1967.

Foucault, M. (1971) *The Order of Things: An Archaeology of the Human Sciences*. A translation of *Les mots et les choses*. Pantheon, New York.

Foucault, M. (1972a) *Histoire de la folie à l'âge classique*. Gallimard, Paris.

Foucault, M. (1972b) *The Archaeology of Knowledge*. A.M. Sheridan Smith (trans.). Tavistock, London.

Foucault, M. (1973) *The Birth of the Clinic: An Archaeology of Medical Perception*. A. M. Sheridan Smith (trans.). Tavistock, London.

Foucault, M. (1976a) *La volonté de savoir. Histoire de la sexualité*, vol. 1. Gallimard, Paris.

Foucault, M. (ed.) (1976b) *Généalogie des équipements de normalisation: Les équipements sanitaires*. CERFI, Fontenay-sur-Bois.

Foucault, M. (1977) *Discipline and Punish: The Birth of the Prison.* A. Sheridan (trans.). Pantheon, New York.

Foucault, M. (1978) *The History of Sexuality. Vol. 1: An Introduction.* R. Hurley (trans.). Pantheon, New York.

Foucault, M. (1980a) *Herculine Barbin: Being the Recently Discovered Memoirs of a Nineteenth Century Hermaphrodite.* R. McDougall (trans.). Vintage Press, New York.

Foucault, M. (1980b) *Power/Knowledge: Selected Interviews & Other Writings, 1972–1977.* C. Gordon (ed.). Pantheon, New York.

Foucault, M. (1982) The subject and power. L. Sawyer (trans.). *Critical Inquiry* **8**(4), 779–95.

Foucault, M. (1983) How we behave. *Vanity Fair* **46**(9), 66–7.

Foucault, M. (1984) Le retour de la morale, entretien avec G. Barbedette et A. Scala. *Les Nouvelles* **28 June–5 July**, 36–41.

Foucault, M. (1985) *The History of Sexuality. Vol. 2: The Use of Pleasure.* R. Hurley (trans.). Pantheon, New York.

Foucault, M. (1986) *The History of Sexuality, Vol. 3: The Care of the Self.* R. Hurley (trans.). Random House, New York.

Foucault, M. (1988a) *Politics, Philosophy, Culture. Interviews and Other Writings 1977–1984.* L.D. Kritzman (ed.). Routledge, New York.

Foucault, M. (1988b) *Technologies of the Self: A seminar with Michel Foucault.* L.H. Martin, H. Hutton, and H. Gutman (eds.). Tavistock, London.

Foucault, M. (1989) *Foucault Live: Collected Interviews 1961–1984.* S. Lotringer (ed.). Semiotext(e), New York.

Foucault, M. (1991a) *The Foucault Effect: Studies in Governmentality.* G. Burchell, C. Gordon, and P. Miller (eds.). Harvester Wheatsheaf, Harlow, Essex.

Foucault, M. (1991b) *Remarks on Marx: Conversations with Duccio Trombadori.* R.J. Goldstein and J. Cascaito (trans.). Semiotext(e), New York.

Foucault, M. (1994a) Critical theory/intellectual inquiry. In: Kelly, M. (ed.) *Critique and Power: Recasting the Foucault/Habermas Debate.* MIT Press, Cambridge, MA, 109–38.

Foucault, M. (1994b) *Dits et écrits* (4 vols). D. Defert and F. Ewald (eds.). Gallimard, Paris.

Foucault, M. (1994c) Problematics: excerpts from conversations. In: Reynolds, R. and Zummer, T. (eds.) *Crash: Nostalgia for the Absence of Cyberspace.* Third Waxing Space, New York, 121–7.

Foucault, M. (1997a) *"Il faut défendre la société."* Seuil/Gallimard, Paris.

Foucault, M. (1997b) *Essential Works of Michel Foucault. Vol. 1: Ethics: Subjectivity and Truth.* P. Rabinow (ed.). The New Press, New York.

Foucault, M. (1998) *Essential Works of Michel Foucault. Vol 2: Aesthetics, Method, Epistemology.* J.D. Faubion (ed.). The New Press, New York.

Foucault, M. (2000) *Essential Works of Michel Foucault. Vol. 3: Power.* J.D. Faubion (ed.). The New Press, New York.

Foucault, M. (2001) *Dits et écrits* (2 vols). D. Defert and F. Ewald (eds.). Gallimard, Paris.

Foucault, M. (2003a) *Abnormal: Lectures at the Collège de France, 1974– 1975.* G. Burchell (trans.). Picador, New York.

Foucault, M. (2003b) *"Society Must Be Defended": Lectures at the Collège de France, 1975–1976.* M. Bertani and A. Fontana (eds.), D. Macey (trans.). Picador, New York.

Foucault, M. (2004a) *Naissance de la biopolitique.* Seuil/Gallimard, Paris.

Foucault, M. (2004b) *Sécurité, territoire, population.* Seuil/Gallimard, Paris.

Foucault, M. (2005) *The Hermeneutics of the Subject: Lectures at the Collège de France 1981–1982.* G. Burchell (trans.). Palgrave Macmillan, New York.

Foucault, M. (2006) *History of Madness.* J. Khalfa (ed.), J. Murphy and J. Khalfa (trans.). Routledge, London.

Foucault, M. (2007) *Security, Territory, Population: Lectures at the Collège de France, 1978–1979.* M. Sellenart (ed.), G. Burchell (trans.). Palgrave Macmillan, New York.

Foucault, M. (2008a) *Le gouvernement de soi et des autres.* Seuil/Gallimard, Paris.

Foucault, M. (2008b) *Psychiatric Power: Lectures at the Collège de France, 1973–1974.* G. Burchell (trans.). Picador, New York.

Foucault, M. (2008c) *The Birth of Biopolitics: Lectures at the Collège de France, 1978–1979.* M. Sennellart (ed.), G. Burchell (trans.). Picador, New York.

Foucault, M. (2009) *Le gouvernement de soi et des autres II: le courage de la vérité.* Seuil/Gallimard, Paris.

Foucault, M. (2010) *The Government of Self and Others.* G. Burchell (trans.). Palgrave Macmillan, New York.

Foucault, M. (2011) *The Government of Self and Others II: The Courage of Truth.* G. Burchell (trans.). Palgrave Macmillan, New York.

Foucault, M. and Stone, L. (1983) An exchange with Michel Foucault.

New York Review of Books (http://www.nybooks.com/articles/ archives/1983/mar/31/an-exchange-with-michel-foucault/?page=2) (last accessed March 26, 2012).

Friera, S. (2004) Auquel filósofo que escribía ajas llenas de herramientas. *Página 12* (http://www.pagina12.com.ar/diario/cultura/index-2004-06-25.html) (last accessed December 15, 2012).

Galloway, A. and Thacker, E. (2007) *The Exploit: A Theory of Networks*. University of Minnesota Press, Minneapolis.

Galston, D. (2010) *Archives and the Event of God: The Impact of Michel Foucault on Philosophical Theology*. McGill–Queen's University Press, Montréal.

Geertz, C. (1983) *Local Knowledge: Further Essays in Interpretive Anthropology*. Basic Books, New York.

Gehring, P. (2004) *Foucault: die Philosophie im Archiv*. Campus Verlag, Frankfurt.

Genette, G. (1980) *Narrative Discourse: An Essay in Method*. J. Lewin (trans.). Cornell University Press, Ithaca.

Gialourakēs, M. (1959) *Cavafy of the Capital "T": Conversations with Timos Malanos*. N.P., Alexandria (in Greek).

Gialourakēs, M. (1975) *From Priapus to Marx*. Oikos, Athens (in Greek).

Giddens, A. (1979) *Central Problems in Social Theory: Action, Structure, and Contradiction in Social Analysis*. Macmillan, London.

Giroux, H. (2007) *The University in Chains: Confronting the Military-Industrial-Academic Complex*. Paradigm Publishers, Boulder.

Giroux, H. and Myrsiades, K. (eds.) (2001) *Beyond the Corporate University*. Rowman & Littlefield, Lanham.

Goffman, E. (1961) *Asylums: Essays on the Social Situation of Mental Patients and Other Inmates*. Doubleday, New York.

Grace, W. (2009) Faux amis: Foucault and Deleuze on sexuality and desire. *Critical Inquiry* **36**, 52–75.

Gurian-Sherman, D. (2008) *CAFOs Uncovered: The Untold Costs of Confined Animal Feeding Operations*. Union of Concerned Scientists (http://www.ucsusa.org/assets/documents/food_and_agriculture/ cafosuncovered.pdf) (last accessed November 25, 2010).

Gutting, G. (2005) Michel Foucault: a user's manual. In: Gutting, G. (ed.) *The Cambridge Companion to Foucault*, 2nd edn. Cambridge University Press, Cambridge, 1–28.

Haag, M. (2004) *Alexandria: City of Memory.* Yale University Press, New Haven.

Habermann, M. and Uys, L. (eds.) (2006) *The Nursing Process: Nursing Discourse and Managerial Technologies.* Churchill-Livingston, London.

Hacking, I. (1975) *The Emergence of Probability.* Cambridge University Press, Cambridge.

Hacking I. (1981) How should we do the history of statistics? In: Foucault, M., *The Foucault Effect: Studies in Governmentality.* G. Burchell, C. Gordon, and P. Miller (eds.). Harvester Wheatsheaf, Harlow, Essex, 181–96.

Hacking, I. (1982) Biopower and the avalanche of numbers. *Humanities in Society* **5,** 279–95.

Hacking, I. (1990) *The Taming of Chance.* Cambridge University Press, Cambridge.

Hacking, I. (1995) *Rewriting the Soul.* Princeton University Press, Princeton.

Hacking, I. (1998) *Mad Travelers.* Harvard University Press, Cambridge, MA.

Hacking, I. (2004) *Historical Ontology.* Harvard University Press, Cambridge, MA.

Hacking, I. (2006a) Foreword. In: Foucault, M., *History of Madness.* J. Khalfa (ed.), J. Murphy and J. Khalfa (trans.). Routledge, London, ix–xii.

Hacking, I. (2006b) Genetics, biosocial groups, and the future of identity. *Daedalus* **135**(4), 81–95.

Hacking, I. (2006c) *The Emergence of Probability.* Cambridge University Press, Cambridge.

Hardt, M. and Negri, A. (2000) *Empire.* Harvard University Press, Cambridge, MA.

Hardt, M. and Negri, A. (2004) *Multitude: War and Democracy in the Age of Empire.* Penguin Books, New York.

Hardt, P. (2005) *Genealogie der Gnade: eine theologische Untersuchung zur Methode Michel Foucaults.* Lit, Münster.

Headrick, D. (2000) *When Information Came of Age: Technologies of Knowledge in the Age of Reason and Revolution.* Oxford University Press, Oxford.

Hegel, G.W.F. (1977) *Phenomenology of Spirit.* A.V. Miller (trans.). Oxford University Press, Oxford.

Hegel, G.W.F. (2010) *Philosophy of Mind*. W. Wallace and A.V. Miller (trans.). Oxford University Press, Oxford.

Heintz, M. (ed.) (2009) *The Anthropology of Moralities*. Berghahn, Oxford.

Heller, J. (1962) *Catch-22*. Simon & Schuster, New York.

Heyes, C. (2007) *Self-Transformations: Foucault, Ethics, and Normalized Bodies*. Oxford University Press, Oxford.

Holloway, L. and Morris, C. (2012) Contesting genetic knowledge-practices in livestock breeding: biopower, biosocial collectivities and heterogeneous resistances. *Environment and Planning D: Society and Space* **30**, 60–77.

Howell, S. (ed.) (1997) *The Ethnography of Moralities*. Routledge, London.

Huffer, L. (2010) *Mad for Foucault: Rethinking the Foundations of Queer Theory*. Columbia University Press, New York.

Humphrey, C. (2007) Alternative freedoms. *Proceedings of the American Philosophical Society* **151**, 1–10.

Huntington, S. (1993) The clash of civilizations? *Foreign Affairs* **72**(3), 22–49.

Inda, J.X. (ed.) (2006) *Anthropologies of Modernity: Foucault, Governmentality, and Life Politics*. Blackwell, London.

Inglehart, R. and Norris, P. (2003) The true clash of civilizations. *Foreign Policy* (http://www.glapn.org/sodomylaws/world/wonews037.htm) (last accessed August 4, 2012).

Jacob, F. (1970) *The Logic of Life: A History of Heredity*. B.E. Spillman (trans.). Random House, New York.

Jaschik, S. (2011) Rejecting double bind. *Times Higher Education Supplement* (http://www.timeshighereducation.co.uk/story.asp?/sectioncode+26&storycode+416353&c+1) (last accessed December 15, 2012).

Jeffreys, P. (2006) "Aesthetic to the point of affliction": Cavafy and English aestheticism. *Journal of Modern Greek Studies* **24**, 57–89.

Judovitz, D. (1989) Derrida and Descartes: economizing thought. In: Silverman, H. (ed.) *Derrida and Deconstruction*. Routledge, New York, 40–58.

Jusdanis, G. (1987) *The Poetics of Cavafy*. Princeton University Press, Princeton.

Keeley, E. (1996) *Cavafy's Alexandria*. Princeton University Press, Princeton.

Kelly, M. (2009) *The Political Philosophy of Michel Foucault*. Routledge, London.

Kleinman, A. (1999) Moral experience and ethical reflection: Can ethnography reconcile them? A quandary for "the new bioethics." *Daedalus* **128**, 69–97.

König, A. (2006) *Splitterflüsse: der Einfluss jüdischer Mystik auf die Philosophie Benjamins, Foucaults, Derridas und Deleuzes*. Mertz & Solitude, Stuttgart.

Koopman, C. (2012) *Genealogy as Critique*. Indiana University Press, Bloomington.

Koopman, C. (forthcoming) Two uses of Michel Foucault in political theory: concepts and analytics in Giorgio Agamben and Ian Hacking. *Constellations*.

Koopman, C. and Matza, T. (2013) Putting Foucault to work: analytic and concept in Foucaultian inquiry. *Critical Inquiry* **39**(4), 817–40.

Kristof, N. (2010) Cleaning the henhouse. *The New York Times*, September 1 (http://www.nytimes.com/09/02/opinion/02kristof.html) (last accessed September 3, 2010).

Kristof, N. (2011) When food kills. *The New York Times*, June 12, Week in Review, 10.

Lacan, J. (1998) *Le séminare V: Les formations de l'inconscient*. Seuil, Paris.

LaCapra, D. (2009) *History and Its Limits: Human, Animal, Violence*. Cornell University Press, Ithaca.

Laidlaw, J. (2002) For an anthropology of ethics and freedom. *Journal of the Royal Anthropological Institute* **8**, 311–32.

Laidlaw, J. (2010) Social anthropology. In: Skorupski, J. (ed.) *The Routledge Companion to Ethics*. Routledge, London, 369–83.

Laing, R.D. (1960) *The Divided Self*. Tavistock, London.

Lambek, M. (ed.) (2010) *Ordinary Ethics: Anthropology, Language, and Action*. Fordham University Press, New York.

Laplanche, J. (1961) *Hölderlin et la question du père*. Presses Universitaires de France, Paris.

Laqueur, T. (2003) *Solitary Sex. A Cultural History of Masturbation*. Zone Books, New York.

Larrinaga, M. and Doucet, M. (eds.) (2010) *Security and Global Governmentality: Globalization, Governance and the State*. Routledge, London.

Lazzarato, M. (2002) From biopower to biopolitics. *Pli* **13**, 100–11.

Le Brun, J. (2002) *Le pur amour, de Platon à Lacan*. Seuil, Paris.

Lee, K. (2012) *Reading Descartes Otherwise: Blind, Mad, Dreaming, and Bad.* Fordham University Press, New York.

Lemke, T. (2007a) An indigestible meal? Foucault, governmentality and state theory. *Distinktion* **15**, 43–66.

Lemke, T. (2007b) *Biopolitics: An Advanced Introduction.* New York University Press, New York.

Lévinas, E. (1961) *Totalité et infini. Essai sur l'extériorité.* M. Nijhoff, The Hague.

Lewin, E. (1993) *Lesbian Mothers: Accounts of Gender in American Culture.* Cornell University Press, Ithaca.

Lewin, E. (1998) *Recognizing Ourselves: Ceremonies of Lesbian and Gay Commitment.* Columbia University Press, New York.

Lewin, E. (2009) *Gay Fatherhood: Narratives of Family and Citizenship in America.* University of Chicago Press, Chicago.

Liddell, R. (1976) *Cavafy: A Biography.* Schocken, New York.

Lightbody, B. (2010–11) *Philosophical Genealogy: An Epistemological Reconstruction of Nietzsche and Foucault's Genealogical Method* (2 vols). Peter Lang, New York.

Lightbody, B. and Dalvi, R. (eds.) (2012) *Studies in the Philosophy of Michel Foucault: An Alternative to Anglo-Americanism.* Edwin Mellen Press, Lewiston, NY.

Mader, M.B. (2011) *Sleights of Reason: Norm, Bisexuality, Development.* SUNY Press, Albany, NY.

Mahmood, S. (2005) *Politics of Piety: The Islamic Revival and the Feminist Subject.* Princeton University Press, Princeton.

Malanos, T. (1935) *About Cavafy.* Serigiadēs, Athens (in Greek).

Malanos, T. (1957) *The Poet C.P. Cavafy: The Man and His Work.* Boukoumanēs, Athens (in Greek).

Malanos, T. (1981) *Cavafy Untwisted.* Prosperos, Athens (in Greek),

Markula, M. and Pringle, R. (2006) *Foucault, Sport and Exercise: Power, Knowledge and Transforming the Self.* Routledge, New York.

Martin, C.R. (2004) *Framed! Labor and the Corporate Media.* Cornell Univeristy Press, Ithaca.

Martin, R. (2002) *Financialization of Daily Life.* Temple University Press, Philadelphia.

Martin, R. (2011) Taking an administrative turn: derivative logics for a recharged humanities. *Representations* **16**(1), 156–76.

Maturana, H. and Varela, F. (1992) *The Tree of Knowledge: The Biological*

Roots of Human Understanding, rev. edn. R. Paolucci (trans.). Shambala Press, Boston.

McFalls, L. (2008) Les fondements rationnels et sociaux des passions politiques: vers une sociologie de la violence contemporaine avec Weber et Foucault. *Anthropologie et Sociétés* **32**(3), 155–72.

McFalls, L. (2010) Benevolent dictatorship: the formal logic of humanitarian government. In: Fassin, D. and Pandolfi, M. (eds.) *Contemporary States of Emergency: The Politics of Military and Humanitarian Interventions*. Zone Books, New York, 317–34.

McGushin, E. (2007) *Foucault's Askēsis: An Introduction to the Philosophical Life*. Northwestern University Press, Evanston.

McKinlay, A. and Starkey, K. (eds.) (1998) *Foucault, Management and Organization Theory*. Sage, London.

McNay, L. (1992) *Foucault and Feminism*. Polity, Cambridge.

McNay, L. (2000) *Gender and Agency: Reconfiguring the Subject in Feminist and Political Thought*. Polity, Cambridge.

McWhorter, L. (2009) *Racism and Sexual Oppression in Anglo-America: A Genealogy*. Indiana University Press, Bloomington.

Mill, J.S. (1864) *Essays on Some Unsettled Questions of Political Economy*. J.W. Parker, London.

Miller, J.-A. (1989) Michel Foucault et la psychanalyse. In: *Michel Foucault: Philosophe*. Rencontre internationale, Paris, 9, 10, 11 janvier 1988. Seuil, Paris, 77–84.

Miller, P. (2007) *Postmodern Spiritual Practices: The Construction of the Subject and the Reception of Plato in Lacan, Derrida, and Foucault*. The Ohio State University Press, Columbus.

Miller, P. and N. Rose (2008) *Governing the Present: Administering Economic, Social and Personal Life*. Polity, Cambridge.

Miller, T. (1994) Althusser, Foucault and the subject of civility. *Studies in Twentieth Century Literature* **18**(1), 97–117.

Miller, T. (2007) *Cultural Citizenship: Cosmopolitanism, Commercialism and Television in a Neoliberal Age*. Temple University Press, Philadelphia.

Mokaddem, S. (2004) *Michel Foucault: une vie philosophique*. Théétète éditions, Nîmes.

Morar, N. and Koopman, C. (2012) The birth of the concept of biopolitics – A critical notice of Lemke's *Biopolitics*. *Theory & Event* **15**(4).

Morton, S. and Bygrave, S. (eds.) (2012) *Foucault in an Age of Terror: Essays on Biopolitics and the Defence of Society*. Palgrave Macmillan, Basingstoke.

Nealon, J. (2007) *Foucault Beyond Foucault: Power and Its Intensifications Since 1984.* Stanford University Press, Stanford.

Nehemas, A. (1983) Memory, pleasure, and poetry: the grammar of the self in the writing of Cavafy. *Journal of Modern Greek Studies* **1**, 295–319.

Nietzsche, F. (1956) *The Geneaology of Morals: An Attack.* In: *The Birth of Tragedy and the Genealogy of Morals.* F. Gollfing (trans.). Doubleday, Garden City, NY, 147–299.

Nietzsche, F. (1974) *The Gay Science: With a Prelude of Rhymes and an Appendix of Songs.* W. Kaufmann (trans.). Vintage, New York.

O'Grady, H. (2005) *Woman's Relationship with Herself: Gender, Foucault and Therapy.* Routledge, New York.

Oksala, J. (2010). Foucault's politicization of ontology. *Continental Philosophy Review* **43**(4), 445–66.

O'Leary, T. (2006) *Foucault and the Art of Ethics.* Continuum, London.

Ortner, S.B. (2006) *Anthropology and Social Theory: Culture, Power, and the Acting Subject.* Duke University Press, Durham.

Palmer, M., Boyd-Barrett, O., and Rantanen, T. (1998) Global financial news. In: Boyd-Barrett, O. and Rantanen, T. (eds.) *The Globalization of News.* Sage, London, 61–78.

Pandolfi, M. (2003) Contract of mutual (in)difference: governance and humanitarian apparatus in Albania and Kosovo. *Indiana Journal of Global Legal Studies* **10**(1), 369–81.

Pandolfi, M. (2011) Humanitarianism and its discontents. In: Bornstein, E. and Redfield, P. (eds.) *Forces of Compassion between Ethics and Politics.* School for Advanced Research Press, Santa Fe, 227–48.

Pandolfi, M. and McFalls, L. (2009) Intervention as therapeutic order. *AM. Rivista della società italiana di antropologia medica* **27–28**, 91–111.

Papoutsakis, G. (1963) *Cavafy: Prose Works.* Fexēs, Athens (in Greek).

Patterson, C. (2002) *Eternal Treblinka: Our Treatment of Animals and the Holocaust.* Lantern Books, New York.

Patton, P. (2007) Agamben and Foucault on biopower and biopolitics. In: Calarco, M. and Steven DeCaroli, S. (eds.) *Giorgio Agamben: Sovereignty and Life.* Stanford University Press, Stanford, 203–18.

Patton, P. (2011) Life, legitimation and government. *Constellations* **18**(1), 35–45.

Peridēs, M. (1948) *Cavafy: Prose.* Ikaros, Athens (in Greek).

Peters, M. and Besley, T. (eds.) (2007) *Why Foucault? New Directions in Educational Research.* Peter Lang, New York.

Peters, M., Besley, T. and Olssen, M. (eds.) (2009) *Governmentality: Studies in Education*. Sense Publishers, Boston.

Pew Research Center (2009) *Covering the Great Recession: How the Media have Depicted the Economic Crisis* (http://.www.journalism.org/analysis_report/story_lines_banks_stimulus_and_detroit_dominate_narrative) (last accessed December 15, 2012).

Philip, M. (1985) Michel Foucault. In: Skinner, Q. (ed.) *The Return of Grand Theory in the Human Sciences*. University of Cambridge Press, Cambridge, 65–82.

Pieridēs, G. (1943) *Cavafy: Conversations, Characterizations, Vignettes*. Eleventh Hour, Athens (in Greek).

Polanyi, K. (2010 [1944]) *The Great Transformation: The Political and Economic Origins of Our Time*. Beacon Press, Boston.

Quadflieg, D. (2006) *Das Sein der Sprache: Foucaults Archäologie der Moderne*. Parodos Verlag, Berlin.

Quiggin, J. (2010) *Zombie Economics: How Dead Ideas Still Walk Among Us*. Princeton University Press, Princeton.

Rabinow, P. (1989) *French Modern: Norms and Forms of the Social Environment*. MIT Press, Cambridge, MA.

Rabinow, P. (1992) Artificiality and enlightenment: from sociobiology to biosociality. In: Crary, J. and Kwinter, S. (eds.) *Incorporations*. Zone Books, New York, 234–52.

Rabinow, P. (1999) *French DNA. Trouble in Purgatory*. University of Chicago Press, Chicago.

Rabinow, P. (2003) *Anthropos Today: Reflections on Modern Equipment*. Princeton University Press, Princeton.

Rabinow, P. and Bennett, G. (2012) *The Accompaniment: Assembling the Contemporary*. University of Chicago Press, Chicago.

Rabinow, P. and Rose, N. (2006) Biopower today. *BioSocieties*, **1**, 195–217.

Rabinow, P. and Stavrianakis, A. (2013) *Demands of the Day: On the Logic of Anthropological Inquiry*. University of Chicago Press, Chicago.

Rancière, J. (2004) Who is the subject of the rights of man? *South Atlantic Quarterly* **103**(2/3), 297–310.

Reardon, J. (2005) *Race to the Finish: Identity and Governance in an Age of Genomics*. Princeton University Press, Princeton.

Revel, J. (2008) *Dictionnaire Foucault*. Ellipses, Paris.

Richter, G. (1986) *Gerhard Richter (October Files)*. H. Buchloh (ed.). MIT Press, Cambridge, MA.

Ritzer, G. and Jurgenson, N. (2010) Production, consumption, prosumption: the nature of capitalism in the age of the digital "prosumer." *Journal of Consumer Culture* **10**(1), 13–36.

Roilos, P. (2009) *C.P. Cavafy: The Economics of Metonymy*. Harvard University Press, Cambridge, MA.

Rorty, R. (1991) Moral identity and private autonomy: the case of Foucault. In: *Essays on Heidegger and Others. Philosophical Papers*. Vol. 2. Cambridge University Press, Cambridge, 193–8.

Rose, N. (1999) *Powers of Freedom: Reframing Political Thought*. Cambridge University Press, Cambridge.

Rose, N. (2006) *The Politics of Life Itself: Biomedicine, Power and Subjectivity in the Twenty-first Century*. Princeton University Press, Princeton.

Saregiannēs, I.A. (1964) *Notes on Cavafy*. Ikaros, Athens (in Greek).

Sartre, J.-P. (1958) *Being and Nothingness*. H. Barnes (trans.). Routledge, London.

Sartre, J-P. (1981) *The Family Idiot: Gustave Flaubert, 1821–1857*. Vol. 1. C. Cosman (trans.). University of Chicago Press, Chicago.

Savidis, G.P. (ed.) (1983) *Cavafy: Unpublished Notes Political and Ethical*. Ermēs, Athens (in Greek).

Savidis, G.P. (ed.) (1985) *Small Cavafiana, Vol. 1*. Ermēs, Athens (in Greek).

Savidis, G.P. (ed.) (1987) *Small Cavafiana, Vol. 2*. Ermēs, Athens (in Greek).

Sawicki, J. (1991) *Disciplining Foucault: Feminism, Power, and the Body*. Routledge, London.

Sedgwick, E. K. (1990) *Epistemology of the Closet*. University of California Press, Berkeley.

Seferis, G. (1966) C.P. Cavafy and T.S. Eliot: parallel lives. In: *On the Greek Style: Selected Essays in Poetry and Hellenism*. Th.D. Frangopoulos and R. Warner (trans.). Bodley Head, London, 119–62.

Shoemaker, M. (2008) *Genealogy, from Nietzsche to Foucault: Tracing the History of the Present*. VDM Verlag, Saarbrücken.

Sibilia, P. (2009) *El hombre postorgánico: Cuerpo, subjectividad y tecnologías digitales*, 2nd edn. Fondo de Cultura Económica, Buenos Aires.

Solomon, D. (2009) Big man on campus. *New York Times*, September 27

(http://www.nytimes.com/2009/09/27/magazine/27fob-q4-t.html)
(last accessed December 17, 2012).

Stoler, L.A. (1995) *Race and the Education of Desire: Foucault's* History
of Sexuality *and the Colonial Order of Things.* Duke University Press,
Durham.

Storr, R. (2000) *Gerhard Richter: October 18, 1977.* The Museum of
Modern Art, New York.

Storr, R. (2009) *Cage: 6 Paintings by Gerhard Richter.* Distributed Art
Publishers, New York.

Sykes, K. (ed.) (2009) *Ethnographies of Moral Reasoning: Living Paradoxes of
a Global Age.* Palgrave Macmillan, New York.

Szasz, T. (1961) *The Myth of Mental Illness.* Holber-Harper, New York.

Tanke, J. (2009) *Foucault's Philosophy of Art: A Genealogy of Modernity.*
Continuum, London.

Taylor, D. (ed.) (2011) *Foucault: Key Concepts.* Acumen Publishing,
Durham, UK.

Thompson, G. (2009) What's in a frame? How the financial crisis is
being packaged for public consumption. *Economy and Society* **38**(3),
520-24.

Tran, J. (2011) *Foucault and Theology.* T. & T. Clark, Edinburgh.

Tribe, K. (2009) The political economy of modernity: Foucault's Collège
de France lectures of 1978 and 1979. *Economy and Society* **38**(4),
679–98.

Tsirkas, S. (1958) *Cavafy and his Period.* Kedros, Athens (in Greek).

Tsirkas, S. (1971) *The Political Cavafy.* Kedros, Athens (in Greek).

Tuchman, G. (2009) *Wannabe U: Inside the Corporate University.* University
of Chicago Press, Chicago.

Valdivia, A. (2001) Rhythm is gonna get you! Teaching evaluations
and the feminist multicultural classroom. *Feminist Media Studies* **1**(3),
387–9.

Venegas, J.M. (2003) ¿Yo pro qué?, insiste Fox; ¿qué no somos 100 millones de mexicanos? *La Journada*: Politica 3.

Veyne, P. (2010) *Foucault: His Thought, His Character.* J. Lloyd (trans.).
Polity, Cambridge.

Vigo de Lima, I. (2010) *Foucault's Archaeology of Political Economy.* Palgrave
Macmillan, New York.

Wang, Y. (2003) *China's Economic Development and Democratization.*
Ashgate, Farnham.

Weston, K. (1991) *Families We Choose. Lesbians, Gays, Kinship.* Columbia University Press, New York.

West-Pavlov, R. (2009) *Space in Theory: Kristeva, Foucault, Deleuze.* Rodopi, New York.

Williams, B. (1985) *Ethics and the Limits of Philosophy.* Collins, London.

Wittgenstein, L. (1958) *Philosophical Investigations.* G.E.M. Anscombe (trans.). Macmillan, New York.

Zigon, J. (2007) Moral breakdown and ethical demand: a theoretical framework for an anthropology of moralities. *Anthropological Theory* **7**, 131–50.

Zigon, J. (2008) *Morality: An Anthropological Perspective.* Berg, Oxford.

Zigon, J. (2009) Within a range of possibilities: morality and ethics in social life. *Ethnos* **74**, 251–76.

Zigon, J. (2010) Moral and ethical assemblages: a response to Fassin and Stoczkowiski. *Anthropological Theory* **10**, 3–15.

Index